Anthony Sattin is a specialist on the Middle East and the author of several highly acclaimed books, including *Lifting the Veil*, *The Pharaoh's Shadow* and *The Gates of Africa*. He discovered and edited Florence Nightingale's letters from her journey of self-discovery up the Nile in 1849-50. He has been a regular contributor to the *Sunday Times* and *Condé Nast Traveller* for many years and his work has appeared in a range of publications in the UK and abroad. He is a broadcaster on both radio and television.

For more information visit his website:
www.anthonysattin.com

Praise for A WINTER ON THE NILE

'Anthony Sattin's study itself has a dreamlike quality . . . he movingly reminds us of how, in the midst of life, those destined for greatness have no more idea where they are going than the rest of us'

Sunday Times

'In this entertaining book Sattin makes some important points on the intellectual, emotional and spiritual development of his immortal subjects'

Mail on Sunday

'It is a tribute to Sattin's knowledge of Egypt and his skill as a writer that he makes this counterpoint narrative seem so effortless. His protagonists circle without ever touching in a dance through the desert'

Independent

'Running beneath this cavalcade of visionary incidents and skilfully realised tablea   cal dislocation'

Telegraph

'Sattin offers a probing assessment of two very different figures whose preoccupations are unexpectedly similar'

Times Higher Education

'Remarkable'

Scotsman

'Sattin has written a brilliantly assured experiment in biography, a triumph of the historical imagination. Convincingly researched, informed by an unobtrusive first-hand knowledge of Egyptian places, compellingly skilful in the writing, the whole story is illuminated by Anthony Sattin's delicately perceptive sense of character in action'

Literary Review

'Sattin tells his travellers' tales with fluency and wit. He interweaves the stories skilfully'

The Tablet

'Sattin's account is authoritative, thoroughly researched and pacy . . . this book is a treat'

Time Out

'Fascinating'

The Resident

'A highly readable, informative and enjoyable book'

Country Life

'Beautifully counterpoints the spiritual travel experiences of the soon-to-be-famous nurse fleeing an arranged marriage, with the much more lubricous ones of the then-unpublished novelist. If this book doesn't win a major book prize, I will eat my sola topi'

Condé Nast Traveller

'A beguiling and impressively researched book . . . a compelling snapshot of two of the most celebrated figures of the age, before their fame, and of a time when travel was leisurely and scholarly. And it sings with the romance of Egypt'

Traveller

A Winter On The Nile

Florence Nightingale, Gustave Flaubert and the Temptations of Egypt

Anthony Sattin

✦ WINDMILL BOOKS

Published by Windmill Books 2011

2 4 6 8 10 9 7 5 3 1

Copyright © Anthony Sattin 2010

First published in Great Britain in 2010 by Hutchinson

Windmill Books
The Random House Group Limited
20 Vauxhall Bridge Road, London SW1V 2SA

Addresses for companies within The Random House Group Limited can be found at:
www.randomhouse.co.uk/offices.htm

The Random House Group Limited Reg. No. 954009

www.rbooks.co.uk

A CIP catalogue record for this book
is available from the British Library

ISBN 9780099534082

The Random House Group Limited supports The Forest Stewardship
Council® (FSC®), the leading international forest certification organisation.
All our titles that are printed on Greenpeace approved FSC® certified paper
carry the FSC® logo. Our paper procurement policy can be found at:
www.randomhouse.co.uk/environment

Typeset by SX Composing DTP, Rayleigh, Essex, SS6 7XF

Printed and bound in Great Britain by
CPI Cox & Wyman, Reading, RG1 8EX

In memory of my beloved parents,
Mona and Gerald Sattin,
who encouraged me in this as
in so much else.

'One wonders that people come back from Egypt and live lives as they did before'—

Florence Nightingale, Luxor, New Year's Eve, 1849

'The Orient, Egypt especially, smoothes away all the little worldly vanities. After visiting so many ruins, one doesn't think of building shacks' —

Gustave Flaubert, Cairo, February, 1850

Contents

Acknowledgements

The author would like to thank the following for permission to quote from their works:

Professor Lynn McDonald, Professor Gérard Vallée and Wilfrid Laurier University Press for permission to quote from *The Collected Works of Florence Nightingale*.

Éditions Gallimard for the right to quote from Jean Bruneau's edition of *Gustave Flaubert: Correspondance*.

Grasset publishers and M. Pierre-Marc de Biasi for permission to quote from *Voyage en Egypte*.

The American Philosophical Society, Philadelphia, for permission to quote from *Florence Nightingale in Rome*, edited by Mary Keele.

Yvonne Neville-Rolfe for permission to quote from the unpublished letters of Edward Stanley Poole.

Mark Bostridge and Viking Publishers for permission to quote from *Florence Nightingale, The Woman and Her Legend*.

Michael D. Calabria and the State University of New York Press for permission to quote from *Florence Nightingale in Egypt and Greece: Her Diary and 'Visions'*.

List of Illustrations

1. Florence Nightingale aged about 25 (pencil on paper) by Bonham-Carter, Hilary (1821–65). (Florence Nightingale Museum, London, UK/ The Bridgeman Art Library)
2. Gustave Flaubert (1821–80) in Cairo, 9th January 1850 (b/w photo) by Du Camp, Maxime (1822–94). (Bibliothèque de l'Institut de France, Paris, France/ Archives Charmet/ The Bridgeman Art Library)
3. Embley Park, c.1856 (litho) by Nightingale (Lady Verney), Parthenope (1819–90) (after). (Florence Nightingale Museum, London, UK/ The Bridgeman Art Library)
4. Study of Gustave Flaubert (1821–1880) in the pavilion of Croisset, near Rouen (Seine-Maritime), c. 1840. (Photo by Harlingue/Roger Viollet/Getty Images)
5. Florence Nightingale with Charles Holte Bracebridge and Selina Bracebridge in a Turkish street. Oil painting by Jerry Barrett, 1859. (Wellcome Library, London)
6. A luggage label from the Coulomb brothers' Hôtel d'Orient. (Author's collection)
7. Maxime Du Camp, c.1852 (photo) by French Photographer,

(19th century). (Musée de la Ville de Paris, Musée Carnavalet, Paris, France/ Archives Charet/ The Bridgeman Art Library)

8. Kanga on the Nile at Luxor (w/c on paper) by Prisse d'Avennes, Emile (1807–79). (Victoria & Albert Museum, London, UK/ The Bridgeman Art Library)

9. 'Karnak: View Across the Hall of Columns' by David Roberts. (Mathaf Gallery, London)

10. 'View From Under the Portico of the Temple of Edfou, Upper Egypt' by David Roberts. (Author's collection)

11. Maxime Du Camp's view across the Nile to Esna, home to Kuchuk Hanem (Christopher Wahren Fine Photographs of New Haven, CT)

12. The Hypaethral Temple at Philae, 1850 (w/c) by Lewis, John Frederick (1805–76). (Private Collection/ © The Fine Art Society, London, UK/ The Bridgeman Art Library)

13. Colossal statue of Ramesses II at Abu Simbel, 1850 (b/w photo) by Du Camp, Maxime (1822–94). (Private Collection/ The Stapleton Collection/ The Bridgeman Art Library)

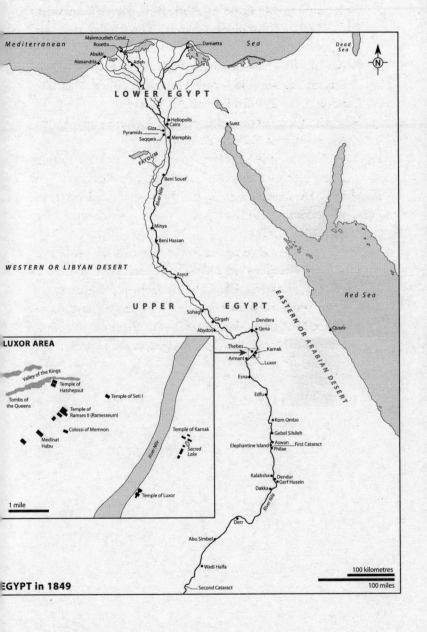

Mediterranean
Sea
Dead
Sea
Mahmoudieh Canal
Rosetta
Damietta
Abukir
Alexandria
Atfeh

LOWER EGYPT

Heliopolis
Cairo
Suez
Pyramids
Giza
Saqqara
Memphis

FAYOUM

Beni Souef

River Nile

Minya
Beni Hassan

WESTERN OR LIBYAN DESERT

Asyut

UPPER   EGYPT

Red Sea

Sohag
Girgeh
Abydos
Dendera
Qena
Quseir

EASTERN OR ARABIAN DESERT

Thebes
Karnak
Armant
Luxor

Esna

Edfu

Kom Ombo

Gebel Silsileh

Elephantine Island
Aswan
Philae
First Cataract

Kalabsha
Dendur
Gerf Husein
Dakka

Derr

Abu Simbel

Wadi Halfa

Second Cataract

100 kilometres

100 miles

N

EGYPT in 1849

LUXOR AREA

Valley of the Kings
Temple of
Hatshepsut
Tombs of
the Queens
Temple of Seti I
Temple of
Ramses II (Ramesseum)
Colossi of Memnon
Medinat
Habu
Temple of Karnak

River Nile

Sacred
Lake

Temple of Luxor

1 mile

Introduction

Discovery

I first came across this story in the British Library's old Reading Room. The catalogues there were large, heavy, leather-bound albums, their thick pages covered with hand-pasted strips. These strips were clues to the whereabouts of millions of books, pamphlets and documents – an irresistible invitation to roam around the written world. In the late-1980s, I spent months under the library's soaring nineteenth-century dome researching material for a book I was writing about travellers in Egypt. One morning, flicking through the catalogues, I came across an entry that simply read, 'Nightingale, F., letters from Egypt'.

It is not always easy to recognise eureka moments, but I knew instantly that this was one. I knew that Florence Nightingale had risen to fame during the Crimean War and then fought a lifelong battle to improve health care in Britain, but I had no idea that she ever went to Egypt or that she wrote about it. Yet it never once occurred to me that the Nightingale F. of the catalogue could be anyone other than Florence. I filled in the request slip, returned to my desk and waited.

Time can be infuriatingly inconsistent. The moments we want to treasure can often pass impossibly quickly. In this case they did not. Service at the old library was a regular, if slow, affair. An hour might have passed, but it seemed like a day. Then one of the silent librarians laid a slender volume on the desk beside my pile of travellers' tales.

Letters from Egypt arrived as 23 sections of unbound, printed pages and carried the name of no author on either its cloth box or title page. The letters were written during the winter of 1849–50 and had been printed four years later, around the time that Nightingale went to the Crimea, a journey that would bring her enduring fame. The volume was marked *For private circulation only*. Since then, some long-gone librarian had identified the author as Nightingale, F.

Florence Nightingale believed that destiny plays a large part in deciding what becomes of us. Living in a time of peace and advanced public welfare, a person with similar talents, strength and desires would not necessarily scale the peaks that she did. Had she lived now, she might have worked in health-care management, putting in a lifetime of efficient and anonymous service before collecting a pension on retirement. Maybe she would have married and worried about how to juggle the work/life balance. Perhaps she would have been happy.

At another time, I might have passed by that entry in the catalogue or done no more than mention it in the book that I was writing, as I eventually did. But I knew an editor who was setting up a publishing company and whose list was still open. When I explained what I had found, she was interested. When she saw some of the letters, she was as excited as I was. Whatever we had read or been told about Florence Nightingale, no one had ever suggested that she could write so well, or be so lively, entertaining and passionate, or that the journey to Egypt was so full of temptations, so rich in possibilities, so significant in her struggle to fulfil herself.

Cecil Woodham-Smith's 1950 biography devotes less than three pages to the Egyptian journey and makes no mention of the letters. Recent biographers have acknowledged the letters, but few have recognised the significance of the journey itself to her, the exception being Professor Gérard Vallée, editor of the *Collected Works of Florence Nightingale*, Volume 4, who wrote of her achieving clarity in the direction her life should take and intensity in her dialogue with God during that interlude. The transformative nature of the journey was immediately obvious to Nightingale herself; at the beginning of her five months in Egypt, she wrote that she wondered how 'people come back from Egypt and live lives as they did before'.[1]

I had no great interest in either the angelic Lady of the Lamp or the grumpy reformer who, for much of the last 50 years of her long life, agitated for better health care, much of that time from within the confines of her bedroom. But I found and continue to find this young Florence fascinating. She is serious and spiritual, but also full of life and wit. She is a young woman getting over a disappointment in love and searching for her own path in life, battling her family and prepared to give up an existence of great comfort and privilege to do something she thinks is worthwhile. Determined and independent, she is a Florence for our time.

Florence Nightingale's Letters from Egypt was published in London and New York in 1987 and was well received in the press. The *New York Times* was most enthusiastic and described it as 'a major publishing coup, and, simultaneously, in its own way, a major Egyptian discovery'. The reviewer also thought that it was 'perhaps the best personal travel account of Egypt ever written'. Sales boomed.

That might have been the end of the story, the royalty

payments dwindling over the years, the memory a happy one. But destiny, fate, luck, had not finished with the story.

I returned to the book I was originally writing and to other accounts of travelling in Egypt. Among them was that of the great nineteenth-century French novelist Gustave Flaubert. A selection of his writings from Egypt was available in English, chosen and translated by the American author Francis Steegmuller. The *New York Times* had called Nightingale's account 'more satisfying even than Flaubert's roistering letters and journals. Well, actually, Flaubert is better on the brothels, Nightingale on the temples, and her writing is no less accomplished.' The critic Edward Said attacked Flaubert for being imperialist and for not taking Egyptians on their own terms. (Said does not mention Nightingale, perhaps because he did not know that she travelled in Egypt.) But even he acknowledged that the Frenchman was scrupulous in the way that he reported events, people and settings. Said also noted that Flaubert delighted in *bizarreries*.[2]

I knew that Flaubert went to Egypt in the 1840s, around the same time as Nightingale. But it wasn't until I came to write about them, under the British Library dome in 1987, that I realised Flaubert had arrived in Alexandria just a few days before Nightingale, in November 1849. When I compared their descriptions of leaving Alexandria, I discovered that they boarded the same boat to Cairo on the same day.

I wrote about this at the time and some perceptive reviewers picked up on it. One pointed out that I had managed to get them on to the boat but could take them no further. That challenge has nagged at me ever since. This book is my attempt to answer it.

Consequences

Florence Nightingale feared fame. Wary of its consequences, of the guilt and impositions that would inevitably follow, she wanted to work without recognition. She would do things for the joy of them, for the satisfaction of doing them well, of fulfilling her calling. But reputation came all the same and within five years of her return from Egypt, and one year of her arrival in the barracks hospital at Scutari, across the Bosphorus from the Topkapi Palace, she had become one of the most famous women in the world.

Her mythical status was first embroidered in newspaper articles and then summed up by the American poet Longfellow:

> A Lady with a Lamp shall stand
> In the great history of the land,
> A noble type of good,
> Heroic womanhood.

While her name inspired people, her presence often terrified them, as Lady Emilia Hornby discovered during the Christmas of 1855. At a reception held by the British Ambassador in Constantinople, her ladyship watched in awe as Lady Stratford, the ambassador's wife, led in the angelic young woman. 'Yes,' she wrote in a letter home, 'it was Florence Nightingale, greatest of all now in name and honour among women. I assure you that I was glad not to be obliged to speak just then, for I felt quite dumb as I looked at her wasted figure'.[3]

Months later, in the summer of 1856, peace returned to the Crimea. After the nurses she had brought with her had been sent home and the last of the official papers filed, the 'wasted' Florence Nightingale and her aunt Mai, who had been looking after her while she was looking after so many others, made plans to return to England. Nightingale declined the British government's offer of a warship to bring her home. Instead, she and Aunt Mai booked passage anonymously on a ship called the *Danube*, stopping at Athens and Messina on the way to Marseille. The only clue to Nightingale's special status was the presence of a messenger sent by Queen Victoria to ease her passage across borders.

On 5 August 1856, while the government and army still hoped to bring her home in triumph and the press devoted itself to speculating as to her whereabouts, 'Mrs and Miss Smith' left Paris and reached London unnoticed. Nightingale spent that night in the south of the city, keeping a promise she had made to visit the Bermondsey Convent, five of whose nuns had worked with her in Turkey. The following afternoon she took a train to the family house, Lea Hurst, in Derbyshire. She made it as far as the local station before she was recognised by a family acquaintance, Lady Auckland.

The Nightingales had known their younger daughter was on her way, for they had already received what her mother called Florence's 'spoils of war'. First there was a one-legged orphan sailor boy, who had spent ten months in Nightingale's Scutari hospital. He was followed by a Russian orphan named Peter and a Crimean puppy, a gift from some soldiers. And then came Florence herself. Aunt Mai had written to warn of the dread her niece had of the proposed heroine's welcome, so her return was a quiet one. 'A little tinkle of the small church bell on the hills,' her sister Parthenope wrote, 'and a thanksgiving prayer at the little chapel next day, were all the innocent greeting.'[4]

But Queen Victoria had not forgotten her. A little over two weeks after Nightingale's return, Sir James Clark, the royal physician, wrote inviting her to stay at his house in Scotland. The air would be good for her, he suggested, and, in case she was missing the point, added that his house was very close to the royal estate at Balmoral, where the Queen would shortly be in residence: Her Majesty knew of Sir James's invitation.

Queen Victoria wished to hear Nightingale's story first-hand and without any generals or ministers present. The two women met at Balmoral on 21 September and the Queen was later quoted as saying that: 'I wish we had her at the War Office.' Prince Albert recorded in his diary that 'she put before us all the defects of our present military hospital system, and the reforms that are needed. We are much pleased with her.'[5]

Nightingale was commanded to remain in Scotland. Over the following days she attended a church service with the Queen, a ball at which she was seated with the royal family, and a meeting with Lord Panmure, Secretary of State for War. When she returned south with a promise that a Royal Commission would look into the health requirements of the army, Nightingale knew something she did not know in Egypt: that all the struggle and tribulation she had suffered over the past few years had not defeated her. She had triumphed.

Two years after meeting the royal family, Nightingale published one of her key works, *Notes on Matters Affecting the Health of the British Army*, in which she laid out her thoughts and observations on the spread of infection in army hospitals. She followed this in 1860 with her most famous work, *Notes on Nursing*, which established the role and responsibilities of nurses in a way that remains relevant today. That same year she also opened the Nightingale School of Nursing at London's St Thomas' Hospital, paid for by a public subscription that had raised over £50,000 (more than £2.5 million today) in her name while she was in the Crimea. The school and the publications were the foundations on which the modern nursing profession was built.

While Florence Nightingale was in Scotland attending Queen Victoria, Gustave Flaubert was in Paris, as he described it, losing his virginity as a writer.

For as long as he could remember, and he was now thirty-four years old, he had wanted to write. More than that, he wanted to be a great writer. The son of an eminent surgeon,

Flaubert, a failed law student, an epileptic, a loner, had devoted himself to the pursuit of literary perfection. For the five years since his return to France from Egypt, he had been at work on a novel which related the tragic tale of a doctor's adulterous wife in Normandy. For years he had retreated to his family home beside the Seine outside Rouen. When he was not at work on this story, he was writing long letters to friends, telling them about the difficulties he was having. He suffered in his relative isolation, sharing a house with only his mother and his young niece whose upbringing he supervised. Writing from lunchtime to late at night, he was so deeply immersed in his work that it was difficult for him to do anything else. Then, on 1 October 1856, while Florence Nightingale was still in Scotland, Flaubert went into print.

His novel was published in instalments in a literary magazine called *La Revue de Paris*, part-owned by Maxime Du Camp, the writer with whom Flaubert had travelled to Egypt. Their friendship had cooled since their return to France, in part because Flaubert had dragged his feet over getting into print: Du Camp was more the 'publish and be damned' sort of writer. In the event, Flaubert was the cause of their both being damned. When his novel appeared, the State Prosecutor accused him and his publishers of immorality. Public attention intensified after a French court threw out the case. When critics looked at the work, they recognised *Madame Bovary* as being one of the finest of all novels. Its author was set on the course he had always wished for himself. He could not have imagined a better storyline.

Nor could he have imagined that more than a century after his death, he would still be regarded as one of the great writers of his age. In 1853, while at work on *Madame Bovary*, Flaubert identified that the greatness of fiction lay not in its ability to amuse or arouse us, but in the way that it could make us dream.

His achievement, in *Madame Bovary* and in parts of his later works *Salambo* and *Sentimental Education*, was that he succeeded in doing all three. In the process, he transformed the novel.

So here were two of the most celebrated people of the nineteenth century making parallel journeys. There were obvious differences: she was more sophisticated, more experienced, better connected and came from a wealthier family. As a man, he enjoyed the sort of freedom she longed for. Her instincts led her towards the dead world of tomb and temple, his towards the living in cafes and brothels. But the similarities are more striking, for they were at the same stage in their lives, both in their late twenties, both in despair of ever fulfilling their dreams, but on the cusp of achieving more than even they had dared hope. Of course neither knew what fate had in store for them. But we know that Florence Nightingale goes to the Crimea and returns a heroine. We know that Gustave Flaubert goes home and begins to write *Madame Bovary*, and that the scandal and the brilliance of the book make him one of the best-known novelists of any age.

Part of the fascination of writing this story has been in thinking about all the 'what ifs?' Florence Nightingale and Gustave Flaubert make a deliciously unlikely couple, but they only ever lie together between the sheets of this book. At times I imagine them roaming up the Nile together, concocting scenes of seduction and outrage, of love in Luxor and unbelievable nights behind pyramids, watching them jointly face the temptations of Egypt, revelling in their common fascination with the past and the lessons it has to teach us. But just as I once turned down a serious offer from a serious publisher to write a biography confirming that Nightingale was gay (she was not), so I could not bring myself to take them further than they chose to go. Florence Nightingale never spoke to Gustave Flaubert and, as far as I know, was never even aware of his presence. He seems to have observed but not approached her. Why would it have been otherwise? At this point, they were mere faces in a crowd. Had they made the journey six or ten years later, things might have been different. But there is no need to change the historical record, especially when I have such eloquent witnesses.

Florence Nightingale and Gustave Flaubert both wrote lengthy and frequent letters home to their families and friends, and kept diaries or journals. Much of the Nightingale material has long been available, though not as accessible as it is now. Twenty years ago, there was no other available version of her Egypt letters than the one I found in the British Library and later put into print. These letters were the story that she wished to tell her family. A small blue pocket diary, also held in the British Library but obviously intended for her eyes only, gives an insight into her most private thoughts and frequently tells a different story: one of personal anguish. Curiously, there is also a second pocket diary, a red one, begun on 1 November 1849, the day she took the train from London to Folkestone, and ended on 15 July 1850, when she was on her way home to England. As a result of a radio programme I made in 2000 about Nightingale in Egypt, it was sent anonymously to Claydon House, the home of Nightingale's sister. This second diary gives details of Nightingale's movements and has many notes that she later worked up into long letters home. All this material has now been gathered into one of the many volumes of the *Collected Works of Florence Nightingale*, overseen by the dedicated Professor Lynn McDonald, with the Egypt volume expertly edited by Professor Gérard Vallée.

Gustave Flaubert never intended to publish his travel journal and was even more against the idea after 1851 when Du Camp, his travelling companion, published an account of their

Egyptian journey while omitting any mention of Flaubert's presence on it. When Du Camp suggested that Flaubert might also write up a portion of their journey, he replied that travel writing was a low form of literature. 'Incidents gleaned abroad,' he insisted, 'might be used in a novel, but not in a straight account.'[6]

Flaubert wrote long letters home on a regular basis, even though the opportunities to post them were few and far between. He also kept a journal, part of which he worked into a narrative, *Le Cange*, after his return. Francis Steegmuller published a selection from Flaubert's letters, journal and *Le Cange* in 1972, but the full version of the original 240-page autograph manuscript of Flaubert's travel journal was not available to him, only emerging after a sale in Paris in April 1989. Neither the full journal nor the complete letters have been translated into English, so for most quotations in this book I have returned to the original French and made my own translations.

I have also made my own judgments on spelling. There is no universally agreed convention on the transliteration of Arabic, but I have attempted to be consistent in my spelling of Arabic and Turkish words, using -a not -eh (so *dahabiya* not *dahabeeyeh*), -sh not -ch (so pasha not pacha).

With a book this long in gestation, it is impossible to thank all the people who have helped or inspired me, but I must start at the beginning with Anne Furniss, who commissioned the original volume of *Florence Nightingale's Letters from Egypt*, and David Fordham, who designed it. I have had generous advice, guidance and encouragement from Sue Baxter and the staff at the National Trust's Claydon House, and from Deborah Manley, Dr Robert Morkot and the many enthusiastic members of the Association for the Study of Travel in Egypt and the Near East (ASTENE), who travelled with me on the Nile and answered my queries online. Professor Lynn McDonald approached me many years ago, at the beginning of her vast, ongoing publishing project, and has been supportive ever since and I thank her, Professor Gérard Vallée and the Wilfred Laurier University Press for allowing me to reproduce passages from Florence Nightingale's writing. Thanks also to Dr Jason Thompson who has provided information over the years, to Emily Weeks, who was generous in sharing information on J. F. Lewis, and to her father, Professor Kent Weeks, ever an inspiration. The University of Rouen's Flaubert Centre has made much of the great man's writing easily accessible, I am grateful to M. Pierre-Marc de Biasi for access to his important new work on Flaubert's eastern journey and to Yvonne Neville-Rolfe for allowing me to quote from papers in her family archive. Mark Bostridge has kindly allowed me to quote from his excellent biography of Miss Nightingale. I would also like to thank the American Philosophical Society, Philadelphia, the State University of New York Press, Grasset and Gallimard publishers, all of whom have allowed me to quote from their original material.

I owe thanks to the librarian and staff at the British Library, who first brought me the Nightingale letters and many other books and papers, and to the librarian and staff at the Victoria & Albert Museum, the Birmingham Museum and Art Gallery, and the Wellcome Institute Library. I owe a huge debt of gratitude to Christopher Phipps, former librarian, and staff at the London Library where I have conducted research, read, written and sought refuge all my writing life. Caroline Worthington, director of the excellent Florence Nightingale Museum, and Kirsteen Nixon, her helpful assistant, kindly allowed me to see some of the personal possessions that survived Nightingale's journey in Egypt. I am also extremely grateful to Christine Walker of the *Sunday Times* and Sarah Spankie at *Condé Nast Traveller*, who sent me back to Egypt.

Many friends have helped in many ways and to all of them I am extremely grateful, especially to Brigid Keenan and Alan Waddams, who lent me a house where I wrote a considerable part of this book; to Adrienne Gaha, Tim Maguire and Brooke Fitzsimmons, who provided essential space and understanding in London; and to Mark Skeet and Max Mulhern, who took the manuscript apart at an early stage. My agent Gillon Aitken of Aitken Alexander has provided guidance and sound judgment from the beginning. I owe Caroline Gascoigne endless thanks for commissioning the book for Hutchinson, as well as being so solid in her support and so thorough in her editing. Tess Callaway, my copy editor Lynn Curtis, and the designer Glenn O'Neill have all been enthusiastic and inspired in their suggestions and help, and to them and all at Hutchinson I wish to express my gratitude.

My mother Mona and my late father Gerald Sattin always supported my writing projects and I am forever grateful for their help. But of all the people who have lived with this project, none have lived closer than my two sons, Johnny Paris and Felix, who have been dragged into tombs and temples in Luxor, bookshops in Paris and libraries in London, and my wife Sylvie, who has had to share me with the shades of Flaubert and Nightingale. They have all seen more of my back than my front during the writing of this book. Only they know how much it has meant to me to shake this idea out of my head and give it life on the page.

Footfall

'Flo is in such a state of enchantment, it would do your heart good to see her' – Selina Bracebridge to Fanny and William Nightingale from Alexandria

Alexandria, 18 November 1849

Charles Bracebridge Esquire believed that men were best at making decisions on these matters. Although it was only nine o'clock in the morning, he had decided it was too far and already too hot to have the three women walk to their hotel. Instead he ushered them into a horse-drawn carriage. Their luggage would be sent after them.

The omnibus drove out of the port gates, the travellers inside it relieved to be on dry land again. They rattled along narrow dirt streets, through the crowded huddle of shops and houses in the Turkish town, and emerged on to a road that traced the great arc of the harbour. They turned east. Behind them now were the cream, crenellated towers of a fifteenth-century fort and the remains of the ancient lighthouse. Ahead, halfway around the bay and at the edge of the city, lay their destination.

Frank Square, the heart of Alexandria's European quarter, was larger than anything they knew of in England. Its centre was a straggling open space, which, when not filled with camels or donkeys carrying bales of cotton or bundles of goods off the boats, was used as a parade ground for the pasha's troops. Perhaps out of respect for the Christians who lived or worked around the square, the parade was never held on a Sunday, so today it was quiet and empty.

The square stood open on one side to the harbour and the Mediterranean beyond; the little English party had seen enough of that for now. On the other sides it was enclosed by tall, palatial buildings. Some were occupied by foreign consulates, several housed the offices of international trading companies and two served as hotels. One of these carried the sign of the Hotel d'Europe. In spite of the Francophile name, it had been opened a few years earlier by Mr Hill, an Englishman, and was the hotel of choice for the British traveller. The French generally stayed across the square at Monsieur Coulomb's Hotel d'Orient. The cooking at the d'Europe was quite good and the proprietor civil, which was about as much as one could expect from a hotel in such a place at this time. So at half-past nine on the morning of 18 November 1849, this is where Mr Bracebridge led the three women in his care: his wife Selina, a servant by the name of Trautwein, and the Bracebridges' friend, twenty-nine-year-old Florence Nightingale.

Miss Nightingale stepped into the Hotel d'Europe's court-yard and stood between the baggage being brought in from the street and the washing hanging in the backyard. She was 5'8", tall for a woman at that time, and slender. In a photograph taken a few months after her arrival in Alexandria, she is shown with her head down and her eyes lowered towards a book. It is as though she is trying to hide the full force of her character and its increasingly steely determination behind a demure, retiring façade. A hint of a smile on her lips, she looks as enigmatic as a sphinx. She wears her chestnut hair in the fashion of the day, parted in front and pulled into a bun behind. Her neck is bare, her collar open, a string of stone beads hangs over her bosom and a striped silk shawl – perhaps bought in Egypt – is wrapped around her shoulders. She appears thoughtful, powerful and determined.

A little before ten, another Englishman arrived at the Hotel d'Europe. An air of importance hung about this gentleman like the most pungent of perfumes from the souk. Heads turned as he passed. This was Mr Gilbert, Her Britannic Majesty's representative in the port, and he had come to pay his respects to the new arrivals. This was an uncommon event: the consul did not turn out for just anyone, especially given the number of British travellers arriving in Alexandria these days. The visitors, however, were friends of his sister, Lady d'Oyley, and he had come as a courtesy.

Mr Gilbert met the new arrivals in the courtyard, where they were waiting for some India-bound travellers to leave so that they could move into their rooms. He stayed only as long as form dictated, which was long enough to welcome them, enquire after their journey and offer the protection of one of his Turkish janissaries. This young man was called Ali. Not, the consul assured them, that they needed a guard or had anything to fear. True, there had been some incidents – only a few weeks before the British clergyman in Alexandria, Mr Winden, had had something thrown at him in the street – but Gilbert knew how to deal with that sort of behaviour. He had summoned the headman of the district in which the outrage had been committed and, although he knew the man was innocent, had had him tied up and prepared for a flogging. Then he let him go. Gilbert had made his point and the headman had understood it: when he left, he kissed the consul's feet and promised that this sort of incident would never happen again. If Ali were not needed to protect the new visitors, however, he would at least be of use in escorting them to the places they wished to see: an elegant protector in long flowing robes, with an embroidered waistcoat and carrying a large stick.

The travellers had spent the best part of a week on the Mediterranean: three days' sailing from Marseille, a six-hour stopover at Malta – time to do no more than change ships – and then a run of almost four days to Alexandria. The *Merlin* had been crowded. The men, Mr Bracebridge among them, had spent much of the voyage up in the saloon, talking, smoking and drinking. With that sort of behaviour going on above deck, the women spent more time below than they would have wished. With 17 people occupying bunks in that long, narrow cabin, both privacy and comfort were elusive. Even washing had been difficult. Now that their bags were safely in the hotel, what the women most wanted was a bath. In Alexandria, that meant leaving the hotel.

Soon after Mr Gilbert left for the consulate, a small procession emerged from the d'Europe's gate with Ali and his stick at its head. Behind him walked the three European women. Selina Bracebridge at forty-nine years old was shorter and stouter than her friend, but not as large nor as stout as Trautwein, Florence's German maid, known as Trout. The morning was sunny and, although it was the beginning of winter and Egyptians were already wrapped in several layers of clothing, the women felt the heat as they walked away from the sea and the now busy square. At the end of an avenue of palms, bananas and trellised petunias, they came to a quiet garden. In it was a long, low building, the *hammam*.

There were public baths in Britain, but women of Nightingale's class would not have needed to use them. Perhaps Selina Bracebridge had visited a *hammam* on earlier visits to Beirut or Istanbul, but Nightingale had not. All she could compare it with were the baths she had seen at Pompeii. She was later to describe it as 'the joy of the East'.¹ Now she walked with a light step into the first large, marble-clad chamber and undressed.

Victorian painters made much of this kind of scene, their fantasies allowed full rein by the steam, the party atmosphere, and above all by the imagined ease of a group of naked women. The *hammam* emerged from their paintings as the ante-chamber to an Eastern brothel, a visual feast of flowing tresses and generous, pert breasts, a place that reeked of sensuality and that promised sexual licence. The reality, of course, was more than a little different: it was unusual for people to go naked in a *hammam* and the young Englishwoman would have followed custom and covered herself with a towel.

A marble-tiled passage led to the high-domed, octagonal hot room, where she sat and waited. It being considerably warmer than an English June inside the *hammam*, she began to perspire. Rivulets of sweat ran down her back. When the attendant was available, she was taken, flushed, into a side-chamber for what she called 'the process'. Sitting on the marble floor, she was scrubbed with a handful of palm fibres, massaged with oil, and had her limbs manipulated. It is easy to imagine her emerging, slowly and carefully on the wet floor, clean, glowing, relaxed. She must have felt as though she had stepped into a tale from the *Arabian Nights*.

After the *hammam*, since it was Sunday and their journey had ended happily, the whole party joined Mr Gilbert for a service at the solemn little English church.

*

The following morning, long before daylight, Florence Nightingale went to the table in her room, lit a candle and began to write a letter home. 'Yes, my dear people, I have set my first footfall in the East and oh! that I could tell you the new world of old poetry, of Bible images, of light and life and beauty which that word opens.'[2]

She knew her parents and elder sister Parthenope were longing to hear about the journey and her reaction to it. She also knew that they would carefully weigh her words for their enthusiasm, for the excitement they expressed. The Bracebridges were travelling to Egypt for pleasure and out of curiosity, but Nightingale had been sent abroad for far more complicated reasons. She had been unhappy for years.

This misery had grown out of a clash between her family's expectations of the life she would lead and her own idea of her destiny. They wanted her to marry while she wanted to do something useful with her life: to work. In particular, she wanted to nurse. But she lived in an age when it was unthinkable for a woman of her position to do so. It had been bad enough when she was still a teenager; it was worse now she was twenty-nine and had long been of marriageable age. But how could she marry when marriage meant agreeing to obey a husband? It was no easier staying single, however. Like other women of her time, she was not free to do as she pleased and her family had steadily refused to allow her to pursue her dreams.

The conflict had come to a head in the months before her departure and she had become ill with grief, tension and worry. She hoped a trip to Egypt would restore her health and spirits; her family hoped it would allow her to reconcile herself to the idea of marriage. There was also undoubtedly the desire just to have her out of the way for a while, to bring an end to the daily confrontations, the shouting and tears. The expectation she felt is apparent in a note she wrote to her mother, at the beginning of November 1849, while waiting at Folkestone for a boat to cross the Channel: 'I hope I shall come back and be more of a comfort to you than ever I have been.'[3]

There are two distinct images of Florence Nightingale. There is the popular one constructed by newspaper reporters and embellished by public sentiment, the sugar-sweet heroine of the Crimean War, the Lady of the Lamp who tirelessly walked the wards of wounded soldiers, both literally and figuratively bringing light to their darkness. The other is a cantankerous old woman – old, by her own admission, long before her time – who campaigned on health care and public welfare reform from the privacy of her home, badgering politicians and advising medical professionals. Florence Nightingale lived to be ninety and in some ways, at certain times, both of these images of her were correct. But the bright young woman who stepped on to the Alexandria dock four years before the Crimean War, who was fussed over by her German maid, who undressed to be scrubbed and oiled in the *hammam*, and was awake before anyone else in the hotel because she was too excited to sleep, this Florence Nightingale is neither of them.

The person who inhabits the pages of this book is young and fun, girlishly slim with striking good looks. She loves opera and likes to dance. She is disarmingly bright and endlessly, sometimes tiresomely, questioning. She is a woman with a quest, fighting to make a place for herself in the world and yet at times desperate enough to want to leave it. She is stubborn and opinionated, but also damaged and now very vulnerable.

We tend to think of travelling on the Nile as a pleasurable experience, and for most modern tourists that is precisely what it is. But the campaigning English writer Harriet Martineau, who was in Egypt just a few years before Nightingale, had found her journey up the Nile 'as serious a labour as the mind and spirit can be involved in'.[4] It was no less strenuous for Florence Nightingale. She described the physical journey to Cairo and up the Nile to Abu Simbel in long, eloquent letters to her family. But there was also a more dramatic, more extraordinary, interior journey, a mental voyage that we can trace in the tortured observations she recorded in notes and a diary that she intended to be for her own eyes only. These private thoughts reveal that while on this journey, more than anywhere else and at any other time, Nightingale came to understand the nature of the service to which she had been called. Her travels in Egypt allowed her to define that calling, to build up the mental reserves she needed to face further conflict with her family and, by the end of it, to take instruction in nursing.

She had wondered for many years why she was not satisfied with the comfort, privilege and love in which she had been nurtured. By the time she left the Nile she understood why this was. Moreover she was reconciled to the fact that she could never be satisfied with that life, no matter how hard she tried. Once the question was settled in her own mind, it was only a matter of time before she changed her circumstances.

But for now, during these first days in Alexandria, she was content to think about nothing more than passing her time here agreeably. They had a week to wait before the next boat left for Cairo – a week in which to do some shopping and see the sights.

Most cities grow from the seeds of smaller settlements, but Alexandria was always destined to be a metropolis. The man who gave it his name wanted it to be the hinge that would hold together two very different worlds: the old one of Ancient Egypt and the brash new world of Hellenistic Greece. To achieve that, Alexandria needed to be ambitious and innovative, and it succeeded. Just a couple of hundred years after its founding, at the time of its most famous ruler, Cleopatra, it was second in size only to Rome. Its glory was eclipsed soon after, but the rot did not set in until the seventh century CE, when the city fell to the Arabs. Its new conquerors wanted as little as possible to do with the place; they preferred to be on the eastern – Arabian – side of the Nile and for that reason they created a new capital, Cairo. They condemned Alexandria to a long, slow slide into decay that was only halted a few years before Nightingale arrived, when Muhammad Ali Pasha, ruler of Egypt since 1805, developed the port to encourage trade with Europe.

Twelve hundred years after the Arab conquest, Florence Nightingale did not exaggerate when she wrote that 'there is not much to see here, nothing but the perpetual feeling of being in the East, the eastern colouring and eastern atmosphere'.[5] In 1849, as now, most of the ancient city was covered by modern buildings or by rubble, and there was nothing left standing above ground that conjured up the magnificence of the past in the way that the Pantheon or Colosseum did in Rome.

The city's iconic Pharos, the lighthouse that had been one of the Seven Wonders of the Ancient World, had crumbled away over centuries. When it was finally completely levelled by an earthquake at the beginning of the fourteenth century CE, it served as an eloquent symbol of the city's decline. Nightingale does not even mention the large fort that the Sultan Qait Bey built on its foundations in the 1480s, now one of the modern city's main attractions. The only remnant of the nearby ancient palace complex with its *museion* and library was a pair of obelisks. These had originally stood in Heliopolis, near Cairo, but were moved in the first century BCE to the façade of a temple Cleopatra built to honour the memory of Mark Antony. By the 1840s, the temple had disappeared and one of the obelisks had fallen. In 1819, Muhammad Ali Pasha gave it as a present to Britain, although the British government was loath to pay for its removal and it was not until 1878 that it was brought to the Thames where it still stands. So there it lay, alongside its twin, which was later moved to New York's Central Park. Consul Gilbert escorted them to see 'Cleopatra's needle', as Nightingale called it, the day before they left for Cairo. But she did no more than list the visit in her diary.

Four days after her arrival, she made the 15-mile journey east along the coast to Abukir Bay, but the site of Nelson's great victory over Napoleon's fleet also failed to stir her British heart. She made no effort to hide her disappointment, describing 'a dreary plain of white sand covered with white stones, a scanty fringe of palm trees in the distance, the broken wall of Nicopolis, built by Augustus; in the foreground, a road, many inches deep in sand, through which we waded – it looked like the shroud of an empire's body'.[6] She went for a walk along the beach to see the breakers roll in and watched the sun setting over the distant prospect of Alexandria.

She was not alone in failing to become excited about Abukir. The British historian Sir John Gardner Wilkinson, who had just published the first English-language guidebook to Egypt, his *Hand-Book for Travellers*, warned that 'the only distinction now enjoyed by that place is, its being the abode of state prisoners sent by Mohammed Ali [the late pasha], to repent of their misdeeds in this lonely spot'.[7] Even Alexandria's ancient catacombs, which Nightingale saw the following day and which Wilkinson thought were remarkable in size and elegant in design, she found 'rather a farce'[8] after the ones she had seen in Rome. Pompey's Pillar, the city's most famous attraction, fared no better, though she was clearly amused by the way she reached it. 'The donkey is very small and you are very large (the Egyptian is a very tall race), and you sit upon his tail . . . After mounting – a feat which is effected by curling your right leg round your saddle bow (the saddles are men's and nothing but the fear of men would have prevented me from riding astride) – you set off full gallop, running over everything in your way, and the merry little thing runs and runs like a velocipede.'[9]

She rode on towards the pillar, which she had identified from the boat, but before she reached it came upon something she described as the end of the world. She had ridden into a Muslim cemetery that had spread around the base of the pillar. Small mounds of white mud broke the flat earth, each decorated with a stone and a stem of dry aloe. She watched a woman walk among the graves, 'a single figure . . . clasping her hands, her black robe over her head, in the middle of all this desolation. There being no enclosure, but the tombs stretching every way, makes it so striking, and Pompey throws his immeasurable shadow over the plain.'[10]

If the ancient city failed to excite Nightingale's interest, she found the living one fascinating. The *hammam* had met with her approval, as had the Armenian garden they visited afterwards, where she watched children eating 'like little gods, with infant dignity slowly and majestically dipping their sop in the dish and conversing'.[11] Her curiosity about life in the city mounted until, on her last day, she asked Mr Gilbert if she could attend prayers in a mosque.

The consul was discouraging. As far as he knew, no European woman had ever been to the mosque in Alexandria. It was dangerous because it was forbidden; non-Muslims were not allowed into the main mosques, especially during prayer time. The only chance Florence had of getting inside, he explained, was to go disguised as a local woman. If Gilbert thought this would discourage her, he was wrong: she was not the sort of person to be deflected by a little sartorial inconvenience. After the deed was done she wrote home:

> First an immense blue silk sheet (the head comes through a hole in the middle); then a white stripe of muslin which comes over your nose like a horse's nose bag, and is fastened by a stiff passementerie band, which passes between your eyes and over and behind your head like a halter; then a white veil; and lastly, the black silk balloon, which is pinned on the top of your head, has two loops at the two ends through which you put your wrists in order to keep the whole together. You only breathe through your eyes.[12]

When the women were thoroughly covered, the consul warned them not to show their hands or to speak. If there were trouble, Mr Bracebridge and the consul would be nearby.

The three foreign women were only in the mosque for 15 minutes, but they had entered during noon prayers, so the place was crowded and they were led first to an upper gallery and then up the minaret, where the *muezzin* was calling the faithful to pray. From there they had a view out across the city and down into the mosque.

'Some were at their prayers; but one was making baskets, another was telling *Arabian Nights* stories to a whole group of listeners, sitting round him – others were asleep.'[13] Selina Bracebridge considered it irreverent for people to behave in such a way in a place of prayer, but Nightingale was charmed. She thought behaviour in London churches was worse. She loved the sense of ease in the mosque, and recognised something honest and also noble in the behaviour of the men. If you were tired, you went to sleep in a corner; if you wanted to talk, you leaned against a pillar with a friend. But when the faithful heard the call, they all bowed down together. 'The hour comes, the Muslim falls on his knees and for five minutes the world is nothing to him.' The only problem – and, as far as she was concerned, it was insurmountable – was the way women were treated: no better, she thought, than animals. 'If I could have said where any *woman* may go for an hour's rest, to me the feeling would have been perfect.'[14]

The *hammam* had amused her, the mosque had both fascinated and enraged, and the square in front of the hotel impressed her. Yet the place she found most rewarding in Alexandria was one that few visitors had any desire to see.

On her way out from England, travelling from Paris to Marseille, she had struck up a conversation with two sisters from the order of St-Vincent-de-Paul. These women – *les Filles de la Charité*, known in English as the Sisters rather than Daughters of Charity – were dedicated to working among the poor. When Nightingale mentioned that she was going to Alexandria, they suggested she should visit their order there. 'Was that not curious?' she wondered in a letter to her parents, although they, who had hoped to dissuade her from nursing, would doubtless have found it more frustrating than anything else.

In Alexandria, the Sisters of Charity ran a school and a *Miséricorde* or hospital for the poor; in practice, this was more of a clinic or dispensary than anything we would now call a hospital. The school impressed Nightingale, knowing how little education was available to the city's poor. But what interested her most was the clinic, where she reckoned the 19 sisters were doing the work of 90.

She told her parents she had spent 'a great deal of time with them',[15] and that was no exaggeration. On Wednesday, three days after landing, she and Mr Bracebridge had gone shopping for some things they would need for their boat and had then made a preliminary visit to the sisters. On Thursday Nightingale went back to the dispensary with Selina Bracebridge. On Friday she went with Trautwein. On Saturday she was there again. She made no mention of being accompanied, so perhaps she went alone that time. In her diary she noted she was at the *Miséricorde* at 8 a.m. on Saturday: 'the 300 patients this time served by the three sisters alone: discipline, quickness and kindness; beautiful'.

Selina Bracebridge seemed to approve of them too, for she wrote to the Nightingales in England that 'they are the most elevated sort of sister we have seen; they leave the drudgery of the household work to servants and under the direction of the physician bleed and dress wounds, dispense medicines and compound them; the poor flock by hundreds to them for advice and medicine, and with no fixed revenue it is wonderful how much they do'.[16]

On Saturday, after her call on the *Miséricorde*, Nightingale visited the mosque in disguise and later that day a relieved consul took her for a drive along the shore to see the obelisks. After that, she had to arrange her bags and tin box because Mr Bracebridge had had confirmation that the Cairo ferry would leave the following morning.

'We have not been able to leave before,' Nightingale explained in a letter home, 'because there was no intermediate steamer.'[17] Others in Alexandria had had the same problem: no boats to Cairo. That evening the Hotel d'Europe was full of guests and servants hurrying to prepare themselves for travel. There were bags to pack, banking to be done, bills to settle, letters to finish and send.

Across the square at the Hotel d'Orient, two Frenchmen and their Corsican servant were also preparing to leave.

2

The Cairo Ferry

Alexandria, 25 November 1849

Gustave Flaubert, his friend Maxime Du Camp and Du Camp's valet Louis Sassetti had arrived in Alexandria three days before Nightingale and had endured the same unvarying ritual that awaited all new arrivals. They had made the whole voyage from Marseille on *Le Nil*, a three-masted packet ship with a steam-driven paddle and single funnel. A large *tricolore* hung from her stern. Unlike the Bracebridges and Miss Nightingale, the Frenchmen had had a rough crossing; *Le Nil* had 'rolled like a drunk'.[1] The storm became so violent as they left Malta that the captain had ordered them back to port where they waited for three days.

Once they were underway Du Camp took to his bed, Sassetti was no steadier on his feet, and only Flaubert, a man known for his delicate constitution, who was travelling in part for his health, enjoyed the crossing. Well, there had been a bad moment as they left Marseille . . . he had drunk a glass of rum to ward off seasickness and to give him courage for the journey, and that had quickly come back up. Since then, as he gleefully wrote to his mother, 'I've spent my time walking on deck, dining with the ship's officers, standing on the gang-way between the two paddle-wheels with my cap on one side and cigar in my mouth . . . When it grows dark I watch the sea and daydream, draped in my pelisse [cloak] like Childe Harold. In short I'm on top of the world.'[2]

The two friends and their servant had come to Egypt to travel up the Nile, seeing the sights and the country as they did so. Like so many people before and since, they had long dreamed of making the trip. Du Camp had planned the journey and prepared the necessary documents, which was fortunate. Flaubert was neither well travelled nor well connected. Twenty-eight years old, living outside Rouen with a domineering mother and yelping baby niece, he considered himself a failed writer and found the idea of a journey to Egypt by turns terrifying and liberating. His mother found it merely terrifying, but she was sufficiently anxious about her son's health to agree to let him go when the family doctor said it would do him good.

Wealthy and independent, Du Camp was significantly more experienced than his friend. He had already travelled to Algeria and Turkey. His account of that journey, *Souvenirs et Paysages d'Orient*, had won him some recognition as a writer and earned him membership of the Academy of Arts. More important for the prospects of their Nile journey, Du Camp had also been elected a Chevalier of the highly esteemed Légion d'Honneur, a distinction he had won after being shot at a barricade during the previous year's revolution in Paris. To ease their passage and to open doors in Egypt, he had arranged official commissions for them both.

Du Camp's was the more glamorous: the Ministry of Public Instruction had asked him to produce a photographic record of the monuments of Egypt, which they hoped would be a useful teaching aide in French colleges. The Institut de France, which advised him on his mission, went further and thought that this first thorough photographic record of the pharaohs' treasures would be extremely important. For his friend Gustave, Du Camp had secured an assignment from the Ministry of Agriculture and Commerce: the young writer was to report on Egypt's agricultural and industrial output, its system of taxation, and the trade carried on at river ports and caravan centres. It is hard to imagine a less suitable person for such a mission. But however unfit for purpose they were, they had steamed into Alexandria's harbour that November morning, storm-tossed and happy, with no idea of the chaos and fuss that was about to overtake them.

While still some distance out, Flaubert had watched the outline of the pasha's palace emerge between the morning sun and the silvery sea. Now, as they came into harbour, 'the first thing we saw on land was a pair of camels led by their driver; then, on the dock, some Arabs peacefully fishing. Landing took place amid the most deafening uproar imaginable: negroes, negresses, camels, turbans, cudgellings to right and left, and ear-splitting guttural cries. I gulped down a whole bellyful of colours, like a donkey filling himself with hay.'[3]

In the large square, which Flaubert characterised as architecturally 'bastard, half Arab, half European',[4] they avoided the very British Hotel d'Europe and took rooms in Monsieur Coulomb's Hotel d'Orient. This segregation by nationality was to continue: as soon as they had refreshed themselves after their journey, they hurried off to present their credentials to the French community. They found themselves in the middle of a gathering of some of the most powerful people in the country.

Flaubert was introduced to Hakakim Bey, brother-in-law of the Egyptian Prime Minister, and to General Gallis and Princeteau Bey, two senior French officers come to Egypt to advise, respectively, on how best to build fortifications and how to use artillery to knock them down. And there was Soliman Pasha, the man who turned out to be the most welcoming and of the most use to them.

Despite his name, this pasha was French not Egyptian, a man from Lyon not Cairo. He was born in 1788, christened Octave Joseph Anthelme Sèves, and had served with the artillery of Napoleon's *Grande Armée* during the march on Moscow. He had survived the 1812 retreat and the downfall of his leader three years later. But the change of regime that followed blighted his prospects and so, with a captain's rank, he decided it was time to find a new field of engagement. Persia looked promising and he was on his way to Teheran when he stopped in Egypt. He was still there more than 30 years later, persuaded to stay by Muhammad Ali Pasha.

Sèves had thrived. Converted to Islam, renamed Soliman and married to a woman named Mariam Hanem, he had helped to build and command the army that defeated the Ottoman Emperor. As the victories piled up, so did the honours: first colonel, then general, than pasha. He also founded a dynasty that lasted as long as the monarchy: his great-granddaughter was the wife of King Fouad and mother to the last Egyptian king, Farouk. In Flaubert's estimation, in 1849 Soliman Pasha was 'the most powerful man in Egypt'[5] and therefore a most useful person to have as a friend. He was to provide great assistance as the travellers made their way up the Nile.

Flaubert was surprised by the welcome he and his companions received in Alexandria. 'It's unbelievable how well we are treated here,' he bragged to his mother, perhaps exaggerating just a little to ease her anxiety about the journey. 'It's as though we were princes, and I'm not joking. Sassetti keeps saying: "Whatever happens, I'll be able to say that once in my life I had ten slaves to serve me and one to chase away the flies," and that is true.'[6]

The two friends and their servant had hatched a plan to ride across to the mouth of the Nile at Rashid, which Europeans called Rosetta, where the famous stone had been found. From there, they would continue along the coast and then south along the river to Cairo. But Soliman Pasha had advised them to change their plan; the ride to Cairo across the sands would be too tiring. Instead, they were going to ride to Rashid and back, and then take the Cairo ferry.

Before they went, they took in the traditional sights: the obelisks and Pompey's Pillar. Like Florence Nightingale, they were especially struck by the tombs around the pillar, 'the colour of grey earth, without a hint of green', Flaubert noted, while Du Camp wrote of 'a sterile barrenness, a grey earth, ugly and tiring to the eyes, the graves all alike, in brick or mud, and, at nightfall, the plaintive howling of jackals hungry for corpses. If you lift a rock, you find scorpions; huge bats fly here at sunset and lost girls practise their prostitution among the dead.'[7] Then they went to the *hammam*. Nightingale had compared it to something out of the *Arabian Nights*, but Flaubert found it funereal, 'as though you are being embalmed'.[8]

At 7 a.m. on Sunday 18 November, just as the crowd of port officials and porters in the harbour were reading the name

Merlin on the side of an incoming steamer and Mr Gilbert was preparing to visit the friends of his sister who had recently arrived from England, four men emerged from the Hotel d'Orient and approached a huddle of animals grazing in the centre of the square. With Du Camp, Flaubert and the Corsican Sassetti was Joseph Brichetti, their *dragoman*, officially a translator but in practice the person responsible for smoothing their way through the country. Brichetti was a thin man in his fifties, with a greying beard and an idiosyncratic way with words. Originally from Genoa, he had lived so long in Egypt that he now spoke a mix of Italian, French and Arabic. To this, he added a few words of his own invention, which made his translations something of a challenge to understand. Flaubert described him as a man of unparalleled vanity.

The two Frenchmen and Sassetti, an ex-cavalryman, mounted horses, which looked like old nags, but turned out to be perfect for riding on the sand. Brichetti, for all his vanity, was riding a donkey, on which he also carried the coats and supplies they would need to get them to Rosetta. Behind him ran four men, sent to protect them, although the horsemen also were armed.

They made their way east around the harbour, beneath violet clouds, passed the obelisks and then rode along a broad sandy track that has since become Alexandria's eight-lane waterfront highway. For a while there was a scattering of villas and groves of fruiting palms. Flaubert, finally set loose in the Orient, remembered a passage in *Don Quixote* in which Sancho Panza compares a beautiful girl with heavy earrings to a palm laden with dates.

The sand began beyond the old gates of Alexandria. They followed the coast for a few hours across a rolling landscape and then stopped to rest at a small fortress that overlooked Abukir Bay. The sentry sent out his dogs, but called them off when he heard the name Soliman Pasha. They ate the chicken they had brought, sitting in the shade of the fort, while the guards looked over their weapons and talked about war between Turkey and Russia. The conflict that was to sweep Nightingale to fame was already looming.

After another hour in the saddle, they rode past planks and ropes and other wreckage. Flaubert thought he was looking at the remains of the French fleet that Nelson had sunk 50 years earlier. The beach was covered in shells and there were several sharks visible close to shore. 'We shot cormorants and water-magpies,' he noted in his journal, 'our Arabs (all children, except the old one with a little turban) ran like hares and with great joy picked up the ones we killed – for the first time in my life I killed a bird – grand solitude – the sea is immense – the sinister effect of the light, which has something black about it.'[9]

They took all day to cover the 45 miles from Alexandria and, as they approached Rosetta, were treated to a spectacular sunset. 'A sky of melted crimson, then clouds of a deeper red in the shape of huge fish bones (there was a moment when the sky was a plaque of crimson and the sand was inky) – ahead, and to our left, over the sea and Rosetta, the sky was a tender, pastel blue – the shadows of the two of us on horseback are gigantic – regularly moving ahead of us – like two grand obelisks walking through the countryside.'[10] The gates were already closed, but once again Soliman Pasha's name worked like Ali Baba's 'Open sesame' and they rode into the darkening town.

A hundred years earlier, Rosetta had been Egypt's main Mediterranean port, but Alexandria's revival under Muhammad Ali had been its neighbour's undoing. Without its former international trade it was a sleepy place, but Flaubert found it more interesting than Alexandria for that reason. 'We cross the narrow streets with trellis-work *mashrabias* [carved wooden window screens] – they are dark and narrow – the houses seem to be touching each other – shops in the bazaars are lit by glasses full of oil, hung from a wire – if we had left our rifles across our saddles, they would have been broken, because of the narrowness of the streets."[11]

The local pasha, Hussein, received them sitting on cushions. Soliman Pasha's letter of introduction helped once again and servants were ordered to bring them supper and make up beds with good mosquito netting. The next morning, the pasha's medical officer, an Italian who spoke French, showed them his hospital and a nearby rice factory run by a Frenchman. This was an early, extremely rare and not particularly successful attempt by Flaubert to fulfil his mission. Even if he wanted to report on trade in Rosetta, there was little to write home about.

He was more successful at recording the details that caught his eye, in particular the pasha's ten black attendants who served lunch. 'They wore silk jackets and some had silver bracelets,' he wrote, as he might have done in one of his oriental tales, 'and a little black boy waved away the flies with a kind of feather-duster made of rushes; we ate with our fingers; the food was brought one dish at a time on a silver tray; about 30 different dishes were served this way. We were in a wooden pavilion, all the windows open, on divans, with a view of the sea.'[12]

In the afternoon, they sailed on the Nile to see more sights, among them a tree that was worshipped as a holy man. It is a sign of Flaubert's lack of interest in antiquities that he fails to mention in his letters or notes that he was in the place where the so-called Rosetta Stone had been found (by a Frenchman), the stone which had allowed Champollion (another Frenchman and the father of Du Camp's sister-in-law) to decipher hieroglyphic writing. Instead, being as far from home as he had ever been in his life, he watched a passing boat with a tartan sail

– '*voilà* the real Orient' – and was suddenly extremely sad. He felt lost in the middle of something immense and pitiless.

The following night they were back in Alexandria in the more familiar surroundings of the Hotel d'Orient and Flaubert was dressed in white tie and tails, ready to meet the Egyptian Foreign Minister, Artim Bey. For the next four days he and Du Camp rested, dined with Soliman Pasha, the French general and other functionaries, played whist, went to the opera, used their best manners and prepared their bags. Early on Sunday 25 November, the Frenchmen left the Hotel d'Orient with Sassetti and Joseph, crossed Frank Square and made their way to the landing for the Cairo ferry.

There was nothing remarkable about the crowd gathered on the dusty bank that morning. Under a gloomy autumn sky, there was the usual crush as 70 passengers squeezed on to the Cairo-bound boat, a barge-like construction intended for 25. There was the usual babble of Arabic, English, French, Greek, Italian and Turkish as passengers fought for space: men in the forward cabin, women to the rear. Then, at 8 a.m., the steam tug began to pull them slowly through the Nile delta.

'The canal perfectly uninteresting,' Florence Nightingale recorded, 'the day gloomy. I was not very well.'[3] 'The banks flat and dead,' Flaubert wrote of the same journey, 'several naked Arabs running . . . from time to time, a traveller passes on horseback, wrapped in white and trotting in his Turkish saddle.'[4]

Nothing unusual, then, about this boat cutting through the flatlands of the Nile delta in November 1849, except that it was carrying a twenty-nine-year-old Florence Nightingale and a twenty-seven-year-old Gustave Flaubert. Within a few years, both would be celebrated throughout Europe. But as they sat on the barge bound for the Nile, both were tormented by their inability to follow the course in life that they had chosen for themselves. This struggle had had an effect on their health, which was the main reason why their families had agreed to – and paid for – a winter in Egypt. They were about to make the same journey – to Cairo, Luxor, Aswan and Abu Simbel. They were about to write two of the finest accounts of travel in Egypt. But, for now, they were simply Miss Nightingale of Embley, Hampshire, and Monsieur Flaubert from Croisset outside Rouen, in Normandy.

They reached the end of the canal by late afternoon and there, just ahead of them, the river of legend appeared: fat, dark and hemmed in by mud banks and canals. This was not the moment to wax lyrical or savour their first view of the Nile, though, because they had to change boats. Nightingale and Selina Bracebridge jumped on to the bank before the gangplank was laid and ran ahead of Mr Bracebridge, Monsieur Flaubert and the rest of the crowd, hoping to find the best places on the *Marchioness of Breadalbane*, the overnight ferry to Cairo. But it made no difference. The others caught up, there was still not enough space, and even in the 'ladies' cabin', they were so squeezed together that some found it best to sit on the floor. The men were no more comfortable up front, but as the weather was calm and not cold, some of them moved on to the open upper deck.

'Then I first saw the solemn Nile,' Nightingale wrote home, 'flowing gloomily, a ray just shining out of the cloudy horizon from the setting sun upon him. He was still very high; the current rapid. The solemnity is not produced by sluggishness, but by the dark colour of the water, the enormous unvarying character of the flat plain, a fringe of date trees here and there, nothing else. By 6 o'clock p.m. we were off, the moon shining and the stars all out.'[15] She laughed at the strange scene of Greeks, Turks, Levantines, Italians and British all spread out on the floor, talking through the small hours, scratching as the fleas bit.

At some point during the night, Flaubert went below and saw them. Nightingale made no mention of it in her diary, but Flaubert did and in his journal recorded seeing 'an English family: hideous, the mother looking like a sick old parrot (because of her green eyeshade attached to her bonnet)'.[16] So there she was, Selina Bracebridge, caught in time, one of Flaubert's parrots. Florence, always so observant, would have looked up as the Frenchman came in. She too was part of this menagerie.

This silent moment is as close as the two travellers come to meeting each other. Or at least it is the closest encounter we know about – perhaps there were other moments in Cairo, a brief nod of the head at they crossed the Ezbekiya or passed in the souk. But if they did, these moments are lost forever and we can only be sure of this brief encounter on the night ferry. If they had talked, they would have found much in common. Both loved opera, both were known in some of Paris's finest salons, both had been introduced to Madame Recamier, the doyenne of Parisian society who had died six months earlier, and both had an interest in the esoteric side of Ancient Egyptian religion – Flaubert had read some of the Gnostics while Nightingale knew of them through her reading and discussions with her friend Baron Bunsen. They also shared character traits: they were uncompromising to a degree that had caused much pain to their families. Both were also certain that they were put on earth to serve a greater purpose.

Nightingale wrote nothing about the Frenchman, but she did record meeting Madame Rosetti, wife of the Tuscan consul, and a newly-wed though by no means young Greek woman from Lemnos, covered in diamonds and pearls, wearing a blue velvet, fur-trimmed jacket and attended by several servants. There was also a Turkish woman in tight jacket and trousers, a sash round her waist – 'the prettiest woman I ever saw' – who took offence at Mr Bracebridge's coming into the women's quarters to see how they were. She 'rose in her wrath, adjusted her black silk veil, and with her three slaves, who all put on theirs which were white, sailed out of the cabin like a Juno in her majestic indignation, and actually went for the night on board the baggage steamer which followed us'.[17]

Among the passengers on the top deck besides the two young French gentlemen and their servants were Monsieur Duval de Beaulieu de Blaregnies, secretary to the Belgian Ambassador in Constantinople, and the ruler of Egypt's personal physician. Flaubert also mentioned an Arab engineer who spoke English and wouldn't stop talking once he started drinking beer. Once they had set up beds on deck, Du Camp wrapped himself in his pelisse and went to sleep. But Flaubert was too excited to do the same. 'I gesticulate, recite lines from [their friend the poet] Bouilhet, cannot bring myself to go to bed – I think of Cleopatra – the water is yellow – it is very calm – there are stars – well wrapped in my pelisse, I fall asleep on my camp bed, on deck – and with what joy!'[18]

Things were less peaceful below deck. At two o'clock, Florence Nightingale was still unable to sleep because of the crowd, the crying children, the fleas, the endless questions as to why she wasn't married, why she hadn't gone to the opera in Alexandria, and what on earth she was going to do in Upper Egypt. At some point, she looked out of the window and saw the moon set and the stars brighten.

The gentleman's daughter who could have been a writer but longed to become a nurse, and the doctor's son who was trying to write novels, were spending their first night on the Nile, beneath a diamond-studded sky. Alexandria had been a transit station, a first glimpse of Egypt. They had found it too

Europeanised – too many hats, Flaubert had complained – and yet both had thought of the *Arabian Nights* while they were there. Now, as they dreamed, the ferry pushed slowly up the fast-flowing, yellow river towards Cairo, the city the *Arabian Nights* narrator had called 'the mother of the world', the next step on a journey that was to change the lives of both of them.

3

Words of God

When did Florence Nightingale first think about Egypt? Perhaps upon hearing the Bible story of Joseph, sold into slavery by his brothers and emerging as the pharaoh's trusted adviser. Or else the story of Moses confronting the pharaoh, his magician and the Angel of Death, to bring his chosen people out of Egypt. No one ever accused Florence Nightingale of lacking imagination and these stories are powerful enough to conjure up an imaginary landscape of river and bulrushes, palace, pyramids and desert. If that was the case, then her earliest impressions of the country that was to have such a profound effect on her were intricately connected with the Bible. It was a land of beauty but also one of struggle; a place where people and beliefs could be tried and tested.

She certainly knew of Egypt from childhood. For her fifth birthday, her mother gave her *Fruits of Enterprize Exhibited in the Travels of Belzoni*, a book that retold the adventures of Giovanni Belzoni, who found an entrance into the second pyramid at Giza, opened the fabulous tomb of Seti I in the Valley of the Kings, and shovelled his way into Ramses' great temple at Abu Simbel. Belzoni was most famous for bringing the granite head of 'the young Memnon', Ramses II, to the British Museum. He removed it from the temple in July 1816. Between then and its installation in the museum's Egyptian Sculpture Room in January 1819, the story of its removal captured London's imagination and inspired Shelley to write his poem 'Ozymandias', with its warning to: 'Look on my works, ye Mighty, and despair!' Nightingale still knew Shelley's poem by heart in her old age.

If from no one else, Nightingale had heard first-hand stories about Egypt from Richard Monckton Milnes, a British poet and politician who had visited Egypt in the winter of 1842. He had had two reasons for travelling there. He wanted to see the sights and to interview its ruler, Muhammad Ali Pasha, who had defeated the Ottomans in Syria three years earlier. The pasha would have moved on Istanbul and disturbed the delicate balance of this volatile region had Britain and the European powers not stopped him. Milnes' interview with him was quick and inconclusive, the sightseeing more time-consuming and rewarding.

He rented a boat in Cairo and sailed up the Nile in the company of Mansfield Parkyns, an eccentric friend of his from Cambridge who was later to earn some notoriety for going native in Ethiopia. For the Nile excursion, Parkyns packed an extensive arsenal of weapons. Milnes, who had a very different idea about the journey they were going to make, compiled a list of 'luxuries to take up the Nile' that included a chisel – handy for hacking interesting hieroglyphs and paintings off the walls of tombs and temples – and extra panes of glass to stop the draughts in his cabin. More worried about defending his reputation as one of London's great hosts than saving himself from wild tribesmen or animals, he had also brought recipes 'for making everything that can be made of mutton, pigeons, chickens, eggs and rice'.[1]

The Nile worked its magic. Milnes was surprised by how 'autumnal' and cold the weather could be, but greatly impressed by the antiquities he saw. He spent weeks moored off Karnak Temple; days sitting under its columns, a turban on his head, reading Dante. The nights were long, so he was happy to entertain whenever he found company along the river. Between the sightseeing, the tomb hacking, the sketching and visiting, the shooting at crocodiles and arguing with Parkyns over whether they would make it beyond the First Cataract (they wouldn't), he also found both the time and the inspiration to write verse:

> When you have lain for weeks together
> On such a noble river's breast,
> And learnt its face in every weather,
> And loved its motions and its rest, –
> 'Tis hard at some appointed place
> To check your course and turn your prow,
> And objects for themselves retrace
> You passed with added hope just now.[2]

Milnes turned out to be the main catalyst for Nightingale's journey to Egypt – but that had nothing to do with either his anecdotes or his verse.

*

Florence Nightingale was born into wealth and privilege, but lived in an age when women, however elevated their background, had no personal freedom. Her childhood was spent in the very close confines of her extended family, between the Nightingale mansions in the north of England, where they went for the summer, and the south, where they moved to escape the worst of the winter. In between, they stayed in the houses of cousins and grandparents in the country, or took a suite at a London hotel for the 'Season'. Her adult life would be controlled by her parents until she married, when she would in turn be subject to the wishes of her husband. *If* she married, that is . . . Florence Nightingale had other ideas, other desires.

Her father, William Shore, came from a long line of Sheffield traders and bankers. The Shores were also Unitarians and, like many in his family, William rejected Church of England dogma in favour of a more liberal and inclusive spiritual life. The wealthiest member of the family, William's great-uncle Peter Nightingale, had also been a Unitarian. But however radical he was in matters of religion, Great-uncle Peter was a traditionalist when it came to his view on women and, like many men of his time, didn't believe that the female of the species should inherit money. So when it became obvious that he would die childless, he decided to leave his fortune, some £100,000 (around £7 million today), to his nearest male relative, his great-nephew, William Shore. Peter Nightingale attached two conditions to his bequest. The first stipulation was that William should change his surname to Nightingale. The second was that if he had no son, the money and property should pass to another male of the family on his death.

William Shore had already finished his studies at Trinity College, Cambridge by 1815, when he turned twenty-one, changed his name to William Nightingale and became a very

wealthy young man. Three years after this change of circumstances, he married Fanny Smith, the sister of an old school
friend. He did not invite his parents to the wedding, in spite of
his father's protests, perhaps because he was worried that they
were unfashionable and would embarrass him. His sister Mai,
whom he did invite to the wedding party, did just that:
unprepared for the grandeur of the occasion, she arrived
inappropriately dressed. Soon after the wedding, the newly-
weds took themselves off for a long, slow, Grand Tour of the
Continent, specifically of Italy.

Their first child was born in Naples in April 1819 and given
the Greek name for the city. Although there was great joy and
jubilation at Parthenope's birth, not even Fanny's proud father
could suppress the thought that, 'As for the sex, perhaps it
might have been better; but I am disposed to give the little
female a most cordial welcome.'[3] That grandfatherly welcome
would have to wait, though, because the tour was far from
over. Not that they were going anywhere for a while: Fanny
had developed a swollen breast while William had gone down
with malaria. They didn't leave Naples until the following
February and then only reached Florence before another
pregnancy forced them to settle there for longer than planned.

Their second daughter was born on 12 May 1820 at Villa
Columbaia, a house they had rented near the city's Porta
Romana. At a christening ceremony some seven weeks later,
the younger Nightingale was named after the great
Renaissance city in which she had been born. There are no
references in surviving correspondence to the fact that a son
'might have been better', but disappointment must have
mounted as it became clear that Fanny could have no further
children. After her death, William Nightingale's fortune would
pass to a nephew, Mai Shore's son. However soothing the
knowledge that the fortune would stay within the extended

family, Fanny Nightingale was acutely aware that Parthenope and Florence would have to make their own way in the world. The only means she knew for them to do that was to make a good marriage.

Florence Nightingale's earliest schooling was left to French maids and strict English governesses, and was an extensive and enthusiastic affair. At the age of eight, she was already studying 'figures, music...Latin, making maps of Palestine (and such like about the Bible) & then we walk, & play, & do patchwork, & we have such fun'.[4] She enjoyed watching her garden grow and caterpillars turning into chrysalides. When Florence was eleven, Parthenope twelve, their strict governess left to get married. Had they not been Unitarians, the girls might have been sent away to boarding school, but their father was a Cambridge graduate with time on his hands and only too happy to supervise his daughters' education at home.

William Nightingale taught his girls what he knew of maths, geography, chemistry and physics, history and philosophy. They also studied no fewer than five languages – Latin, Greek, Italian, German and French – and later Florence added a smattering of Hebrew, as well as even learning some hieroglyphs for the Egyptian trip. Home tutoring was no holiday: Mr Nightingale expected his daughters to apply themselves, and Florence in particular put in long days over her schoolbooks.

A Miss Hawkes was taken on to give art and music classes, and Fanny Nightingale instructed the girls in the more ladylike skills of needlework and dancing. She also expected them to know about household management: just because staff were employed to run the houses did not mean the girls could not also be involved. She took responsibility for their religious education besides. Still very much a Unitarian's daughter, Fanny did not want the girls taught church dogma and preferred 'all doctrinal points to be left alone till our pupils are of an age to judge for themselves'.[5]

Although born within a year of each other and brought up in this close family, the sisters had very different temperaments and interests, and nowhere did this reveal itself more clearly than in their schooling. Parthenope showed a passion for the piano, for drawing, and for the feminine graces her mother could teach her. Florence, on the other hand, was a determined, attentive and devoted student. From an early age, she had been a list-maker with an innate ability to sift and order information. Under her father's care, these talents were harnessed to a wider education. 'I had the most enormous desire of acquiring,' she wrote about those years, on her way back from Egypt, 'for seven years of my life, I thought of little else but cultivation of my intellect.'[6]

Fanny and William Nightingale were as different in character as Florence and her sister. Her mother was socially ambitious; we can see something of her in Jane Austen's Mrs Bennet, always thinking what was to be done for her daughters and how she might best marry them off. She loved the Season in London and parties at big houses in the country. William Nightingale, on the other hand, was happiest on his Derbyshire estate, surrounded by books in his library or out visiting his tenants.

In January 1835, when Florence was almost fifteen, her parents found common purpose when her father decided to stand for Parliament. He seems to have done so out of conviction, not, as was true for so many at the time, because it was something for a gentleman to do. Fanny encouraged him, relishing the prospect of becoming a political hostess, especially with Lord Palmerston, Foreign Secretary and future Prime Minister, as their friend and neighbour. But Florence was unhappy with the prospect, fearing that her father's election would deprive her of her tutor and lead to 'the break-ing up [of] our pleasant country life'.[7] She need not have worried. He was decisively beaten and, however great his interest in politics, never stood again. In the end, it was Florence herself who shattered their calm family existence.

If there was one specific event, one moment that can be pinpointed as having triggered this new discord, it occurred on 7 February 1837. The family were at Embley, their house in the Hampshire New Forest. A 'flu epidemic had swept across southern England that January, and Embley did not escape. The big house resounded, as Fanny Nightingale wrote at the end of the month, to a chorus of coughing. Florence's parents, her nurse and 15 of the servants fell ill. Florence herself was sixteen years old at the time and in her element: she took charge of all the nursing, dispensing various salts, senna tea, saline mixtures, spirits of nitre and fever draughts, as well as doses of the intriguing-sounding Ipecacuanha wine, made from a Brazilian plant with emetic properties. It was, she later wrote, the only 'real activity'[8] she ever had in her childhood.

At the end of the first week of February, as the epidemic passed, something more momentous happened, something she was to celebrate on 7 February each year for the rest of her long life. In a note written years later, she recorded that on this day 'God spoke to me and called me to His service'.[9]

It is impossible to know where she was or what exactly happened when this call came. Some biographers have suggested she was sitting on a bench beneath a cedar in the garden at Embley, but it seems more likely that she was in her bedroom. It is also not clear whether this 'call' was something she heard as an external sound. Later in life, Nightingale was sceptical about the physical apparitions recorded by earlier Christian mystics. So perhaps what she 'heard' was a voice inside her head. Or maybe it was less even than that, nothing more defined than a sense of awakening, a discovery that her life held a purpose only God knew about. Whatever it was, it changed her and their 'pleasant country life' forever.

The change did not come about all at once. She had heard the call and was ready to obey, but God still had not told her what her 'service' to Him should be. The problem Florence Nightingale now faced was how, or where, to discover that.

4

Coming Out

'A woman is continually thwarted. Inert, compliant, she
has to struggle against her physical weakness and legal
subjection' – Gustave Flaubert, *Madame Bovary*

William Nightingale never thought of travelling to Egypt, but in
September 1837 he did take his family south again, this time for
a tour of the Continent. He found travel a chore, but hoped it
might also provide a cure. Of several good reasons he had for
making the journey, one of the most pressing was his need for a
project now that he had given up hope of becoming a politician.
So he devoted himself to the twin tasks of arranging this
extended tour of Europe and planning for Embley to be
transformed in their absence from an unassuming Georgian
house to a large, imposing, neo-Elizabethan mansion with new
kitchens and six extra bedrooms.

Fanny Nightingale had reasons of her own for agreeing to
travel. One of the most important to her, as a mother wishing

to marry her daughters well, was that travel would add to their accomplishments. Parthenope had been presented at court the previous year, but her mother knew that she was not the most beautiful of young women and hoped that a veneer of European glamour would help better her prospects. She also hoped that a spell in the south would improve her daughters' health because, from early childhood, both Florence and Parthenope had suffered colds, chest infections and sore throats, and were bedridden for weeks almost every winter. Parthenope's chest had been so bad the previous February she had had to be bled frequently and there had been the very real possibility that she might not fully recover. A dose of Mediterranean heat would do them all good.

It is on this journey, more than at any other time, that we glimpse how lively and fun-loving the seventeen-year-old Florence could be. She was slender and relatively tall and, according to Lady Palmerston, who knew some of the most beautiful women of the period, she was also extremely feminine. Her ladyship particularly liked the 'graceful way in which her small head was set on her shoulders'.[1] Florence, in other words, had presence. Her mother, who was often her sternest critic, admitted that she was 'much admired for her beauty and . . . is reckoned very clever and amusing'. But Fanny also saw how Florence's 'stately manners keep people at a distance'[2] and, when they came closer, how her wit and intellect often overwhelmed them. The novelist George Eliot, who met Florence in London before the Crimea and fame, found that 'there is a loftiness of mind about her which is well expressed by her form and manners'.[3]

The four Nightingales left England with their old nurse and a French maid. They travelled in their own large carriage but, covering some 35 miles a day, it was a long and tiring journey south. In December they stopped for a while in Nice among a group of British expats who remembered the Nightingales from their honeymoon tour almost 20 years earlier. There was a round of parties and dances to celebrate Christmas and, while Florence still struggled to understand the precise nature of the call she had heard in Embley back in February, she also found time to dance and to complain that there was 'nothing but quadrilles and waltzes . . . alas!'

The following spring and summer the Nightingales were in Italy and the girls were busy with parties, art classes, Italian lessons and musical encounters. Parthenope was the better pianist, but Florence had a passion for music. She loved Mozart, loved dancing at the Grand Duke of Tuscany's ball, and loved opera so much she persuaded her mother to take her several times a week. Later, she wrote that 'if I could have sung, I should have wished for no other satisfaction. Music excited my imagination and my passionate nature so much.'[4]

However much she learned in Italy, whatever influences she picked up – and she became increasingly interested in politics during this journey – there was to be a more formative encounter still for Florence in the autumn, when they reached Paris. There, the Nightingales looked up an Englishwoman long settled in the city and to whom they had an introduction, a Miss Mary Clarke.

Clarke presided over one of the city's most brilliant salons. She had acquired her skills, and some of her reputation, under the guidance of Madame Recamier. The Nightingales met many of the intellectual elite and political establishment of Paris at Clarke's salons, including the medieval scholar Claude Fauriel, whom Clarke adored, the Oriental scholar Julius Mohl, whom she eventually married, and the revered novelist Chateaubriand, whom Flaubert also knew.

Clarke was 28 years older than Florence, but both women recognised that they had much in common. Nightingale respected Clarke for having broken out of the restrictions of her well-to-do English background and found social freedom in the more liberal atmosphere of Paris. They both longed, as Clarke once put it, 'to work for the public good, and have a busy life, instead of sitting by the fire'.[5] Clarke's refusal to conform to the traditional female role, and her inability to stay silent, were an inspiration to her new young friend as she prepared herself for the return to England.

The Nightingales crossed the Channel early in April 1839. They had been away for a year and a half, but the work of remodelling Embley was still not finished, so they went to London for the Season and settled into rooms on Regent Street at the Carlton Hotel.

One day at the beginning of May, around her nineteenth birthday and ten years before her arrival in Egypt, Florence emerged from the Carlton in her finest white Parisian dress. She and her mother stepped into a waiting carriage for the short ride through Green Park to Buckingham Palace.

Florence had had no trouble discussing art and literature in Italy, or politics with the great and the good in Parisian salons. She had been delighted to meet members of the finest families of Europe. But the prospect of an audience with Queen Victoria terrified her. The Queen was just a year older than her and had been on the throne for two years. As Britain's first female ruler for more than a century – and as a young, single woman – she had instantly acquired an aura of regal mystery. No wonder Florence was anxious about the meeting as they drove through the palace gates. But once inside, as she later told her grandmother, she was 'not nearly so much frightened as I expected ... The Queen looked flushed and tired, but the whole sight was very pretty.'[6]

The palace visits – they attended a second audience, 'the Queen's birthday drawing room', on 19 May – and the events that surrounded them, confirmed the arrival in society of the Nightingales' younger daughter. Florence was bright, attractive and sophisticated. She shone at court and, as far as her mother was concerned, had brilliant prospects as a bride. Unlike twenty-year-old Parthenope, who had failed to attract a single proposal of marriage, Florence had no shortage of suitors.

That summer, Mary Clarke went to stay at Lea Hurst, the Nightingales' home near the River Derwent in Derbyshire. Parthenope later remembered her as:

[A]lways bright, lively, and witty, without effort, very keen yet full of kindly sympathies, interested in everything (except gossip, which she could not 'abide'); reading all the new books, of which there were many, at my father's house, or, if there were none she fancied, burying herself in Montaigne, Horace Walpole, Thiébault's *Frederick the Great*, etc. I can see her now, lying curled up in a great armchair, or in a corner of the sofa, with a large quarto on her knees.[7]

Nightingale's cousin Henry Nicholson was also a regular visitor at Lea Hurst. A year older than Florence, reading maths at Trinity College, Cambridge, he eventually sounded her out on the prospect of marriage. She did not respond. A more direct proposal came from Marmaduke Wyvill. The Nightingales had met the Wyvills, a prominent Yorkshire family, during the Christmas they spent in Nice. Now that Florence had 'come out', Marmaduke wrote asking her to confide herself 'to my care'.[8] Wyvill's intention to become her 'protector and guardian' suggests that he understood even less about the nature of the woman he claimed to love than he did about her 'manner & looks': he was convinced she looked at him with affection, but she confessed to feeling nothing more than pity for him.

What Wyvill had failed to understand was that Florence was not looking for a guardian or protector and that she objected to the unequal nature of most marriages. 'To her [the wife],' she wrote in 1846, 'marriage is *the* thing, while to the husband it is only *one* of the things which form his life.'[9] If there were ever to be a husband, he would need to allow this determined young woman to have something other than her marriage in her life. He would have to give her the freedom to follow her calling. Maybe he would even have to share it with her. At a time when her calling was still vaguely formed and the idea of following it, whatever it was, seemed an impossibility, how could she even think of accepting a marriage proposal?

Florence Nightingale's early nursing experiences are enveloped in myth but they include her bandaging dolls and caring for injured dogs and sick relatives. In early 1837 she had nursed the family and household through the 'flu epidemic. She was only too happy to leave home to comfort ailing friends and relatives, and she attended the deathbeds of tenants throughout her teenage years. But in her twenties, with her education complete, she needed something more important and fulfilling to do.

Nightingale seems to have reached some loose definition of her calling while still in her early twenties. During those first years of the 1840s, Britain was hit by a severe economic crisis and, even in Florence's enclosed world, there was no way of ignoring the effects of the downturn. The Nightingale household might not itself have felt the pinch, but people in the villages around their estates were suffering. Florence sympathised with their problems. In the summer of 1842 she wrote that, 'All that poets sing of the glories of this world seems to me untrue. All the people I see are eaten up with care or poverty or disease.'[10] She decided to do something to help and now believed that she understood her calling: she would train to become a nurse.

It was an impulse that she thought ought to have been applauded by her family and friends. After all, it was expected that a young woman of her status should show some interest in those who were less fortunate. But there was a huge difference between supporting charitable causes or visiting poor retainers on one's estate, as her mother and sister did, and actually caring for the sick oneself. Nursing was not considered a suitable activity for a young lady; nursing in a hospital, as Florence was hoping to do, was simply unthinkable.

There were several reasons for this, but the most obvious one, in an age when appearances were so important, was that nurses had a reputation for drunkenness and promiscuity. A head nurse at London's Westminster Hospital would later tell Nightingale that 'she had never known a nurse who was not drunken, and that there was *immoral* conduct practised within the very walls of the ward'.[11] And while that was doubtless an exaggeration, it was not entirely untrue: there was drinking in hospitals, and there was also the problem of having female nurses obliged to stay overnight in a building occupied by male doctors and patients. Undesirable things did happen. But then nurses and hospitals performed a very different function in the 1840s from the one they fulfil today.

Women of Nightingale's class were unlikely ever to have entered a hospital. However sick they became, they were most likely to be treated at home. The poor also were nursed at home, as Nightingale had seen in the villages around Embley and Lea Hurst. Only in extreme cases were they taken to an infirmary or hospital, and then only when recommended by someone attached to the institution. Once there, they would be seen by a trained doctor. Most nurses had little or no training and were treated no better than domestic servants, which would have seemed appropriate at the time as their job mostly involved cleaning both patients and wards. The Nightingales had raised Florence to be accomplished and educated. She had met the Queen, seen some of the glories of Western civilisation, and been welcomed into some of the finest houses in Europe. If she were going to be of use to the world, her family argued, surely she could do something more appropriate to her station than dressing wounds and cleaning bedpans?

Among the many guests who stayed at Embley in the summer of 1844 were a couple of newly-weds from Boston, Dr and Mrs Samuel Howe. Mrs Howe – Julia Ward Howe – was later to become known for an unlikely combination of achievements: she was an early women's rights activist and the author of 'The Battle Hymn of the Republic', with its rallying cry to 'die to make men free'. In 1844, however, it was the doctor, not his wife, who interested Miss Florence more, for he was director of the Perkins Institution and State School for the Blind, whose annual reports she had already read.

One evening during their stay, Nightingale asked for a moment alone with Dr Howe in the library. Although there is no reference to this among her own papers, according to Howe, she asked him whether 'it would be unsuitable and unbecoming for a young Englishwoman to devote herself to works of charity in hospitals?'[12]

'My dear Miss Florence,' Howe apparently replied, 'it would be unusual, and in England whatever is unusual is apt to be thought unsuitable; but I say to you, go forward if you have a vocation for that way of life; act up to your inspiration, and you will find that there is never anything unbecoming or unladylike in doing your duty for the good of others. Choose, go on with it wherever it may lead you, and God be with you.'[13]

The following month, Nightingale forced the issue with her

parents. The catalyst was the arrival at Embley of the elderly Dr Richard Fowler and his wife. Fowler was a physician at the nearby Salisbury Infirmary. Nightingale found him a kindred spirit: she described him as a man 'who seems to finish all your half-formed thoughts for you'.[14] While the doctor was at Embley, Florence raised the idea of studying nursing at Fowler's infirmary, a mere 13 miles from home. Her parents objected, of course, for the familiar reason that it would be improper for Florence to associate with nurses. Mrs Fowler agreed with her parents and, to Florence's dismay, Dr Fowler stayed silent. Why? Because, Mrs Fowler explained, nurses came from a very different background and they would feel uncomfortable to have her working among them, even if Florence did not.

Two months later she tried again, writing to ask her father's permission to spend a few months in Dublin at St Vincent's, a hospital run by the Sisters of Charity. Surely, she wrote, 'there would not be the same objections as in an English hospital'.[15] In Dublin, no one need know who she was or where she came from. But if he could not give his permission, she assured him, 'I had rather know it at once, & then, let us never speak on this subject again.' The answer, as she must have expected, remained no.

Unable to persuade her parents and Parthenope out of their objections, Florence stuck to her promise. Or at least, if she did speak of it, she only did so when it was absolutely necessary. And she refrained from asking questions to which she knew the answer would be negative.

By October 1846, twenty-six years old and single – *available* as far as her parents were concerned – she was up-to-date with the latest developments in maths and other sciences and buzzing with ideas of her own. She devoured whatever she could find to read about advances in medicine and institutional care, and she heard first-hand about the latest political issues from the Palmerstons and other family friends. It was now also almost ten years since she had received her calling and she despaired of ever realising her ambition. It is hard for us now to understand the restrictions she lived under. But as a single woman, even at twenty-six she was bound by her parents' decisions and, without any legal rights or financial independence, simply could not leave home.

Ada Lovelace, Lord Byron's daughter, was among the many who fell for Florence's charms during this time; she marvelled at her 'soft and silver voice', 'her grave and lucid eye'.[16] A drawing by a Nightingale cousin, Hilary Bonham-Carter, captures the attraction: viewed from close up, sideways on, while looking down, her brown hair is pulled into a small bun at the nape of her neck, those 'grave and lucid' eyes are averted, brows pencil-fine, the nose strong, lips slightly pouting.

A more significant meeting for Nightingale that month was with Chevalier Bunsen, the German Ambassador to London, who was also a philanthropist and Egyptologist. With poverty a growing problem, with more suffering in the villages near her homes, with the potato famine killing thousands in Ireland, she opened those brown eyes in supplication and asked him, 'What can an individual do towards lifting the load of suffering from the helpless and miserable?'[17]

Bunsen's answer has not survived, nor has Nightingale's immediate response to it, but she must have known what he would say. Like Dr Samuel Howe, he encouraged her. Four months earlier, in June, she had gone to London to visit his new German Hospital in London's East End. This appears to have been the first time she stepped inside such a place. It was also the first time she met the people who were to have such a profound effect on her life: the hospital was staffed by Lutheran deaconesses from the Institution of Kaiserwerth in Germany.

In October, Bunsen sent Nightingale something he thought might help her to find a way forward. It was the Kaiserwerth Institution's yearbook, and he was right. She thought it was the answer she had been looking for, a vital clue to the mystery of her calling, and for a while at least it worked as an antidote to the busy emptiness of social life at Embley, a 'refreshment in the midst of this table d'hôte of people'. On 7 October she wrote a private note: 'There [in Kaiserwerth] is my home, there are my brothers and sisters at work. There my heart is and there, I trust, will one day be my body.'[18] She still had years – and many trials – before she got there.

One of the repeat visitors among the Embley 'table d'hôte' was Richard Monckton Milnes, who came to stay three times that summer. The Nightingales had first met him when he was a guest of the Palmerstons. Milnes, then thirty-three years old, was Tory MP for Pontefract and also a poet with several volumes in print. Lord Palmerston, then fifty-eight years old and having recently lost the post of Foreign Secretary, clearly thought more of Milnes' writing than his politics because the invitation to William Nightingale was to 'help us to entertain the poet'.[19]

The dinner was a success and Fanny Nightingale noted that 'we all liked him'.[20] Among the conversation, there was, no doubt, talk of the journey to Cairo that Milnes was about to make. Over the next couple of years, he became a regular visitor to the Nightingale household and, although the entire family was delighted by his wit and entertained by his humour, it was for Miss Florence that he shone. She called him 'the poetic parcel'.[21]

He was a scientific parcel as well, and in this, as in many other things, they found a common interest. Around this time, Milnes joined the Nightingales at Southampton for a meeting of the British Association for the Advancement of

Science. It was the first of several such outings they shared. At another Association meeting, in Oxford the following June, Florence, her father and her suitor went to lunch at Christ Church with a don who kept a tame bear cub in his rooms. Florence was charmed as it 'climbed like a squirrel for the butter on the table'.[22] When the bear became aggressive, it was taken into the garden. 'When we came out,' she wrote to Mary Clarke, 'it was still walking and storming and howling on its hind legs – gesticulating and remonstrating. I spoke to it but Papa pulled me away, fearing it would bite. I said, "Let alone, I'm going to mesmerise it." Mr Milnes followed the suggestion and in ½ minute the little bear began to yawn, in less than 3 min. was stretched fast asleep on the gravel.'[23] Nightingale pressed a white rose, which she kept as a reminder of those happy days. When exactly Monckton Milnes first raised the subject of marriage is not clear, but it may have been in Oxford that summer.

A wedding between her younger daughter and the eminent and eligible Mr Richard Monckton Milnes of Fryston Hall in Yorkshire was exactly the sort of match of which Fanny Nightingale had dreamed. He was a man of fortune, although of course she wanted more than money for her daughter. She had read Milnes' speeches to Parliament and his volumes of poetry, and was certain that he was a poet with a following and politician with a future. (She was right in that; he was later created Lord Houghton for his political work.) He was also one of London's most active socialites. A friend of Tennyson and Alexander Kinglake, he gave Pall Mall breakfasts that were famous for their mix of the elevated and the unexpected; Thomas Carlyle joked that if Jesus were to arrive in London, his first invitation would be to Milnes' breakfast table. So what if he outraged opinion from time to time? The Nightingales were sufficiently worldly to bear a little scandal, and Fanny

Nightingale could see that marriage to Milnes would put her Florence right at the centre of British political and artistic life.

Her daughter stalled. Her issue was not with the man. She admired his mind, enjoyed his company, and later would refer to him as 'the man I adored'. Her objection, as ever, was to the role of women in the institution of marriage. Being married would give her no more freedom than she had at the present time, for she would merely swap one set of constraints and obligations for another. If she married, the legal and financial responsibility for her care would pass from her parents to her husband. And yet, if there were to be a husband, Milnes would do very well indeed . . . She continued to play for time while she weighed up the possibilities.

For as long Milnes persisted in his affection – and his proposal – Nightingale continued to dream that there might be a way to be married to him *and* to fulfil her calling. 'He had,' she wrote later, 'the genius of friendship in philanthropy.'[24] She also knew that she brought out the best in him, for he had confided to her that 'if there is any good in me, it is that I would lay out my life in good service to others'. But would he give up some of his other life, his famous breakfasts, his endless socialising, to join her in answering her call? She must have realised that that would never happen: that she would be mistress of his table more than he would be her co-worker; that she would have to organise big gatherings for breakfast and dinner in London during the Season and in the country during the summer; that she would spend time counting linen and silver when she wanted to be out in the world.

Gustave Flaubert's description of the social constraints on Madame Bovary sums up her dilemma: 'A man is free, at least – free to range the passions and the world, to surmount obstacles, to taste the rarest pleasures. Whereas a woman is continually thwarted. Inert, compliant, she has to struggle against her physical weakness and legal subjection. Her will, like the veil tied to her hat, quivers with every breeze.'[25]

With hindsight, to imagine Nightingale as mistress of Fryston, a large, pedimented white-stone mansion, is to recognise the impossibility of the union. At the time, however, the matter was not so clear-cut. But then, after those happy days spent in Oxford with Milnes, Nightingale received news from Paris of a marriage that gave her pause for thought.

Mary Clarke had always struck Nightingale as an unfettered character who made her own dreams seem possible. Clarke, who was now long past fifty, had achieved both social and financial independence, and was absorbed in the political and intellectual lives of her adopted city. All that, and still single.

This latter situation was not entirely of her choosing: she had long been in love with the brilliant medieval scholar Claude Fauriel. But Fauriel was significantly older than herself and not the marrying kind. In the spring of 1847, less than three years after his death, Clarke proposed marriage to his confidant, Julius Mohl, 16 years younger than herself. In spite of her unconventionality, she was still concerned about what people would think of this age difference, so much so that she went to great lengths to conceal the event. When she left home on her wedding day, not even her maid knew that she was going to be married. When the official conducting the ceremony asked her age, she refused to reply. When he persisted, she told him, 'Sir, if you insist [on knowing], I will throw myself out of the window.'[26]

Nightingale was shaken by the news of Clarke's marriage. 'We must all take Sappho's leap,' she wrote to Paris on hearing what she had done, 'though some take it to death, and some to marriage, and some again to a new life even in this world.'[27] Suicide, marriage to Milnes or 'a new life even in this world': it was still uncertain which way Nightingale would go, and the struggle to reach a decision led to constant conflict with her parents and sister, who despaired at her prevarication with Milnes. As the family settled into Embley for the winter, Nightingale wrote to Clarke that she dreaded 'the prospect of three winter months of perpetual row'. She broke down under the strain, and took to her bed.

The previous autumn, around the time that Baron Bunsen had sent the Kaiserwerth yearbook and just as her relationship with Milnes was becoming more serious, there had been a third change in Florence's prospects: Mary Clarke had introduced her to Selina and Charles Bracebridge, a couple who were to play a decisive role in her calling.

Charles Bracebridge was the last surviving male of a family that traced its origins back 800 years to Lady Godiva and the Earls of Mercia. He was the sort of country gentleman who busied himself with minor political and literary pursuits. Most of this was accomplished in the form of pamphlets and letters to newspapers, although he did occasionally go further, as when he claimed that George Eliot had drawn some material in her novel *Adam Bede* from the writings of a man called Joseph Liggins and some from real-life characters. He even went so far as to travel to Staffordshire to identify the real people behind the fictional ones. Eliot first described him as 'a kind-hearted, patronizing man – of wealth and old family – who once tried to make a figure politically (as a liberal) in his county and succeeded – only the figure was a poor one'.[28] In that she was correct, for he rose no higher than Justice of the Peace. But as his campaign against her continued, so she was forced to revise her opinion of him, deciding that he was 'so nearly an idiot, that it would not be safe to predict his mental processes'.[29]

He had married Selina Mills, a young woman who had

already attracted attention as an artist. She was particularly good at capturing town scenes and at precise architectural detailing, good enough for her work now to be in the collections of London's Victoria & Albert Museum and the Birmingham Museum and Art Gallery. Unable to have children, the Bracebridges devoted themselves to travelling in Europe and to maintaining the family seat at Atherstone Hall in Warwickshire. There was a period when they spent a considerable amount of time in Greece: Bracebridge had been a passionate supporter of the Greek independence movement and had owned a large estate on the island of Evvia, although he had sold it by the time he met the Nightingales.

The Bracebridges did not take long to realise that Florence needed saving, though whether from herself or from her family was not immediately clear to them. Unlike almost everyone else in the Nightingale circle, the Bracebridges had no children and no concerns or pressing projects to occupy them, and consequently had both the time and the inclination to help. Mrs Bracebridge had already taken Nightingale to visit the museum of the Royal College of Surgeons in London and a workhouse near Atherstone. Now, to help defuse the tension building during that autumn of 1847, she suggested to Fanny Nightingale that Florence should join them on a three-month tour of Italy.

The Nightingales took their time considering the proposal. Parthenope had been sickly and was in need of winter sun, so should by rights have been the one to travel, but the Bracebridges had not invited her. When, eventually, it was agreed that Florence might go, she unexpectedly hesitated. It wasn't that she didn't want to go. She loved Italy, the country of her birth. But she recognised that there was an implicit condition attached to her going: her family were hoping she would come home 'cured' of her follies and ready to marry Milnes. She prevaricated over this, as she had over Milnes himself, and only finally decided to go a week before departure.

This was the first long journey she would make without her family, the first Christmas and New Year spent away from them. The Nightingales arranged for their daughters to spend a couple of days alone together at the house before she left. 'It seems to me a very great event,' Parthenope wrote as she helped Florence prepare for the journey, 'the solemn first launching of her into life, and my heart is very full.'[30]

A couple of weeks later, installed in the Hotel Meurice in Paris with the Bracebridges and her French maid, Mariette, Nightingale rushed off to see Mary Mohl, keen to discover whether marriage suited her friend. The eccentric dress sense hadn't changed: she found Mary wearing 'something that looked like part of an old clean duster',[31] with her hair as matted as the coat of the Nightingales' dog. But, thus far, marriage appeared to have suited her. 'Good kind God of Hymen,' Nightingale wrote home, 'how much thou hast done for her mentally, happy she is.'[32]

Good kind God of Travel, how happy Nightingale was as well! Much of that was due to Selina Bracebridge. 'I wonder whether she knows what a difference she has made in my life,' Nightingale confided to her diary. 'The very fact of there being a person with whom one's thoughts are not pronounced fit only for a dream not worth disputing, who does not look upon one as a fanciful spoiled child who ought to take life as it is and enjoy it – that mere fact changes the whole aspect of things.'[33] There was also the fact that she was as stimulated by the sights of Rome as she was by seeing her friends in Paris.

Her letters from Rome buzz with excitement. She described their approach to the Eternal City in a vivid letter home:

I looked out every five minutes to see the lights of the city on the hill, but in vain. The earth was sending forth her fragrance of night like an incense to heaven, for the Campagna is covered with thyme – the stars were all out – there was a solemn silence, not a trace of habitation, all desert solitude, and we were feverish and very tired . . . At last, without the least preparation, not a house, not a suburb, we knocked at a little gate . . . just a little stop during which I heard the sound of the fountains of St Peter's, softly plashing in the stillness of night, and in a moment we were passing the colonnades slowly *au petit pas*. I saw the Obelisk, the Dome, the Vatican, dimly glooming in the twilight, then the Angel of the Last Judgment.[34]

If the first night was full of potent suggestion, the following months were just as charged. They had planned to be away for three months but ended up staying more than four in Rome, and for much of that time the city was in political turmoil as the Pope encouraged an uprising against Austrian occupation. From the Farnese to the Borghese, the Vatican to St Peter's, the Pantheon to the Colosseum, Nightingale was as diligent, as thoughtful and as descriptive as any visitor before or since. She conjured up the sacred fire in the Temple of Vesta at Tivoli and spent a whole day together with Selina Bracebridge in the Sistine Chapel, quite alone, without a *cicerone* or any other visitors present. She rejoiced in everything she saw and had the literary skill to describe it vividly to her family at home. As the political turmoil worsened and people took to the streets, 'your own Correspondent'[35] reported what she saw, with an eye and a pen as lively as that of any Fleet Street hack. On her second full day in the city, she saw the rebellious Pope Pius IX. 'He turned round so gracefully to give us his blessing, not too much and yet quite in earnest, just what a blessing ought to be.'[36]

The sights were wonderful and the events exciting, but it was the people she met in Rome who made the biggest impression. The first was Sidney Herbert, a man of Nightingale's own age who seemed blessed in every way. He had fortune, intellect, wit, good looks and a beautiful wife. Until the previous year, he had been Secretary at War in Sir Robert Peel's government. Nightingale met him within a couple of weeks of her arrival in Rome 'and really,' she wrote to her mother, 'if I were not afraid of being laughed at, I should say [he was] so artless, so full of fun, and so little like a man of the world'.[37] His wife Liz she described as being 'like the sunshine of Italy . . . pure in understanding as well as heart'.[38] The trio took an instant liking to each other and began a friendship that was to mature into a key working relationship: Herbert was back in power at the War Office in 1854 when the Crimean War broke out and it would be he who asked Nightingale to lead a team of nurses to Scutari.

But here, in Rome, it was Liz Herbert who had the greater influence on her. In January 1848, Mr Bracebridge hurt himself falling down the stairs of their palazzo and it was decided that they would stay in the city until Easter. Those extra weeks gave Nightingale time to visit orphanages and convents with Liz Herbert. She thought the French orders most successful, both the Sisters of St-Vincent-de-Paul, whom she was to meet in Alexandria, and the Sisters of the Sacré Coeur, who ran three separate institutions for Rome's poor and homeless. 'There was no impression about this place,' she remembered, 'but of cheerfulness and cleanliness.'[39] It was here that she had her second significant meeting.

One day, while visiting St Peter's, Nightingale started talking to a young girl. Her name was Felicetta Senzi and she was an orphan. Nightingale decided to 'do something' for the unfortunate and arranged for her to be educated at the Sacré Coeur orphanage at the top of the Spanish Steps. On 17 February she wrote telling her parents that she had been to the orphanage because she 'had a little matter of business to settle'.[40] It turned out to be more than a little matter. While arranging payment for Felicetta's schooling – £5 a year, to be saved from Nightingale's dress allowance – she met Laure de Sainte Colombe, the superior in charge of admissions. Sainte Colombe suggested that Nightingale make a retreat in the convent. 'The women of the world in Rome all make *retraites*, generally once a year,'[41] she blithely told her family. She had agreed to spend ten days there.

Nightingale described Sainte Colombe as a warm, plump, jolly, rather plebeian Frenchwoman.[42] She seems to have been somewhat plebeian in thought as well as appearance, for she failed to grasp the complexity, the intelligence and the vulnerability of the young Englishwoman in her care. That did not stop her from having a dramatic effect on Nightingale's life.

At some point during her retreat, she told Sainte Colombe about the call she had had from God and about her 12-year struggle with her family. The sister, whom Nightingale referred to as her *madre*, tried to reassure her. 'What does it matter even if we are with people who make us desperate? So long as we are doing God's will, it doesn't matter at all.'[43] But the words that were to have the greatest effect were not spoken until several days later. As Nightingale was preparing to leave the convent, her *madre* warned her that God 'calls you to a very high degree of perfection. Take care. If you resist you will be very guilty.'[44]

Life was never the same for her after Rome. Strengthened by her friendships with the Bracebridges and the Herberts, spurred on by her *madre*'s call to perfection, Nightingale felt strong enough to face renewed difficulties at home during the summer of 1848. While the family engaged in their usual round of entertaining up north at Lea Hurst, Florence absented herself. Her campaign to do something useful had resulted in her being allowed to spend some hours each week teaching at the local school. She was also allowed to go by herself to visit the Bracebridges at Atherstone.

But as Florence's well-being increased, Parthenope weakened. Her ill health seemed increasingly linked to her sister's absences, as if by taking to her bed in response to these she was trying to exert control over Florence. Whatever the truth, she was so frail by September that her physician ordered her to take the waters at Carlsbad in Germany. The whole family prepared to travel, cheered by the news that Mary Mohl and her new husband would be staying nearby. Florence was especially excited by the prospect of visiting Germany, of seeing Mohl again, and especially by the hope that she would be allowed to slip away for a few days to visit the Deaconesses' Institution at Kaiserwerth near Carlsbad.

So close to realising her dream of learning something about nursing, Nightingale saw her plans overturned by the same political upheaval that had characterised her stay in Rome the previous year: 1848 was a year of uprising and revolution across much of Europe, and Germany did not escape the chaos. When William Nightingale read about riots in Carlsbad, he cancelled their trip. They would instead take the waters at Malvern.

Nightingale was close to despair: 'I cannot go on any longer waiting till my situation should change.'[45] There were several letters from Richard Monckton Milnes waiting for her on her return from Malvern. With her *madre*'s advice about not cutting herself off from her people fresh in her mind, Milnes' proposal must have looked even more attractive. But not everyone approved of him. Mrs Nightingale's childhood friend Fanny Allen wrote, 'I hope Mrs Nightingale does not bother her daughter to accept of Monckton Milnes. He is not worthy of her.'[46]

The reason for this sudden re-evaluation of Milnes' status was a book he had just published on the Romantic poet John Keats. Keats had been much maligned since his death in 1821, for his 'unmanly' behaviour (a synonym for homosexuality) and for his beliefs: it was rumoured that he was a pagan. In his book, Milnes insisted that Keats was a 'misapprehended . . . wayward, erratic genius'.[47] To present the man in a different light, he collected Keats's work and letters and wrote the first biography of the poet. *The Life, Letters and Literary Remains of John Keats* divided literary opinion. Some rejoiced in re-discovering a hero; others thought Milnes' championing of him misguided. 'Making curry of a dead dog' was the damning verdict of Thomas Carlyle.

Mrs Allen clearly sided with Carlyle. 'Have you seen his life of Keats?' she mocked. One 'never knew what religion [Milnes] was of', but now one expected 'to find an altar to Jupiter somewhere in his house'.[48] She was no kinder about his appearance. 'Lively and pleasant' it may be, but he was also 'plain and common-looking', his long brown hair thinning and his belly dropped. The American writer Ralph Waldo Emerson agreed that he was 'fat, easy, affable and obliging; a little careless and slovenly in his dress', but also that he was a man of 'good humour' and 'very liberal of his money'.[49]

Neither her friend's disapproval nor the prospect of having as a son-in-law the first Englishman known to have entered an Eastern harem was enough to deter Mrs Nightingale. Nor was the fact that her elder daughter was still unmarried. Hopes of finding a husband for thirty-year-old Parthe were increasingly remote; a wedding between her younger daughter and the eminent and eligible Milnes would have delighted Fanny.

In fact, it would most probably have been a disastrous union. Lady Ashburton, who knew Milnes well, thought that what he really wanted was 'a Strasbourg goose whom you will always find by the fireside when you come home from amusing yourself'.[50] Nightingale was no goose. And even if Lady Ashburton were wrong, a man with such an appetite for socialising would never be converted to Nightingale's longing for an ascetic life. Nor is it clear how she would have reacted had she discovered that he was one of the great pornographers of the age. He was particularly fascinated by the works of the Marquis de Sade, which he kept in his so-called 'Aphrodisiopolis'. One friend who had been allowed into his sanctuary thought his collection was 'unrivalled upon earth, unequalled I should imagine in heaven'.[51] Nor are his sexual preferences clear; some biographers believe him to have been homosexual. What is certain is that, following in de Sade's footsteps, he was sexually adventurous. The verdict of *The Dictionary of National Biography* seems to come closest when it calls him a man with 'many fine tastes and some crude ones'.[52] However successful their meeting of minds, a physical union between Milnes and Florence Nightingale would have been much more problematic.

The situation dragged on until the summer of 1849. As they did every June, the Nightingales threw a party at Embley to announce their departure for the north. Milnes was there and appears to have pressed Nightingale for a decision. There is no record of what passed between them, but it seems that she prevaricated. In his eagerness to have the matter settled, and to be married, Milnes took this as outright rejection.

But even then the story wasn't finished for, whatever he believed, Nightingale was clearly under the illusion that his offer to her remained open. Eighteen months later, on

Christmas Eve, she weighed the pros and cons in a private note: 'I have an intellectual nature which requires satisfaction, & that would find it in him. I have a passional [*sic*] nature which requires satisfaction, & that would find it in him. I have a moral and active nature that requires satisfaction, & that would not find it in his life. I can hardly find satisfaction for any of my natures. Sometimes I think I will satisfy my passional nature at all events.'[53]

And yet the problem remained: how to secure her freedom so that she could answer her calling? She still hoped it would be possible as mistress of Fryston Hall. She knew that Milnes was intelligent, caring and loving enough to understand her calling. If they could work together to mesmerise a bear, what else might they achieve? 'I could be satisfied to spend a life with him combining our different powers in some great object,' her note continued. 'I could not satisfy this nature by spending a life with him in making society & arranging domestic things.'[54] Of this last point, she was convinced: 'I know I could not bear his life, that to be nailed to a continuation, an exaggeration of my present life without hope of another would be intolerable to me – that voluntarily to put it out of my power ever to be able to seize the chance of forming for myself a true and rich life would seem to me like suicide.'[55]

Later, with hindsight, she must have recognised the impossibility of reconciling her needs to his desires. Milnes also saw the light: in 1862, when she was famous as the Angel of the Crimea and he was about to be given a peerage, the future Lord Houghton happened to stay at Lea Hurst and wrote in his diary, 'Fourteen years ago I asked her to marry me: if she had done so there would have been a heroine the less in the world & certainly not a hero the more.'[56]

Her parents and sister, however, were outraged that she had

apparently rejected his offer of marriage, and her social circle was amazed. There was no other likely suitor, and even if there were, what chance would there be that she would accept a proposal from someone else, having already turned down a prospect like Milnes?

Again the Bracebridges stepped in with a solution. They were going to Egypt for the winter and would visit Greece and Italy on the way home. Travel might help to broaden their friend's mind and ease her sorrows, as it had done before. Why not take her with them?

Her parents' decision wasn't easy to make. Again there was her sister to consider: Florence had been to Italy only two years before, so if anyone were to travel, it should have been Parthenope. There was the cost, too, which was considerable, even for a wealthy family. But there was also the rejection of Milnes to take into account; it would do Florence and everyone else good to put it out of their minds for a while. Arguments and counter-arguments were put forward. Then, finally, Mrs Nightingale wrote, 'We have talked & talked day & a night, dear Mrs Bracebridge, & are come to the decision that if you will take our dear child, for better for worse . . . she shall be yours.'[57] So this was how she came to be gliding towards Cairo in November 1849 on the *Marchioness of Breadalbane*.

What did she think about as the stars shone bright and the bugs bit, while Selina Bracebridge and Trautwein dozed beside her and Monsieur Flaubert dreamed of Cleopatra on the upper deck? She still cherished the thought of Milnes, and regretted the marriage she had given up. For what? She was not sure. One thing she was sure of were her feelings towards him. 'I know that if I were to see him again . . . ' she admitted to herself, at least, '. . . the very thought of doing so quite overcomes me. I know that since I refused him not one day has passed without my thinking of him, that life is desolate without his sympathy.'[58] Desolate, perhaps, but not without its distractions.

Dawn broke, and the pyramids appeared on the horizon.

5

Rabbit Stew

'To write Orientales without having visited the East is like making a rabbit stew without the rabbit' – Chevalier Jaubert to Maxime Du Camp, *Literary Recollections*, Vol. 1

On 14 September 1833, a cargo boat tied up at Rouen's Harcourt quay. The *Louxor* had left the Nile some two years earlier, carrying one of the largest pieces of stonework ever transported from Egypt.

For more than 3,000 years, the obelisk of Ramses II had stood in front of the temple the pharaoh had built beside the Nile at Luxor. Now the 25-metre-high block of granite was on its way to Paris, to the Place de la Concorde, as a symbol of French colonial power. But the Seine was low and the barge would not be able to move until the autumn rains began. While its crew waited, the people of Rouen watched and wondered and talked of little else. Among them was an eleven-year-old schoolboy: Gustave Flaubert.

Twelve years later, in May 1845, while Florence Nightingale was fighting her family for the right to study nursing, this same Flaubert was in Genoa, in the picture gallery of the Palazzo Balbi-Senarega. In front of him was a painting of *The Temptation of Saint Anthony* by Bruegel the Elder. The young man stood for so long in front of the old image that his sister and brother-in-law began to worry about him. All that Flaubert worried about at this stage of his life was how he would write something memorable, a book that would make the world pay attention to his talent.

A few days later he wrote from Milan to his literary confidant, Alfred le Poittevin, 'I am still turning over the idea of my Oriental tale. I saw a painting of Breughel representing *The Temptation of Saint Anthony*, which made me think of arranging [it] for the theatre.'[1] Meanwhile, he dreamed of travelling to the East.

Five years after Genoa and that impulse to write about an Egyptian hermit, and sixteen after the obelisk was delayed in Rouen harbour, Flaubert was in Luxor standing in front of Ramses' temple. As he looked at the empty pedestal from which the obelisk had been removed, he imagined the column on its plinth in Paris, being driven around by the carriages of fashionable Parisians, bored and longing to escape to the Nile.

This dream of a journey to Egypt, and perhaps also of 'my Oriental tale', had first taken shape when the *Louxor* tied up to the Rouen quayside. It was embroidered over the following years until it became a longing that he was compelled to fulfil. The path that led Flaubert to Egypt and a boat cutting through the waters of the Nile towards Cairo was less tortured than Florence Nightingale's, but no more direct.

The Orient had never been as fashionable in France as it was in the autumn of 1833. Over the previous 40 years, French might and French ingenuity had achieved many remarkable things in relation to Egypt, including Napoleon's invasion, the finding of the Rosetta Stone, the creation of the Louvre's stunning Egyptian galleries, publication of the massive collaborative work of scholarship, the *Description de l'Égypte*, and the deciphering of hieroglyphs. But there had never been anything so monumentally triumphant as the transportation of this ancient sculpted stone up the Seine.

The schoolboy who stood watching it was the younger son of a surgeon from Rouen. From an early age, Gustave Flaubert had wanted to write. There was no single moment to pinpoint, no sudden Nightingale-like revelation that this was to be his calling. He was a gifted but ill-disciplined student; a dreamer whose thoughts continuously trailed through a mythical Orient. His first precocious stories celebrated a fantastic land 'with its burning sun, its blue sky, its golden minarets . . . its caravans in the sand; the Orient! with its harems . . . '[2] In December 1836, when those words appeared in a local review, he was fifteen years old and had travelled no further south than northern France, yet his mind was filled with 'white-winged angels who sing verses of the Koran in the Prophet's ears'.

It was no passing fad. In *Memoirs of a Fool*, written two years later, he dreamed of travels far to the south: 'I saw the Orient and its immense sands, its palaces trampled by the camels with their small bronze bells . . . I saw blue waves, a pure sky, silver sand.' He also saw 'women, their brown skin, their fiery look, who speak to me in the language of *houris*'.[3]

Life, meanwhile, was more prosaic. There was school and schoolwork, fun and literary games, good times with friends and with his younger sister Caroline. He seems to have had little in common with his elder brother, Achille, who thought Gustave was gifted but lazy. To celebrate passing his *bac* in the summer of 1840, his parents sent him south to the Pyrenees, the Mediterranean, Corsica. In Marseille, on rue de la Darse, a street up from the port, he had his first overwhelming love affair. The object of his desire was Eulalie Foucauld, an older, married woman who ran the Hotel Richelieu and who was obviously pleased by the attentions of her young lover, for she sent him passionate letters for some time after their affair. The people of Marseille, he would later write in his *Dictionary of Received Ideas*, are 'all great wits'.[4]

Back in Rouen, his Eastern longings continued. On 25 January 1841, he wrote in his diary, 'Today my ideas of a great journey are stronger than ever. It's the Orient, as ever. I was born to live there. Opening a random page in the *Itineraire ABC*, I saw: "A third (a French soldier who stayed on in Egypt and became a Mamluk), a tall young man, thin and pale, had lived many years in the desert among the Bedouin, and he particularly missed that life; he told me that when he found himself alone in the sands on his camel, he was transported by a joy beyond his control." I thought about that for a long time. When I think of it, I would like each day more to fall into the ecstasy of the Alexandrians . . . '[5]

The Alexandrians and their ecstasies would have to wait. In November 1841, the eighteen-year-old went to study law in Paris, where he met Maxime Du Camp who later remembered being impressed by his new friend's imposing appearance. 'With his fair skin and delicate colouring, his soft, flowing hair, his broad-shouldered, tall figure, full beard of pale gold, large eyes grey as the sea, shaded by black eyebrows, his voice like a trumpet, his violent gestures and resounding laughter, he was like one of those young Gallic chieftains who resisted the advance of the Roman legions.'[6]

The 'chieftain' then spent four years studying law and writing stories, and probably expected his life to continue along those lines, but everything changed for him suddenly. During the holiday of Christmas and New Year 1844–5, which

Florence Nightingale spent ill at home in Hampshire, Flaubert went home to Rouen and collapsed. Epilepsy was suspected, although neither his father nor colleagues at Rouen Hospital were happy with that diagnosis. Nor was Flaubert. He talked of being engulfed in flames and blamed the attack on a combination of the visions of 'Saint Theresa, Hoffmann, and Edgar Poe'.[7]

'My illness,' he wrote in the weeks after that first attack, 'has the advantage that I am left to occupy myself as I wish, which is a great thing in life. I can see nothing better in the world for me than a nice, well-heated room with the books I love and the leisure to enjoy them.'[8] The leisure also to write: he was working on a new novel, *The Sentimental Education*.

There had been talk of the family travelling to the Mediterranean, perhaps to Italy, to help Gustave's health and his mother's migraines as well as for the pleasure of it. When his sister Caroline married a young man Gustave had known at school, the Italian journey also became a honeymoon. They left in April 1845.

Flaubert had spent days in his room before departure, reading Italian history and French travel writing, and had drawn up a list of things he wanted to see along the way. Unfortunately for him, his family did not share all of his enthusiasms. 'O dear and tender Alfred,' he wrote to le Poittevin from Marseille, 'I urge you in the name of heaven, in my own name, don't travel with anyone else! Anyone! – I wanted to see Aigues-Mortes, la Sainte-Baume and the grotto where Madeleine cried, the battlefield of Marius, etc. I saw none of it, because I was not alone, I was not free.'[9] Those lines were written by a young man frustrated as much in love as in travel.

In Marseille, before writing that letter, Flaubert had revisited the Hotel Richelieu, scene of his passionate affair five years earlier with Eulalie Foucauld. But now he found the place shut up, the hotelier gone. 'Isn't that a symbol?' he asked le Poittevin. 'For a long time now my heart has had its shutters closed, its steps deserted, formerly a tumultuous hotel, but now empty and echoing like a great empty tomb.'[10]

Two weeks after Marseille, the Flauberts reached Genoa, and Gustave went to the picture gallery of the Palazzo Balbi-Senarega. Here, he stood for a long time in front of Bruegel's painting of St Anthony and his temptations. 'At first this painting seems confused,' he wrote in his notebook, 'then it mostly becomes strange, droll for some, something more than that for others; for me it obscured the rest of the gallery, already I do not remember what else is there.'[11] He had had another kind of vision: he would write about St Anthony.

The law schools in Paris resumed in the autumn of 1845, but Gustave remained in the family house at Croisset, outside Rouen, with its frontage on the Seine, its flower-filled garden, and the room in which he could lie and read on his white bearskin, books and papers arranged on a large round table. In November, calamity struck. His father complained of a pain in his thigh. Achille, who by now was also a surgeon at the same hospital, diagnosed an abscess. The pain became so acute that he was forced to operate, but there were complications. Gangrene set in. On 15 January 1846 Dr Flaubert died. Six days after his death, Gustave's sister Caroline gave birth to a baby girl. The new arrival was healthy, the mother less so.

Gustave was in Paris settling his father's affairs when he heard that his sister had contracted puerperal fever, a post-delivery infection. He was assured that her condition, while serious, was not worrying. When he returned home, it was clear matters were otherwise. 'Hamard [his brother-in-law] . . . sobbing, upright, in the corner by the fire. My mother is a weeping statue. Caroline speaks to us, smiles, caresses us, says

gentle and affectionate things to all of us. She is losing her
memory, everything is confused in her head and she didn't
know if it was me or Achille who had been in Paris . . . The
baby feeds and cries. Achille says nothing and doesn't know
what to say. What a house! [W]hat hell! And me. I have eyes as
dry as marble.'[12] Five days later she died.

The sudden loss of his father and sister changed everything
in Flaubert's life. Hamard, his brother-in-law, barely capable of
looking after himself, was only too happy to hand over care of
the child. So at twenty-four years of age, Flaubert found
himself protector of a household, his mother and a baby niece.

Madame Flaubert did her best to mother the baby, and the
little girl did what babies do: cried and fed and slept.
Flaubert, meanwhile, turned in on himself. His Oriental tale
would be for next year, or the one after, or perhaps never.
First, he told himself, as if these things always come in threes,
there was his mother's death to prepare for: '[M]y plan is
made, I will sell everything and go to live in Rome, Syracuse
or Naples . . . But may Heaven allow me a little peace! A little
tranquillity, dear God! [A] little repose, just that, I'm not
asking for happiness!'[13]

In the event, it was not his mother but Alfred le Poittevin
who was lost to him: at the end of May 1846, he heard that his
friend was to be married. 'As you didn't ask my advice,'
Flaubert wrote to him, 'I shall not give any.'[14] He was certain
that le Poittevin was marrying not for love but to please his
family and for money, and felt there could be no greater
betrayal of the ideals they had cherished. 'So here is another
person lost to me and doubly so, first because he is going to
marry and second because he will live elsewhere. How
everything passes! How everything passes! The leaves are on
the trees but, for us, where is the month of May that will give

us the beautiful flowers and male flavours of our youth? It makes me feel immeasurably old, older even than an obelisk.'[15] But by the end of the summer, Flaubert had a new friend to divert him.

Louis Bouilhet had studied medicine under Flaubert's father, but his skill was with the pen not the scalpel. A poet and a lover of the classics, he gave up medicine after Dr Flaubert's death and began teaching Latin. Once he and Flaubert became friends, Bouilhet spent every weekend at the spacious house in Croisset, translating Greek and Latin.

'Bouilhet, who blushed when he was looked at, was never at ease in a salon,' Du Camp later remembered.[16] 'He was very witty, could be ironical with effect and might have been a comic poet if his early education, his taste for romanticism, and a certain ambition had not diverted his thoughts to lyrical poetry.' Revolted by the commonplace, the dull and ordinary, he was to become one of Flaubert's staunchest supporters and sternest critics.

On Tuesday 28 July 1846, Flaubert met the second person who was to shape this part of his life. Needing a change of air after Du Camp had left Croisset, he went to Paris for a few days. One evening he attended the salon of the fashionable sculptor James Pradier. Several evenings each week Pradier's friends gathered at his studio on the Quai Voltaire to debate the higher precepts of art and to exchange gossip. Celebrated artists and writers mixed with unknown hopefuls, Pradier's clients and some of his models. Flaubert had been a regular visitor to the studio while he was at law school and it was where he had first met one of his literary heroes, Victor Hugo. That July evening, Pradier introduced Flaubert to one of the women at the salon. 'This young man,' he said, 'is going to make a name for himself in literature.'[17] The woman to whom Flaubert was introduced was beautiful, in her mid-thirties, blonde, blue-eyed, voluptuous – and famous. 'Perhaps,' the sculptor said, 'you can be of use to him.'

Disarmed by the attention of a beautiful woman, Flaubert unburdened himself of secrets he had so far only confided in Maxime Du Camp and Louis Bouilhet. He told her that he was a writer, that he was planning an Oriental tale, and that he wanted his first major work to be a thunderclap, something so big, so spectacular, that everyone would have to pay attention. As he talked, he realised with whom he was sharing his confidences.

Louise Colet had won prizes for her poems and no less a figure than Chateaubriand, the great Romantic novelist, had written a letter of praise, which served as a preface to her first collection. But if she was talented with words, Flaubert knew that she was no less gifted in matters of love. She was or had been married: Monsieur Colet, the father of her young daughter, had been a professor of music at the Conservatoire. But whether he was still alive, and living with her, Flaubert did not know; no one ever mentioned him. The person who was talked of in connection with her was Victor Cousin, an older gentleman, a philosopher and politician. What Flaubert didn't know was that Madame Colet had recently ended her relationship with Cousin. When she left Pradier's studio that July evening, she invited Flaubert to visit her. As he was only up in the city for a short while, perhaps, she suggested, he might like to come the following evening.

Colet had pleaded poverty while describing her apartment at 21 rue de la Fontaine-Saint-Georges and Flaubert found it relatively simple for such a celebrity. A maid let him into a small sitting room draped in blue silk, where the poet lay stretched out on a chaise-longue. She had been writing all day, she said, and was fatigued. The room was warm, the lighting soft, she wore a low-cut white gown: the setting was ripe for seduction, if indeed anyone needed to be seduced. They sat together on the couch and read passages from her translations of *A Midsummer Night's Dream*, *The Tempest* and *Macbeth*. Then Colet brought out her latest poems, which Flaubert criticised – something of a liberty given that he was the unknown from the provinces and she the prize-winning poet from the city. What happened next seems inevitable, but he was genuinely surprised that a woman who already had a husband and a lover would allow him to sit so close, to touch her arm, to take her in his, to kiss her . . .

He didn't get as far as he would have liked. However much she was transported by passion – and she was clearly moved – Colet was not sufficiently far from her senses to allow this to continue. She said they must stop 'before it was too late'[18] and that he must leave. But perhaps they might dine together the following evening?

He duly arrived back at her door, having arranged an intimate table for two at a restaurant nearby, only to discover that they would be three: it was 30 July, the anniversary of the downfall of the Bourbon kings, Paris was *en fête* and Henriette, Colet's six-year-old daughter, would be joining them. The maid was out and Colet could hardly leave her daughter home alone or deny her the pleasure of seeing the city on such a night. So they dined and shared intimacies in front of the child. When Flaubert challenged Louise about the rights and wrongs of adultery, she explained that her marriage had been one of convenience, to get her to Paris. Her daughter was the child of her ex-lover, Cousin. Adultery, she insisted, was permissible in a case such as hers.

After dinner, they stepped into the Place de la Concorde. We must excuse Flaubert, at this moment, if he no longer had any thoughts for the obelisk from Ramses' temple in Luxor or even for his Oriental tales. He was a young man on the cusp of a great event in his life and he was blinded, at first by passion for this beautiful woman and then, as they took a carriage towards the Bois de Boulogne, by the fireworks celebrating the downfall of another king. Later he wrote that they were also there 'to celebrate the beginning of our love'.[19] Henriette was asleep by the time they returned to the rue de la Fontaine-Saint-Georges. Flaubert went up to help Colet with her sleeping daughter, and did not come down until the following morning.

He stayed six days and nights in Paris. Around midday on Tuesday 4 August, he left a sobbing Louise behind and travelled back to Rouen where his mother was waiting for him, also with tears in her eyes. Twelve hours later, as the clock struck midnight, he sat at his table in Croisset, his mother and niece asleep upstairs, and remembered that, 'Yesterday at this hour I held you in my arms.'[20] It was the first in a series of wonderfully passionate letters that simultaneously excited and infuriated his new mistress as he outlined the terms of their relationship, along lines that would best suit himself. It was to be an affair of words and opinions as much as of caresses and ecstasies. He loved her, he missed her, he adored her, he was incapable of thinking of anything or anyone but her. 'I want to give you nothing but joy and to surround you with serene happiness to repay you a little for all that you have given me in the generosity of your love.'[21] But he would not be giving her anything directly because he could not return to Paris in the near future and it was simply impossible that she visit him in Croisset.

Louise Colet was disappointed, and with good reason. Most of her letters to him have disappeared, but some of what she expressed can be deduced from Flaubert's responses. She called him selfish, and was angry that he would not return to Paris. He explained that his family situation would not allow it, that he must stay quietly in the country and she must not visit him there. In response, she became even more passionate. When he picked a rose in the garden he would not let her visit, kissed it, and sent it to Paris with a note that she should 'put it quickly to your lips and then you know where . . . '[22] she became incandescent with lust, passion and rage. *He* might be content with just the idea of her, and with an engraving of her that he kept propped against a cushion on his divan: 'My mother . . . thinks you are pretty. Have an animated, open, pleasant expression'.[23] But *she* wanted to love a real man, specifically this one who was eleven years younger than herself and who, she must have realised already, had far greater talent.

As well as coming to visit her in Paris, she thought he should be publishing his writing. He would, he assured her, one day. He had never wanted glory for himself, but now he wanted to do something magnificent for her sake, so that he could toss it to her like a bouquet of flowers – perhaps in return for the medal she had sent him, which she had received from the Académie Française. But a week after his return to Croisset, he was still incapable of writing anything more than a love letter.

A couple of weeks later he did manage a quick visit to Paris and there were passionate, and tumultuous, scenes in his hotel room, which left him wondering whether the next occupant of the room would have any idea of what had occurred there. 'That would be something, to write the history of a bed.'[24] But something else already occupied his mind. 'I unpacked my *Temptation of Saint Anthony* and hung it on my wall. I really love this picture. I have wanted it for a long time. I find its grotesque sadness has an extraordinary charm. It matches the intimate needs of my bitter buffoon character.'[25]

Bitterness and buffoonery, voluptuous indulgence and ascetic retreat, a strong physique and a vulnerability to epilepsy or whatever it was that attacked him . . . he was full of contrasts. By now all the pieces were in place – the mistress in Paris and the friends near at hand, Bouilhet having in some ways replaced the newly-wed Alfred le Poittevin. He had even achieved a certain equilibrium at home with mother and niece and the ever-present dreams of the Orient ('ah, I spent whole days beside my fire, on tiger hunts').[26] Now here too was the image that had so transfixed him in Genoa the previous year.

Louise Colet still was not allowed to come to Croisset and see the picture on the wall for herself. Du Camp and Bouilhet knew there was someone, some woman – everyone who observed the daily exchange of letters between Paris and Croisset would know there was a woman – but did not yet know her identity. Whoever she was, they approved of the effect she was having on their friend because he had finally set to work.

For months he read around the subject, gathering books from the library in Rouen and from a friend in the Royal Library in Paris. Stretched out on his white bearskin, he read the Koran, the writing of St Augustine and other Church fathers, Vedic hymns and Buddhist chants, the *Bhagavad-gita* and Sufi poems, fleshing out his idea. Du Camp, who was a regular visitor at this time, recalled:

> The fire blazed upon the hearth. Flaubert wrote at a round table, and I had a little one to myself. We worked during the day, and in the evening after dinner we talked. When Bouilhet joined the party [each weekend] these talks would be prolonged until three or four o'clock in the morning, and we went to bed so late it was hard to obey the summons of the breakfast bell. Flaubert had begun to write *La Tentation de Saint Antoine*, but to all our questions he only replied, 'You will know all about it by-and-by.'[27]
>
> He would not read us a single line until he had finished

it. That meant a long time to wait, for he reckoned that the book would take him three years. In his preparatory studies for this work he had gone to the original sources. He read the Fathers of the Church, plunged into the archives of the decrees of the Councils by Fathers Labbe and Cossart, studied the scholiastics, and lost himself in a wilderness of books. He could have found sufficient for his purpose in the *Dictionnaire des Hérésies* and in the *Légende dorée*. Once when Bouilhet saw the pile of books upon his table he said, 'Take care; St Antoine was only a simple-minded man; you are about to make a savant of him.'[28]

That winter passed in a flurry of words, in reading for *Saint Anthony* and writing letters to Colet. Sometimes she was happy, even ecstatic. But mostly she was sad and tormented by their arrangement, a feeling that spilled out into long, accusatory letters. Flaubert calmly batted them back to her, spelling out the facts that she refused to accept: that he loved sitting in his room; he loved missing her; he had no need to see her often, perhaps not even at all. He believed that: '[L]ove is not and should not be the main thing in life. It should stay on the back burner. There are other things in the soul, it seems to me, which are nearer the light, closer to the sun. So if you take love to be the main dish in life: no. As a touch of spice: yes.'[29] Then there was the definitive thought of how sweet it would be to be married and for her to die and him to mourn her forever.

By March of the following year, 1848, the whole of Europe was riven by social unrest. Florence Nightingale and the Bracebridges had had to cut short their Roman holiday because of the increased threat of fighting. They had passed through Paris early in April, which raises the delicious prospect that she might have passed through the same rooms, the same salons, the same galleries, as Flaubert. But there is no mention of a common meeting, although Flaubert and Bouilhet were in Paris around that time to watch the revolution as it happened.

He didn't go to see Colet, but while in the capital he wrote her a letter that had a tone of finality about it, a sense of something ending, and yet, perhaps because he was a novelist and always saw other possibilities, there was as always a lifeline: 'Whatever happens, you can always count on me. Even if we no longer write to each other, the bond between us can never be broken.'[30] A couple of weeks later, there was another farewell when his friend Alfred le Poittevin died suddenly. Flaubert might have felt abandoned by him, but that did not stop him grieving. 'I watched over him for two nights, I wrapped him in his shroud, I gave him the farewell kiss, and I saw his coffin nailed shut. I spent those two whole days there. And while watching over him, I read Creuzer's *Religions of Antiquity*.'[31]

On Wednesday 24 May 1848, at a quarter past three in the afternoon, as he recorded precisely at the head of his first sheet of paper, Flaubert began *The Temptation of Saint Anthony*, the book he hoped would launch him into the literary firmament, a work of such brilliance that all his preparatory suffering would be worthwhile. Even Louise Colet, to whom he would toss it as a bouquet, would understand why she had been kept at a distance.

That same day, or rather at one o'clock the following morning, he wrote to Du Camp that he was at work on the book. 'You must drop this illusion that you will hear *Saint Anthony* at the end of August. It will hardly be finished this epoch, and I imagine that the corrections, not for the phrases but for the effects, will be long. For the rest, I know nothing. I haven't written a line since Saturday, stopped by a transition that I can't find a way out of. – I am consumed with anger, impatience, impotence.'[32] The dates on the letter and the manuscript do not tally: if he had started writing that day, he would not be complaining that he hadn't written since Saturday.

But he did write. Du Camp returned to Paris, Bouilhet visited at weekends, and at all times, in Croisset and then in Rouen where they moved during winter, Flaubert poured out words 'like a river', as Bouilhet described it. Some days he didn't even leave the house: pacing his room, lying on the divan, returning to his round table and pens. He divided his time between writing and dreaming, which was a necessary counter-balance to composition. Even he was impressed with how much he could achieve in a day. 'After dinner tonight,' he wrote in his journal that winter, 'I talked with my mother, thought of travel, and dreamed of the various lives I might be leading. Then I wrote almost an entire chorus of *Saint Antoine*, read the whole first volume of Chateaubriand's *Mémoires d'Outre-Tombe*, and smoked three pipes. Now I am going to take a pill . . . and I have not yet gone to sleep!'[33]

Du Camp returned in February, the moment when winter seems eternal, the sun gone forever, the damp and cold cutting to the bone. He had decided to travel in the Orient.

He had already visited Algeria and Istanbul. This time he would make a grander tour: down to Egypt, across to Persia, back to Syria, then up through the Ottoman lands to Greece and Italy. It was part of the long journey that he and Flaubert had often talked of making together. Du Camp had even made a start on his preparatory reading and had brought with him an account of a Nile journey made 20 years earlier by Jean-François Champollion, the man who had first deciphered hieroglyphs. Not only would Flaubert be missing out on the adventure, he would also be losing the company of one of his closest friends . . . and for two years. Flaubert, meanwhile, would be sitting at his table, piling up the pages of *Saint Anthony*.

'I had a restless night thinking of this poor fellow shut up in his solitary existence,' Du Camp later remembered,[34] 'he who dreamt of wide spaces of light and air, of the desert, of rivers of the Bible, and who was condemned, in spite of his youth, to lead the life of some old provincial dryasdust.'

Du Camp claims the credit for what happened next. First he consulted Gustave's brother, Dr Achille Flaubert, who confirmed that a tour of the East would be good for his brother's health. Then he approached Madame Flaubert to say he thought her son should travel, for the sake of his health. Unexpectedly, she agreed.

If he thought Flaubert would erupt with joy at the news of his release, he was wrong: he just turned red. Perhaps he was calculating how much writing lay ahead of him. He insisted that he could not leave before the novel was finished, and that would not be before the end of September. His friend agreed to wait and even offered to make all the time-consuming arrangements for the trip.

Du Camp had been back in Paris just a week when he received an unexpected visitor. 'I wish to have a talk with you,' Madame Flaubert began.[35] 'I am assured Gustave's health requires that he should spend two years in a warm climate, that the long absence would do him good in every way. I have resigned myself to the sacrifice, but there are other warm countries besides Egypt, Nubia, Palestine, Persia, and Asia Minor. It seems to me that such a journey will be very tiring, and I dread its dangers. I am therefore here to ask you to abandon your present plans and to go to Madeira instead.'

He is uncharacteristically brief in describing his response to this suggestion, but he must have been as amused as he was amazed. There were no camels or souks or noble men of the desert there, no grand monuments or biblical associations, and he refused absolutely to consider the option. By the beginning of May, Madame Flaubert had abandoned her resistance to their plan and, while she was silently tormented by thoughts of the coming separation, her son wrote of 'the Orient dancing at the end of my table, and the noise of camels' bells buzzing in my ears alongside the sound of my words'.[36]

Du Camp set to work on the itinerary and also obtained official commissions for himself and Flaubert. These were not necessary in order to make the journey, but they would help open doors in Egypt and give them credentials among the influential French community there. Du Camp was also the sort of person who benefited from having a focus for his endeavours, and the task of taking photographs of the ancient monuments – the commission he was eventually given by the Ministry of Public Instruction – would provide him with one. Throughout the spring and summer, their correspondence and their days were endlessly interrupted by thoughts of things needed for the journey, and in this, as in so much else, Du Camp proved to be far more practically minded than his friend.

He and his valet Sassetti, who would accompany them to the East, began to collect suitable clothes, photographic equipment and supplies for the trip – three beds and saddles, four pairs of boots, two tents, one of which would serve as a mobile darkroom for developing Du Camp's pictures, buckets, boxes of tools, tobacco, knives and scissors intended to be given as presents along the way, piles of books, notebooks, ink, and 101 other things.

On 13 September 1849, around the time that Fanny Nightingale agreed to let Florence go to Egypt, Flaubert wrote to Du Camp, 'I have just completed *Saint Antoine*. Come!'[37] When Du Camp reached Croisset the following day, Bouilhet was already there.

Flaubert had decided to read them the entire manuscript and then listen to their comments. In return for their patience, he promised to bow to their literary judgment. He would read from midday to four in the afternoon and from eight until midnight, for as long as it took. Looking at his two friends sitting in front of him, his voice wavered and his hands shook. He picked up the first of the 541 manuscript pages from his round table and waved them over his head. 'If you do not utter howls of delight, then you are incapable of being moved by anything.'[38] His friends hoped they would howl, but in truth they had no idea what to expect because he had told them nothing more about his project than that it concerned the Egyptian saint. 'We only knew its title,' Du Camp remembered. 'I imagined that Flaubert would write a kind of memoir of the saint who was so severely tempted with his confessions.'[39] Bouilhet was expecting him to bring to life the ancient world of the third century, with the decline of the Roman Empire and the rise of the Christian Church. The book turned out to be something very different.

On a mountain. On the horizon, the desert; to the right, Saint Anthony's hut, with a bench beside the door; left, a small oval chapel. A lamp hangs above a picture of the Virgin; on the ground in front of the hut, baskets made of palm-leaves. In a cleft in the rock the hermit's pig is sleeping in the shade. Anthony is alone, seated on the bench weaving his baskets. He raises his head, looks vaguely at the setting sun. 'I have worked enough: now to prayer!'[40]

The book had taken him sixteen months to write. He now spent the better part of four days, some 32 hours, reading it aloud. Just as Flaubert had said nothing while he was writing, so Bouilhet and Du Camp revealed nothing while listening. Madame Flaubert was not even allowed in the room. But she hovered nearby, and at the end of each reading she appeared and asked the visitors, 'Well, what do you think of it?'[41] Neither gave anything away. Flaubert meanwhile oscillated between excitement at some of his passages and a growing nervousness at his friends' silence. 'Wait! Wait! You'll see!'[42]

They did not see. 'We heard what the Sphinx had to say, the Chimera, the Queen of Sheba, Simon the Magician, Apollonius of Tyanus, Origen, Basiliele, Montanus Manes, and Hermogenus. With even closer attention we listened to the Marcosians, the Carpocrations, the Paternians, the Nicolaites, the Gymnosophists, and the Arcontics; also to Pluto and Diana, and Hercules, and even to the God Crepitus.'[43] He certainly couldn't fault his friends for not paying attention.

On the fourth night, Flaubert read the following lines. 'Here ends *La Tentation de Saint Antoine*, Wednesday, the twelfth of September 1849, twenty minutes past three in the afternoon. Sunny, windy weather.'[44]

He hit the table with his hand and said, 'Now that we three are alone together, tell me, truthfully, what you think.'[45]

They sat in silence for a moment.

Bouilhet and Du Camp had conferred earlier that evening and had agreed what they would say, if not who would say it. Then Louis Bouilhet, the man whose literary judgment Flaubert valued more than anyone else's, pointed at the pile of papers and said, 'We think you ought to throw the whole of that into the fire, and never speak of it again.'[46]

Whatever response he was expecting – and by now he must have had an idea that all was not well – Flaubert had never imagined his friends would damn his work. He leaped to his feet and shrieked, in surprise, pain and frustration.

Du Camp and Bouilhet spent much of that night and all of the next day explaining their criticism. Much of the writing was sloppy, they said. He had not engaged with his subject. But, most important of all, the style was wrong. He had tried to write in the manner of Chateaubriand, but it had come out as pseudo-romanticism. A novelist in the middle of the nineteenth century, a young novelist in the age of revolution and social unrest, should be writing with utmost realism. Bouilhet mentioned Balzac.

Balzac? Flaubert was horrified, for he knew that Balzac took his material not from the glories of antiquity, or the nobility of the Orient with its men of the desert and dark-eyed women, but from the bourgeoisie of France, the middle classes, their little lives and even smaller concerns. What could Flaubert have to do with such a man or such a style of writing?

But his friends insisted that he should think about it, although they recognised the difficulty. 'Three years of labour,' Du Camp wrote, 'all to disappear without any tangible result! There was nothing but smoke to show for it.'[47]

At least he had time. Twenty months to be precise. For that was the length of the journey he and Du Camp had agreed to make. Twenty months to consider his failure, to contemplate romanticism versus realism, Chateaubriand versus Balzac, St Anthony versus the petty concerns of the French bourgeoisie. Twenty months of new sights and sounds.

No wonder he was too excited to sleep as Max and Sassetti lay on their camp beds on the upper deck of the *Marchioness of Breadalbane*, as Florence Nightingale scratched at flea bites and watched the moon from the window of the cabin below. 'Forget work! Enjoy yourself! See all you can!'[48] Bouilhet had advised on leaving him. But how could he forget work? Sixteen years after seeing that obelisk on a boat on the Seine, here he was on the Nile, thinking of Cleopatra and surely also of St Anthony, while sailing slowly towards Cairo.

6

The Rose of Cities

'The rose of cities, the garden of the desert, the pearl of
Moorish architecture, the fairest, really the fairest, place
of earth below' – Florence Nightingale in Cairo, 29
November 1849

The travellers woke to a sight they had often imagined. To
their right, three pyramids rose above a stand of palms, side-lit
by the rising sun. Du Camp, who had slept more soundly than
any of them, was moved to hyperbole. 'Shaded blue by the
distance, bathed in a glorious light that highlighted their
contours, they looked as though they were made of trans-
parent sapphires; a cluster of palms and some cultivated fields
lay green in front of them. All the passengers watched these
mysterious guardians of the desert.'[1] They all watched, but not
everyone was so moved by the view. Flaubert made a brief
mention in his notebook of 'the two pyramids, then the smaller
one'.[2] Nightingale, even less impressed by these 'guardians of

the desert', noticed and noted them – 'three' – but was unable to 'muster a single sensation'.[3] The night on the ferry had taken its toll.

Not long after they had sighted the pyramids, the city appeared to their left. Cairo looked like the setting for a fairytale. Standing at a distance from the river, its flat roofs, generous domes and many minarets were topped by the brooding bulk of Saladin's crenellated citadel and the pencil-thin silhouette of Muhammad Ali's newly-built mosque. Behind it stood the bulk of the Muqattam Hills, where much of the limestone used in the pyramids and the city's palaces had been quarried. Immediately in front of them was the teeming life of the port of Cairo.

Boulaq today is just another area of city-centre Cairo. Its old stone warehouses, landing yards and stables have given way to concrete high-rises; its dirt alleys to asphalt overpasses. The surviving street markets, neighbourhood cafes and nineteenth-century buildings are anomalies beside the looming towers of the Ministry of Foreign Affairs and Cairo World Trade Center. But in 1849, it was, as it had been for many centuries, a landing stage wrapped around by a village, its most prominent landmark a modest but beautiful mosque designed by the imperial Ottoman architect Sinan, whose work transformed Istanbul.

On the busy dockside there was chaos again. The travellers stepped off the ferry into a scene of bag-grabbing and shouting, *baksheesh* and baton-wielding, though Flaubert noticed that there were fewer beatings here than in Alexandria.

By ten o'clock they had all landed and fought their way to camels, donkeys and carriages, which were needed because Boulaq was separated from the rest of the city by a large swathe of farms and gardens – today's downtown Cairo – most of it owned by the ruling pasha and his family. A procession of pack animals and vehicles then moved along the raised causeway, across the fields and between rows of acacias, to Cairo and the Ezbekiya, the city's largest open space.

Like Frank Square in Alexandria, Ezbekiya was where Western travellers were deposited on arrival. As in Alexandria, this was also where the French and the British divided. Their *dragoman* Joseph led Flaubert, Du Camp and Sassetti to the Hotel d'Orient, a flat-fronted, white-washed building in the north-east corner of the square. Like its namesake in Alexandria, this one was also known as *chez Coulomb*. Nightingale, Trautwein and the Bracebridges checked into the Hotel d'Europe, a few doors away. In front of them lay the square, an esplanade and a promenade, an open space in the shape of a vast *tarbush*, or Egyptian fez, planted with trees and bushes, cut through with walks and dotted with benches and a cafe.

Alexandria with its European houses and Mediterranean views had seemed familiar – too familiar for Flaubert's liking. Cairo, this 'second step in the East', was not. It was perhaps a sign of how tired Florence Nightingale felt, and perhaps also of how unfamiliar even this European-friendly area of the city looked, that she stayed in the hotel on her first day there, did nothing more than visit the British Consul-General the next, and did not even start writing a letter home until the third day. It was worth waiting for. 'No one ever talks about the beauty of Cairo,' she told her family, 'ever gives you the least idea of this surpassing city. I thought it was a place to buy stores at and pass through on one's way to India, instead of its being the rose of cities, the garden of the desert, the pearl of Moorish architecture, the fairest, really the fairest, place of earth below.'[4] It was still a place to buy stores and find a boat to take them up the Nile, a place to visit, but it was also a place where the process of her transformation could finally begin.

The British Consul-General helped with both shopping and

sightseeing. Charles Murray had studied at Oxford with Sidney Herbert, whom the Bracebridges knew and whose company Nightingale had enjoyed in Rome two years earlier. By a strange twist of fate, he was also an old friend of Richard Monckton Milnes. These connections helped galvanise the consul; nothing seemed to be too much trouble for him. He lent them books to take up the Nile, gave them little antiquities he had found in Upper Egypt and shells he had brought from the Red Sea, and put a large room in the consulate at their disposal for as long as they wanted. Nightingale sat in this room making notes from the books she was not borrowing and copying out plans of the temples they hoped to visit. When she needed air or refreshment, she had only to stroll into the garden, where the consul's 'slaves' brought coffee or whatever else she desired. In the evenings, she and the Bracebridges sat down to eat at Mr Murray's table. 'He evidently does the consul with a conscience.'⁵

'Doing the consul' conscientiously also involved offering his secretary as their escort around town. Mr Legros, as Nightingale explained to her family, was another of Mr Bracebridge's friends. Was anybody not? On their third day in the capital, when they had strayed no further than across Ezbekiya and seen little more than their hotel and Murray's library and garden, Mr Legros 'wheedled' them out for a donkey ride.

The donkeys had amused Nightingale in Alexandria, but riding them in Cairo was a different proposition. There had been plenty of room for manoeuvre in Alexandria, but the streets of old Cairo were so narrow and busy that she was sure she would run someone down, or be knocked out of her saddle by a cart or a camel coming the other way. 'You address your ass in the tenderest terms and in the purest Arabic; you adjure him by all the names of friendship to stop, but he understands no Arabic except the driver's and on he goes full trot while you are making hair-breadth escapes at every corner.'[6]

They rode through the heart of the city. It was a short but dazzling journey, 'the latticed windows meeting overhead, the pearls of Moorish architecture at every corner, the looking up to the blue sky and golden sunlight from the wells of the streets and in the bazaars, the streets entirely roofed in'.[7] They stopped to visit the fourteenth-century mosque of Sultan Hassan, which Nightingale's guide informed her, correctly, was one of the finest mosques in the city. From there, they rode through the gates of the medieval citadel, up past the palace of Abbas Pasha, current ruler of Egypt, to the mosque and tomb of his grandfather, Muhammad Ali, who had ruled it for almost the first half of the nineteenth century.

Muhammad Ali had originally been sent to Egypt from his native Albania as part of an Ottoman force that was to resist Napoleon's occupation and the subsequent British invasion. He exploited with opportunism and ruthlessness the power vacuum left by the British and French in order to set himself up on the throne. The same army that established him as ruler of Egypt also defeated his nominal overlord, the Ottoman sultan, and the dynasty he founded survived for a century and a half. The grand old man himself had ruled for more than 40 years and had only died a few weeks earlier, at the beginning of August 1849. Although his death had been expected, his tomb was still being decorated. But the structure was complete and its message was clear: it sought to rival the imperial mosques of Istanbul, just as the man buried inside had once dared to challenge the Ottoman Emperor.

Nightingale thought its broad dome and pencil minarets were grand, but found the alabaster-clad interior tawdry. When she came to the burial place, she couldn't resist mentioning how close it was to the place where he had had most of his opponents slaughtered at the start of his reign: 'He sleeps now close to the murdered chiefs and people can forget that murder, and laud Muhammad Ali?'[8]

But no amount of righteous indignation could spoil her enjoyment of what she saw as she walked over to the edge of the terrace standing in front of the mosque. She thought it was simply 'the finest view in the whole world'.[9] This was praise indeed from someone who had looked down on London from Hampstead, on Paris from Sacré Coeur, on Rome from the Pincio.

> Cairo, which is immense, lies at the feet, a forest of minarets and domes and towers. The Nile flows his solemn course beyond, the waters being still out (it is now high Nile), and the three Pyramids stand sharp against the sky. Here Osiris and his worshippers lived; here Abraham and Moses walked; here Aristotle came; here, later, Mahomet learnt the best of his religion and studied Christianity; here, perhaps, our Saviour's mother brought her little son to open his eyes to the light. They are all gone from the body, but the Nile flows and the Pyramids stand there still.[10]

It was a fine evocation, if not entirely accurate: Abraham never even came close. But we can forgive Nightingale her enthusiasm, for here, a month after she left England, was the Egypt she had imagined as a child while reading the Bible or Belzoni's account of his excavations: below her the fabled river; beyond, the pyramids. These monuments – and the passage of time, of knowledge, of power that they represented – were to be the catalysts of her transformation. After her ecstatic response to this vision, she rode down from the citadel and the scene was transformed.

'Out of this city of noise and bustle and confusion you pass through the gate and come, oh change! oh wondrous change! from the city of the living to the city of the dead.'[11] She had reached the edge of the desert and what was, and still is, the city's great burial ground, a series of cemeteries that over centuries had wrapped themselves around Cairo's northern, eastern and southern walls. She started viewing them enthusiastically enough, declaring that she had never seen anything so wonderful.

> As far as the eye can reach, you see nothing but tombs, and from these streets of tombs, where you walk, and walk, and walk, till you fancy Amina, the Ghoul, sitting on one particular tomb; there is nothing to be seen beyond but the desert, nothing but the sky and the lifeless earth: it is the union with another world – the 'land beyond'.[12]

Her thoughts ranged over visions of life and death, from the crumbling tombs of great medieval rulers she had just visited to the pyramid tombs of the early pharaohs she had glimpsed on the horizon, and the new tomb-mosque of Muhammad Ali, who 'arose and reigned and thought he would be called the Civiliser of the East'. At this point, an incident occurred that darkened her thoughts.

She had already expressed her disgust at the general corruption and the parlous state of politics in the country, besides her shock at the extent of its poverty. Now she found a new focus for her unease. In the distance, not far off, she saw a boy walking past some tombs. While she was watching, a mounted policeman rode up to him and accused him of stealing; he was arrested. This much was familiar enough. But there was no judge, no trial, no weighing of evidence. Instead, the policeman began to flog the boy. Nightingale was not the sort of person to stand by and watch a child being mistreated. When she saw what was happening, she urged Mr Legros to intervene. But there was nothing the consul's secretary could do: he had no jurisdiction here and the policeman was determined to punish the boy.

Whatever the child had done, she thought it was wrong for him to be treated this way. It was sick, corrupt, 'as all the details of government in this horrid country'.[13] The desert, which had looked so fabulous, now seemed to her like a cursed place. Her thoughts ran on. These nineteenth-century Egyptians were descended from the builders of the pyramids. The ancestors of the flogged boy had created an advanced society at a time when Europeans were running around in loincloths and living in mud huts. But something terrible had happened and now, while Britain was developing, Egypt was sliding back into barbarity. She found it difficult to believe that Egyptians were also on their way to a perfect life.

She wanted to understand what had happened. How had they fallen so low? Why had their progress been stopped? What had they done to precipitate this decline? And could such a calamity happen to her own country?

She didn't have any answers, but she did have a reaction to this scene. Her *madre*, the nun in Rome who had guided her in her retreat, had warned against vanity and ambition. Out in the cemetery beyond Cairo's medieval walls, she could see clearly that human greatness was nothing but vanity and that it was something to be devoutly avoided. 'What is *human* greatness when you look at this desolation of the finest country in the world?'[14] Dazed and perhaps confused by the newness, the strangeness, the wonder of Egypt, her thoughts ran on until they came to a question for which as yet she had no answer. If greatness and glory were human vanity, what were we put on this earth to strive for? What was worthwhile? What, she asked now as she had been asking repeatedly since she was seventeen, was she supposed to do with her life?

Du Camp and Flaubert lost no time upon reaching the city: on the day of their arrival they went to pay their respects to the French consul, Monsieur Delaporte. 'A handsome man,' Flaubert noted, though he was both overindulged and overly fastidious. When Flaubert commented that 'you mustn't walk across the sand' in the consul's courtyard, it is safe to assume that he was writing as someone who had done so and suffered the consequences.

With Monsieur Delaporte were some of the French community in Cairo, a mixed bunch of experts and would-be adventurers. Bekir Bey was a Frenchman who had arrived in Egypt as a drummer boy with Napoleon's army. When the army left, he had stayed, converted to Islam and eventually rose to become Chief of the Egyptian Police. Lubbert Bey, a former head of the Paris Opéra, was in charge of royal entertainments in Cairo. Linant de Bellefonds had been Egypt's chief engineer, but had fallen from grace with the regime change following the death of Muhammad Ali. He knew Egypt's topography perhaps better than anyone in the country and was soon to play a significant role in planning the Suez Canal. But however interesting Flaubert found these gentlemen, he had not come to Cairo to spend time with these 'hats'.

He settled into the city in his own inimitable way. 'We are going to visit Cairo carefully,' he assured his mother, 'and force ourselves to do some work every evening, a thing we have not yet done . . . It's at Cairo that the Orient begins. Alexandria is too diluted with Europeans to have kept much local colour. Here one sees fewer hats. We haunt the bazaars, the cafes, the street entertainers, the mosques.'[5] They also saw the sights.

They started, like Nightingale and the Bracebridges, with the mosque of Sultan Hassan. 'Round vestibule, pendentives or stalactites, thick ropes hanging from on high,' Flaubert recorded. 'We put on *babouches* made of palm fibres.'[16] From the mosque they moved to the citadel, where Flaubert seemed more taken by the alabaster fountain, the crystal chandelier and the other decorations than by the structure of Muhammad Ali's mosque. Du Camp, on the other hand, agreed with Nightingale that although the materials were precious, they were so badly designed as to be ugly. 'They have brought together everything that could be thought Turkish bad taste,'[17] he wrote with more than a touch of arrogance.

They walked to the edge of the parapet for the grand view, but the pyramids were in the full glare of the sunshine and they could only just make out their outlines. 'To the right,' as Flaubert saw it, 'the plain of the tombs of the Caliphs – in front of Cairo, a little further to the left, the mass of rubble that precedes old Cairo – behind you, the Muqattam Hills, pitted and sad.'[18]

'This is how I sum up my feelings so far,' he wrote in his first letter to Louis Bouilhet, who was to be his most intimate correspondent during this voyage. 'Very little impressed by nature here – i.e. landscape, sky, desert (except the mirages); stunned by the cities and the people. [Victor] Hugo would say that "I was closer to God than to mankind".'[19] But there was another explanation. When he had dreamed of the Orient as a young boy on the quayside in Rouen, Egypt's architecture was mere background decoration. When, during the months of planning for this trip, he had imagined what was to come, he had thought of landscapes, the river, the temples. Like Nightingale, he had not realised how much else there was to see in Cairo. 'The result is that nature has been a rediscovery and the rest a discovery.'

Among the discoveries was a 'new element which I hadn't

expected to see and which is tremendous here, and that is the grotesque'.[20] There may be no place for grotesques in a Romantic view of the world, but there was no escaping them in Cairo. 'All the old comic business of the beaten slave, of the coarse trafficker in women, of the thieving merchant, is here very fresh, very true, charming.'[21]

Florence Nightingale never seems to have come close enough to Egyptians in Cairo to make this sort of observation. As a woman, she was chaperoned wherever she went and was stopped from going to many of the places Flaubert enjoyed. Even if she had had the freedom to roam the city, she is unlikely to have been as attracted to the sexually grotesque as he was. 'There are some very talented buffoons,' he wrote to his mother, 'whose jokes are more than indelicate.'[22]

The son may have been sufficiently delicate to spare his mother the details, but he lavished them on the pages of his notebook and his letters to Bouilhet. There was the clown at a wedding party they joined their first night, dressed as a woman and telling a joke about a doctor buggering his donkey. There was the story he heard of an idiot, revered as a *marabout* (holy man), who was masturbated by his followers from morning to night. ('O Bouilhet, why weren't you that *marabout*!'[23]) There was the old man in the *hammam* who offered him the full service, with a leer, in return for *baksheesh* (a tip). There was the French consul's friend who ordered a black slave undressed in the market just for the pleasure of seeing her naked. There was Du Camp, who had started chasing women the moment he stepped on to the quay at Alexandria. There were the prostitutes working under the medieval aqueduct, whose services Flaubert bought for his donkey drivers: 'I will never forget the brutal movement of my old donkey driver approaching the girl, holding her with his right arm, caressing her breasts with his left hand and pulling her down, all in one movement, laughing and showing his big white teeth.'[24]

Like the play of brilliant light in the city streets, the noise and movement of the crowds, the inanity of some of the resident French community ('What a stupid dreary life!'[25]), the humour he didn't understand, the syphilitic men in hospital who showed him their anuses, the Englishwoman in his hotel who had converted to Islam and had died a noisy death, over whose body the Christians and Muslims now fought, the bride wrapped so tightly in her gown she couldn't walk, the opium smoker who knew Bonaparte, the overwhelming emotion as he rode up to the Sphinx ('We don't have such po-he-tiques emotions every day, thank God, or it would kill me')[26] . . . none of these or a thousand and one other things that he poured into his letters and notebooks had been seen or even imagined back in Rouen or Paris. And he had only been in Egypt a few days!

And nowhere did the dream of the Orient match the experience of being in Cairo more than in his sexual experiences. In his early writing there had been 'white-winged angels' singing verses from the Koran, and women with 'brown skin, their ardent look, who speak to me in the language of *houris*'.[27] In Cairo there was La Triestina.

Four days after their arrival in the city, while Nightingale and the Bracebridges were safely in their rooms in the Hotel d'Europe – on one of the few evenings they did not dine with Consul Murray – the *dragoman* Brichetti led Flaubert and Du Camp into the darkness behind the hotels. This was the shadier side of town, home to people who lived off whatever they could earn from visiting Westerners. Brichetti was a regular visitor to these dark alleys and dead ends, some so narrow that the carved wooden *mashrabias* almost met in the middle of the street.

He led them into one of these houses and up a narrow flight

of steps to the first floor where there was a large room furnished with divans. Du Camp made no mention of the evening afterwards, but Flaubert described it in detail. He did so using a technique that was soon to become his trademark, building up layers of impartial observation so as to create his effect.

Outside the window stood a palm. Inside, there was a night-light, a bottle of raki and two girls. The girls were stretched out on one of the divans. La Triestina, the woman from Trieste, came down from an upper floor. She told them, in her native Italian, that they must not make any noise. There could be no singing or dancing – otherwise she would have trouble. These days, she explained, the police clamped down on such things on the orders of the pasha. Why? Because Abbas 'loves men'.[28]

She introduced her girls. One was 'thick-lipped, snub-nosed, gay, brutal'[29] and, added La Triestina, 'a little mad'. The other, called Hadely, with large dark eyes, had an air of sadness and fatigue about her. She wore huge, baggy trousers and a tighter green jacket decorated with gold embroidery. Her hair was tied up in a scarf that had coins hanging off it. Flaubert thought she was probably the mistress of a European living in Cairo, suggested perhaps by the fact that she knew a few words of French and enough about France to be impressed that Du Camp was a Chevalier of the Légion d'Honneur.

In spite of La Triestina's anxiety, Hadely struck up a rhythm on the table and the mad-eyed girl tied a scarf low over her hips and began to move. She did a couple of dances. In the second one, she stretched her arms out in front of her, elbows a little bent, her torso absolutely still. Her pelvis quivered. This was enough for Du Camp: he would have the dancer, Flaubert would go with Hadely. 'Before delivering us to copulation, these women performed their preliminary ablutions.'[30]

Flaubert's senses were even more alert than usual. He heard

the rustling of pantaloons and the tinkle of coins on Hadely's scarf as she led him along the corridor. He felt the breeze through the shutters, saw the moonlight, the dancing candle. She shooed a litter of kittens from the mat where he was supposed to lie. He tried to undress her but had never seen such clothes before. 'A Muslim woman is barricaded,' he complained, 'the knotted trousers have no opening and defy all the tricks of the hand.'

The encounter was less romantic than he had imagined and here, as realism set in with a vengeance, his thoughts reverted to the grotesque. 'The whole thing gave the effect of the plague or a leper house.'

Did the girl suspect his thoughts as she helped him get dressed, handing him his clothes and asking questions in Arabic? 'She waited for a reply – our eyes entered into each other, the intensity of our gaze doubled! – and the look on Joseph's face in the middle of all this! – making love by interpreter!'[31] We can only assume that Joseph the *dragoman*, the man of unparalleled vanity, had seen it all many times before.

A couple of days later Flaubert described this 'strange coitus' to Bouilhet. He had been particularly struck by the way they had been 'looking at each other without being able to exchange a word. The exchange of looks doubled by curiosity and surprise. My mind was too stimulated for me to enjoy it much otherwise.'[32] Then he coined a phrase that perfectly expressed his view of all that he had seen so far, all that he had done: '[T]his is where you understand everything by contrast, where splendid things gleam in the dust.'

Splendid things gleamed on the river too, for Cairo was where they would find their *dahabiya*. The name, which translates as *the golden one*, was used to describe the style of Nile vessel preferred by European travellers. Flaubert, who had already thought of

Cleopatra on the ferry from Alexandria, would no doubt have remembered Shakespeare's evocation of her barge, that 'burnish'd throne' with its golden poop and silver oars, the purple sails 'so perfumed that the winds were love-sick with them'.

The Nile was Egypt's highway, as it had been when Cleopatra sat on the throne. There was still no railway (the British built that over the next few decades) and no good road beside the river, just worn tracks that were submerged each summer when the Nile flooded. Nor were there, as yet, any organised tours: Thomas Cook would not lead his first Nile cruise until 1869, the year of the opening of the Suez Canal. To travel before those developments left just one viable option: to go under sail – slow travel – as Egyptians and others had done since the beginning of the river's recorded history. And because they were going to sail, they had to start as soon as possible. The winds blew up the Nile, north to south, in the autumn. So they would go south as fast and as far as they could, making the most of the prevailing winds, and then float back on the current. The captain would not want to stop if the winds were fair, but if they missed something on the way up, they could see it at leisure on the way down.

The season of good wind happened to coincide with the end of the summer heat and the start of a short season of dazzling beauty. This was and still is the period when the light is best, the air clearest, when there is an especial richness to the colours of the landscape: the green of palm and field, the grey and brown of desert and hill, the mercurial shifting of the river shades . . . silver, purple, yellow and black. And all this beneath a sky baked a deep blue by day, but shifting from pink to vermillion to the colour of dried blood at sunset.

Mr Bracebridge had hoped to hire a *dahabiya* back in Alexandria, which was unusual. Nightingale had complained of spending 'rather a tiresome day in looking after *dahabiehs* [*sic*], in which we were not successful; one, which was beautiful, was rather too large and cost £60 a month! That wretch of a Milord has raised all the prices; the only others were too dirty and too small.'[33] The Milord in question was Lord Northampton, President of the Royal Society of Literature and of the Archaeological Institute of Great Britain. He was travelling with a large party, some days ahead of Nightingale and the Bracebridges, and was to incur her wrath several times in Egypt. But she might as justifiably have thanked him for the lack of suitable boats in Alexandria because she knew that people who had rented a boat at the coast had taken twelve days to reach the capital, whereas she had sped to Cairo in two on the *Marchioness of Breadalbane* and then enjoyed 'our lovely week'[34] in the capital.

There were no hotels south of Cairo at that time and no suitable houses available to rent, so the *dahabiya* would be their floating home. And as they were intending to spend three months on the river, their home needed to be large enough for the four of them to live in comfort, which meant at least two sleeping cabins and enough living space for days and nights. But then again, they didn't want the boat to be too big. This wasn't just a question of money. The river was blocked just south of Aswan by the first of a series of cataracts or rapids, and if the boat were too broad, too long, or had too deep a draught, it would not pass on to the upper reaches and they would therefore be unable to visit Abu Simbel.

In this, as in everything else, Mr Legros made enquiries for them. It clearly wasn't a very difficult assignment – in spite of the shortages Nightingale had hinted at in her letter – because two days after their arrival in Cairo, she wrote to tell her parents that they had found a boat. 'Tomorrow the bey, whose property it is and who has behaved very "handsome", comes to smoke the pipe of peace with us after his mosque (it being

Friday, his Sunday) and drink coffee, in order to conclude the bargain.'[35]

Nightingale does not make any further mention of this man, Hasan Bey, but she does give an idea of what his *dahabiya* looked like. 'I have not yet seen the boat,' she admitted. '. . . It has never carried Europeans, being built for his harem . . . It has two sleeping cabins and a sitting room, in which Trout will sleep . . . We shall not be off before Monday, however. Still we trust it will not be low Nile before we reach the first cataract. It is much the best boat they have seen.'[36]

It was Friday and they were hoping to sail on Monday; there was much to be done meanwhile, as the eminent British scholar Sir John Gardner Wilkinson made clear in his 1847 *Hand-Book for Travellers in Egypt*, which Nightingale had brought with her on the journey. 'The first thing . . . after taking a boat is to have it sunk, to rid it of the rats, and other noxious inhabitants it might have.'[37] But there was no time to have the boat sunk and dried, nor to follow some of Wilkinson's other suggestions, such as having the cracks filled with putty to cut out the draughts or having the cabins papered and repainted. 'Paste must not be used [on the wallpaper],' Wilkinson advised, 'as it will harbour insects, and is not likely to hold fast for any time.'[38]

They left the boat in the good hands of Hasan Bey and Paolo, their *dragoman* or interpreter, whom Mr Legros had also found for them, and spent the weekend preparing for their departure. Nightingale went to the bazaar to buy a carpet and then had her body, her mind and spirit attended to: she was scrubbed and oiled in the *hammam*, took the Sacrament at the Prussian Mission church on Sunday, consulted a book on birds, returned to the platform beside Muhammad Ali's mosque in the citadel to watch the sun set behind the pyramids, and dined twice with Consul Murray. She also went twice to visit Dr Abbott.

There was no public museum in Egypt in 1849, nowhere visitors could go to see the objects that Ancient Egyptians had used in their lives and death. This was perhaps as well as Nightingale confessed that, 'I hate a collection.' But there were private collectors and Consul Murray introduced her to one of them. Dr Abbott was a long-time British resident of Cairo who over the years had established a private museum.

Among his treasures were a ring that had belonged to Cheops, the builder of the Great Pyramid, and a necklace of Menes', one of the first recorded Kings of Egypt. More than this or the mummy bulls and ibises Abbott had bought, the object that appealed most to Nightingale was a funerary papyrus. This long scroll kindled her imagination. It was filled with inscriptions and images which, if one knew how to read them, would provide guidance on how to pass safely to the afterlife. But more than 25 years after the deciphering of hieroglyphs, most of the papyrus's inscriptions had yet to be studied.

'I should very much like to have understood [this] funeral papyrus,' she confided to her parents and, unable to read the inscriptions, she began to speculate, assuming that she was looking at some sort of story. 'An Egyptian novel apparently begins with a man's death . . . Then he is standing before Osiris, who sits with his whip in his hand and the dog Cerberus opposite him, and Truth writing down his deeds (with an ostrich feather which is her emblem) and the 40 assessors or judges, all ranged on a shelf above him, each with a different beast's head; another God is holding the scales, and his good deeds look very light.'[39]

She might not have been able to read the inscriptions, but she still managed to grasp one of the central tenets of Ancient Egyptian religion. She was looking at a representation of the judgment of Osiris, that terrifying moment when the dead person was tried by the god of the underworld, their heart weighed in the scales of truth against the feather of justice to decide whether they should be allowed through to eternal life. 'Condemned or justified I could not make out. But I never saw anything more interesting than this supernatural novel.'

Their appetite duly whetted – what new treasures would they see in the south? – Nightingale and the Bracebridges returned to the hotel at Ezbekiya and sent their luggage to the *dahabiya*. Then Nightingale wrote a last letter home and they dined with Mr Legros.

The consul's secretary had had their boat moved upstream, away from Boulaq, with all its noise and bustle, and where, as Nightingale put it, 'the Arabs and the fleas are dreadful'.[40] They left the hotel on a string of donkeys, each of them sitting on top of their mattress, and rode out of the city and over to the Island of Roda. This, as Nightingale knew, was where the child Moses was said to have been found. They rode through thickets of bulrushes towards their boat, so tall they could see nothing but the sky overhead.

The *dahabiya* was tied up on the west side of the island, beside one of the pasha's palaces. They watched the sunset and moonrise, listened to the frogs sing and saw the river run. Nightingale cut a small bouquet of roses and went on board, at peace, moved by the deep quiet of those solemn waters.

They set sail immediately, 'floating up so gently, so smoothly, that you can hardly perceive motion'.[41] It was late on Sunday 3 December 1849, and the pyramids, silent witnesses to their arrival, now loomed large over their departure.

Florence Nightingale spent eight days in Cairo before sailing south; Flaubert and Du Camp lingered for a couple of months. There were several reasons for the delay. The enthusiastic photographer had monuments he wished to record, and that took time. They both wanted to wait and see the return of the caravan of pilgrims from Mecca, one of the city's great annual spectacles. And Flaubert was relishing life in the city.

They began by spending a week at Saqqara and Giza, where they crawled into the Great Pyramid, slipping on bat dung, and then climbed to the top. Du Camp had raced ahead, determined to reach the top first so that he could play a trick on his friend: he had brought a calling card from Rouen, which he rested on a rock at the top. When Flaubert finally got there, he discovered the card of a man called Humbert Frotteur, who worked as a polisher, although Du Camp knew that the word had a slang meaning: wanker. That and Max's 'pathetic state' after having rushed ahead, set the tone for much that was to follow.

They camped at the base of the pyramids and then rode across the desert to visit the scant remains of the ancient capital of Memphis. They shot turtle doves on the edge of the valley and read their notes to each other lying on a rug, 'fleas jumping on the paper'.[42] Flaubert celebrated his twenty-eighth birthday on the day they returned to the city. They were in good spirits, eager, curious, well looked after by their servants and by the owner of the Hotel du Nil, where they had moved on their return from the pyramids. Flaubert recorded the owner's name as Monsieur Bouvaret.

Cairo had more than enough to keep them occupied for a few more weeks and Flaubert's notebook and letters are crammed with stories and impressions. He went to Matariya, where he was told Mary and Jesus had rested. For a week he employed a Cairene teacher to instruct him about Egyptian customs and traditions. He was up one morning before dawn to attend Mass in a Greek church, where he was overcome by the fresh scent coming from under the women's veils. His research for *Saint Anthony* came in useful when he went to discuss liturgy at a Coptic church. And then there was the extraordinary sight of the Mecca caravan, a crowd of travellers arriving at one of the city's medieval gates. Flaubert recorded seeing a naked cameleer, 200 Sufis lying down for their sheikh to ride his horse over them, and a gathering in the citadel palace with the ruler of Egypt. Finally there was a meeting in the French consulate to sign a contract with *Rais* Ibrahim Fergali, the owner and captain of a Nile boat. All of this was rich material and he captured as much as he could of selected moments in pages full of detailed observations. How else could we have known that the Sufi master wore a green turban and rode a dark chestnut horse?

In all this, Flaubert presented himself as many visitors to this extraordinary city have done, both before and since: as a passive onlooker. To his mother he explained it this way: 'I live like a plant, I fill myself with sun, with light, with colours and with fresh air. I eat: that's all. After that, what's left is to digest and to shit – and a good shit! That's the important bit.'[43]

To Louis Bouilhet he confided on a less certain note: 'Everything is mixed up and confused in my sick head',[44] complaining that he struggled to make sense of his experiences. The same day, he wrote a longer explanation of his state of mind to Dr Jules Cloquet, the family friend who had taken him to the Pyrenees and Corsica some years before.

Here we are in Egypt, *land of the Pharaohs, land of the Ptolemies, country of Cleopatra* (as one says in high style). Here we are and here we live, with our heads balder than our knees, smoking long pipes and drinking coffee on divans. What to say? What would you like me to write? I have hardly got over the first bedazzlement. It is like being thrown, fast asleep, into the middle of a Beethoven symphony, when the brasses are ear-splitting, the basses rumble and the flutes sigh. Details seize you, grab hold of you, pinch you, and the more you pay attention to it, the less you can grasp the whole.[45]

But he believed that if he persisted, if he kept on looking, studying, questioning, the pieces would fall into place. He knew he was attentive and he wrote to Cloquet that 'people who are attentive rediscover here much more than they discover. The seeds of a thousand notions that one carried within oneself grow and become more definite, like so many refreshed memories.'[46]

One of those seeds carried the notion that it was futile to strive for fame. When he left France, he could hardly bear to think of how far he was from fulfilling his ambition to write something that would astonish the Paris literary establishment. A couple of weeks in Cairo had reminded him of the futility of such vanity. On the day he and Du Camp boarded their boat, a *cange* or smaller version of the *dahabiya* Nightingale and the Bracebridges had rented, he wrote this to his mother:

When I get home, I shall resume my good and beautiful life of work, in my big study, in my comfortable armchairs, close to you, dear old thing, and that will be all. So don't speak about *pushing myself*: pushing myself towards what? What could satisfy me, if it is not the voluptuous joy of sitting at my round table? Haven't I everything that is most enviable in the world? Independence, freedom of my imagination, my 200 trimmed pens, and the skill to use them. And then the Orient, Egypt especially, smoothes away all the little worldly vanities. After visiting so many ruins, one doesn't think of building shacks. All this old dust makes you indifferent to success. At this precise moment I cannot understand (from a literary point even) the need to have people talk about me. To live in Paris, to publish, to move, all that seems very tiresome, seen from such a distance.[47]

He admitted that maybe, just maybe, he might change his mind in ten minutes, but in the event there was no time to do so, nor to tell his mother about it if he had done so.

'The weather is superb,' he assured the old lady back in cold, wintry Normandy and, omitting to mention that they were being devoured by fleas, added that: '[T]he sun is shining, and there is a good wind. We are off.' He then sealed the letter and handed it to a servant waiting on the bank; the lines were cast off, they floated out into the current.

7

The Stream of Time

'How happy in that cool, bright air to glide
By Esne, Edfou, Ombos! each in turn
A pleasure and to other joys a guide;–
Labourless motion, – yet enough to earn
Syene's roseate cliffs – Egypt's romantic bourn'
– Richard Monckton Milnes, *The Burden of Egypt* [1]

We think of Egypt as a single, unified country with a national identity, but in the 1840s, as now, it was a place of many moods, many different aspects. The north was touched by Europe and the Mediterranean; the south so much more African in character. The *dahabiya* sailed slowly and so the shift between the two was gradual, at first imperceptible.

Two weeks after leaving Cairo, Paolo, *dragoman* to the Bracebridge party, went forward to ask their captain how far they were from a small town called Girgeh.

The old man had spent his whole life on or alongside the

river and certainly knew where his boat was in relation to the town, as he knew every twist and turn of this, the last 1,000 or so miles of the river. And yet, to the *dragoman*, he replied, 'Only God knows.'

Well, Paolo continued, surely the esteemed skipper could at least give them an idea of when they might arrive.

'When God pleases . . . '

'But I ask you how many hours it is,' Paolo pressed on, 'because the master wants to put it down in his journal.'[2] Not even this mention of the man who was paying everyone's wages was enough to extract a figure from the *reis*, however.

To a European mind, especially one of the mid-nineteenth century bolstered by the new certainties of timetables and schedules and almanacs, clinging to a fixed belief in lists and orderliness, all this was a puzzle. Was the captain being bloody-minded? Superstitious? Or, as Florence Nightingale thought, just plain indifferent?

The truth perhaps lay somewhere else, midway between two very powerful forces. On the one hand, there were the number of variables: the captain could not have given a definite answer to the question of when they would arrive because such a thing could not be known with any certainty. All that a man of his experience could know for sure was that these things depended on the wind, the flow of the river, the mood of crew and the availability of food. In addition, you had to factor in any number of unexpected events that could, and inevitably would, overtake them. But more significant even than that was the immutable belief that everything was ultimately down to the will of God. On this journey along the river, as in life, they were in His hands. And He, the Merciful and Compassionate, would deliver them to Aswan, and then up the cataract to Nubia and the southernmost point of their journey, if and when it pleased Him. Looked at like that, there seemed little point in asking the captain when they might reach Girgeh, and none at all in worrying about getting there 'on time'.

Giving up control of the itinerary was just one of the many changes that the journey forced upon Miss Nightingale. She and Mr Bracebridge were used to making plans, and were usually reassured by the idea that they always knew what was coming next in their lives, but they were now obliged to live one moment at a time. (Mrs B. seemed less concerned about these things and more with her sketchbook and pencils.) As the days passed, and Cairo faded from her thoughts just as the minarets and dome of Muhammad Ali's mosque had faded from view, Nightingale learned to measure out her life, or the journey at least, with the meals she ate, the number of villages she walked around, with the tombs or temples she saw or passed, with birds spotted, new sights noted, with people met, purchases made, and letters written and sent.

There were advantages to this way of thinking, as there were in the peace that came from a fair wind and an attentive crew. There are few travel experiences as exciting as pushing out on to the Nile in a sailing boat. Wherever you have come from, however great your experience of sailing, of rivers, of Africa, whatever you have just done or said or thought, if you are in any way alive to new experience, this is a unique moment. For Nightingale, desperate for salvation through new experience, it was irresistibly moving. She was afloat on the river of history, on what she called 'the stream of Time'.

There was a long voyage ahead of them. The captain seemed aware of this; his movements were minimal, as if intent on conserving his energy. He did no more than incline his head a fraction to have the crew run around, cast off lines and loosen the sails. For a moment the current pushed them downstream as if it would carry them to the Mediterranean and throw them back into Europe, but then the wind filled the sail – a massive triangular sheet of cotton strips – the deck timbers creaked, and the captain smiled. Or at least he no longer frowned. His shoulders dropped a fraction and, without turning, he gave a brief instruction to the man at the tiller. Port a little, starboard. Or as they say on the Nile, *bahri* – to the seaside – and *gibli* – to the mountains. Then slowly, almost imperceptibly, they sailed against the current, upstream into Africa.

Florence Nightingale boasted that they had rented the largest *dahabiya* on the river. She had had it renamed the *Parthenope* in honour of her absent sister and had then taken a pair of scissors to her petticoat to cut out letters in Greek for a pennant: '[B]lue bunting with swallowtails, a Latin red cross upon it, and $\Pi AP\Theta ENI\Pi H$ in white tape. It was hoisted this morning at the yardarm, and looks beautiful. It has taken all my tape and a vast amount of stitches, but it will be the finest pennant on the river . . . The Union Jack flies at the stern, Mr B.'s colours half-way up the rigging, all made by ourselves.'[3]

A week after leaving Cairo, she wrote, '[W]e are now thoroughly settled in our house: all our gimlets are up, our divans out, our Turkish slippers provided, and everything on its own hook, as befits such close quarters.'[4] Florence Nightingale had a talent for organisation – this was to be the basis of her later fame – and she had enjoyed getting everything arranged neatly on board: the library of books they had brought from England or borrowed from Consul Murray on the shelves in the wood-panelled, green-painted saloon, clothes and bags stored in large closets in the passage between her cabin and that of the Bracebridges, Trautwein's sleeping things stowed away in the sitting area. Once order had been imposed on the chaos of bags and trunks and tin boxes, she paid attention to the kitchen.

'Our housekeeping is simple,' she wrote to her parents. Two large chests on deck served as storeroom and pantry as well as to separate their part of the deck from the crew's. Food was hung up to keep it away from rats and other pests – the bread in a basket, meat in a safe, oranges in a box. Beyond the storage area, there was another that served as a kitchen, and behind that the large clay jar where their water was filtered. 'So we have kitchen, scullery, still room, larder, safe, and pantry, all in a nutshell, or at least in a walnut.'[5] She enjoyed the simplicity of the arrangement and taunted her mother, 'Ah! would that you could keep house in England so.'[6]

Although the itinerary was beyond their control, a routine on board was soon fixed. However early they woke, they ate breakfast around 8.30 or 9 a.m., dinner at 3 p.m. – on deck if it was warm enough, or not too hot – and supper sometimes as late as 9 p.m. After that, they read, caught up with their notes, Selina Bracebridge worked on her sketches, Trautwein returned to her needlepoint, the captain sat on shore with his pipe, and the crew sang and occasionally danced.

As the days passed and the novelty of being afloat began to wear off, the boat came to seem small. She who longed for revolutions, for seismic shifts and sweeping changes, found it difficult to watch the world pass by so slowly. 'I am no *dahabieh* [*sic*] bird,' she confessed, 'no divan incumbent. I do long to be wandering about the desert by myself, poking my own nose into all the villages and running hither and thither, and making acquaintances *où bon me semble*. I long to be riding on my ass across the plain, I rejoice when the wind is foul and I can get ashore. They [the crew] call me "the wild ass of the wilderness, snuffing up the wind", because I am so fond of getting away. I dearly love our *dahabieh* as my home, but if it is to stay in it the whole day, as we are fain to do when the wind is fair, that is not in my way at all.'[7]

For this reason, the journey upriver was harder than the return. The most important thing on the journey up was to make the most of the wind. If it were blowing, they would not stop, whatever they might miss in passing. But the wind was not always fair and they were becalmed near the town that Paolo had enquired about: Girgeh. No wonder the captain had been reluctant to be pinned down to an arrival time.

The Nile was broad here and split by an island: near this, the town of Girgeh, named after Mari Girgis, St George, patron saint of Egypt as of England, was set well back from the water. Nightingale went out early to walk around what had once been the capital of Upper Egypt and found it to be nothing more than a 'considerable' village. Trout and the Bracebridges were still in bed, but Paolo was attentive beside her as ever. The *khan*, an inn where travellers stayed, caught her attention and she looked in to see 'strings of camels round the walls; a few inner cells behind them, roofless and floorless'.[8] Afraid of attracting attention, she covered her face with her shawl. But however successful she had been at visiting the Alexandria mosque incognito, there was no way to disguise her foreignness in such a place; a tray of 'Turkish thimblefuls of coffee' was brought out to welcome the *hawaga* or white woman. She was delighted by the gesture and its 'refinement'. 'In every village you see a coffee house: generally a roofless cabin built of maize stalks with mud benches round the inside, but always the thimblefuls of coffee, made, not like ours, but pounded, boiled for a moment and poured off directly and drunk black.'[9]

The *Parthenope* had continued tacking across the river while Nightingale and Paolo were on shore, but it had made so little progress that they were able to stroll over to it for breakfast. Back on board, floating lazily on the river, Nightingale sat down with paper and pen to describe the scene to her parents. She wrote that the Nile here:

. . . looks like a great sea, he is so wide – and when the wind freshens, you see a fleet of little *cangias* coming out, like water lilies upon the river (you don't know from where), or like fairy boats, a fleet of *Efreets* [spirits] coming up the Nile, doubling a cape, cutting in among each other. There are islands and headlands and creeks, just like a sea, and sometimes, when the wind blows against the current, it is no longer the solemn Nile, but a most tempestuous lake, with white horses, and turbulent little waves. But he is always beautiful.[10]

At this point, she must have read the pages she had just written and realised how they would read to people back home. All those lilies and horses and spirits made her feel the need to explain this 'very stupid letter'. In doing so, she wrote one of her most revealing ones.

A sort of torpor crawls over one in a *dahabieh*. You feel, as you lie on the divan, and float slowly along, and the shores pass you gently by, as if you were being carried along some unknown river to some unknown shore, leaving for ever all you had ever known before – a mysterious feeling creeps over you, as if it were the passage to some other world, the invisible journey through the valley – not of death, but as the ancients imagined death, a shore where all you have known appear as shades. You feel as if in the power of some unseen spirits, who are wafting you away from all you have ever seen to the far-off land.[11]

A torpor, an unknown shore, shades and unseen spirits, the loss of all one has ever known . . . It sounds like a classic case of what Flaubert called *dépaysement*, a word often translated as 'disorientation' although in this case a better translation would be '*re*-orientation'. Nightingale had come to the Orient – to Egypt – expressly to be carried to an unknown shore, to find salvation or, at the very least, to forget about her troubles. It seemed to be working.

She had recorded many memorable sights in her little pocket diary since boarding the *dahabiya* – the 'citadel of Cairo spectral and white'; the reading of the *Arabian Nights* and the Bible story of Joseph being sold into slavery by his brothers; the Armenian governor of a small town who swore 'eternal friendship' to her; a 'little hot walk on the naked desert'; the 'undescribed misery of an African village'; mounted police; a visit to quarries; monks in a Coptic monastery; a first sight of sugar cane; an hour ('such an hour') spent watching young camels graze; the shooting of an owl; the cry of jackals, and the cemetery where corpses had been dug up by them; sunset on the river; water the colour of 'molten gold'; a sky of sapphire blue. This mass of observation was a sign that for her the process of transformation had already begun.

When she wrote that 'the whole Nile is so unnatural – if one may use the expression – so unlike nature,' she meant that it was unlike any nature she had seen before. 'The descriptions of the gardens in the *Arabian Nights*, with the precious stones, seem no longer here fantastic.'[12] In a place where skies were of molten gold and gardens bloomed with precious stones, surely a person could think, could dream, could *be* whatever they wanted?

But there were challenges. She had been sent to Egypt to recover her health, to get over the end of her relationship with Richard Monckton Milnes and to set aside her ridiculous idea of becoming a nurse. Or so her family had hoped. Her visits to the sisters of St-Vincent-de-Paul in Alexandria had raised eyebrows at home, but there had been no further mention of such places or such work since then. She had not gone to the famous hospital in Cairo, for instance, as Flaubert had done, to inspect the syphilitics with their anal chancres. Since Cairo, she had been overwhelmed by the poverty and deprivation that Egyptians suffered.

When she wrote that no European had the slightest idea of just how miserable an African village could be, it is safe to assume she was writing about herself. Awareness came on this stretch of the river, with a visit to a small village. 'I saw a door about three feet high, of a mud hut, and peeping in, saw in the darkness nothing but a white-horned sheep and a white hen. But something else was moving, and presently crawled out four human beings, three women and a child.'[13] Villages seemed poorer and more derelict the further south they went. Asyut, a provincial capital, looked 'like the sort of city animals might have built, when they had possession of the earth'.[14] In a village to the south, a mud hut would have been a luxury: most people lived surrounded by mud walls beneath a cornstalk roof.

Harriet Martineau had warned that a Nile voyage was a serious labour, and perhaps this was one of the travails she meant. Here was a young woman, soon to be famous for her compassion, struggling to understand how people could live in such circumstances. Worse still, she failed to see how their situation could be improved: she wrote to Dr Fowler, the Salisbury Infirmary physician, of 'the impossibility of doing the slightest good, the feeling of utter helplessness for any future to these miserable Arabs'.[15] The more she struggled, the more she took refuge in her thoughts and in the past.

She had come here for many reasons, chief among them Egypt's antiquities, but it was not until ten days and some 170 miles from Cairo, at a place called Beni Hassan, that Nightingale had what she called her 'first real Egyptian day',[16] her first close encounter with Ancient Egypt.

The previous day they had noticed openings in the ridge of limestone that hemmed in the east side of the Nile valley. From the river these could have been mistaken for caves but were in fact tombs cut into the rock, and she prayed for the wind to drop so that she could go and visit them. She must have prayed too earnestly because the wind dropped so instantly and so completely that it took until sundown to reach the landing nearest the tombs; it was too late to visit then. She prayed again that there would be no wind in the morning and again her prayers were answered.

The party was ready before dawn: the Bracebridges, and Paolo, and Trautwein, who brought her knitting. This area was known for its thieves as well as its tombs, so the captain sent some of the men from the boat, who came wearing red *tarbushes* and swinging heavy sticks. 'At sunrise we put off in the little boat, crossed the Nile, and landed just below those magic holes,' she wrote with breathless enthusiasm. Then she checked herself. 'Holes did I call them, with their square entrances as fresh as if they had been chiselled yesterday.'[17]

They had six glorious hours to scramble up the cliff and climb into the openings. In her diary, Nightingale noted '30 caves' and a 'glorious day, a curious contrast to my first sight of the Sistine Chapel, this day two years ago'.[18] She believed the tombs were the oldest monuments in Egypt after the pyramids and therefore also among the oldest surviving monuments anywhere in the world. She was wrong. They were cut around 2000 BCE, so although they were old, they were not the oldest monuments. But their supposed antiquity added a frisson to the visit.

If you visit out-of-the-way Beni Hassan today, you may be lucky enough to find a person with a key to open the tombs and turn on the lights. You will only make the effort to reach them, braving armed convoys and police checks, if you

FLORENCE NIGHTINGALE

aged about 25   drawn by J.H.B.C.

Florence Nightingale by her cousin, Hilary Bonham Carter, four years before Egypt.

A rare photograph of Gustave Flaubert, taken by Maxime Du Camp in the garden of the Hotel du Nil, Cairo, on 9 January 1850.

Embley, in Hampshire, the Nightingales' winter home. It was here, on 7 February 1837, that Florence Nightingale was 'called to service'.

Flaubert's study, with its white bearskin, at the family house in Le Croisset, outside Rouen. He wrote *The Temptation of Saint Anthony* and *Madame Bovary* at the round table.

Nightingale and the Bracebridges. Jerry Barrett's painting captures the closeness of their relationship.

HÔTEL D'ORIENT AU CAIRE

COULOMB FRÈRES

The Coulomb brothers' Hôtel d'Orient was favoured by French travellers.

Maxime Du Camp, Flaubert's friend and travelling companion. Writer, Chevalier of the Légion d'Honneur and publisher of *Madame Bovary*.

A *cange*, the smaller Nile boat used by Flaubert and Du Camp, passing Luxor Temple.

David Roberts' view
of the hypostyle
hall at Karnak as
it appeared when
Flaubert and
Nightingale saw it.

David Roberts' view from under the portico of the Temple of Edfou, Upper
Egypt.

Maxime Du Camp's view across the Nile to Esna, home to Kuchuk Hanem.

Philae, which Florence Nightingale called the Holy Isle and where she experienced a religious epiphany.

One of four colossal sculptures of Ramses II at Abu Simbel, still buried in sand, photographed by Maxime Du Camp.

already know of the joys ahead of you. Most of the 30 rock-cut tombs had already lost their decoration when Nightingale went to visit, victim of the slow deterioration of time or the random destruction of robbers. But the ones that had survived were among the finest painted tombs to be seen anywhere in Egypt.

The eastern sun did not shine into their doorways (looking west), still we could see plainly enough; all civilised trades were there – glass, iron – all the rest of it; also the trade – shall I call it civilised or not? – of opera dancing; Pierrot, making a *jet d'homme*, with extended leg, showing that precedent is not always good, we have so closely followed our Egyptian antecedents. Ships, with rudders exactly like those on Lago Maggiore, the men rowing, standing. The colours and even drawing of these things showed them to be good chemists and good draughtsmen at this day. The dress of the women was civilised – the ornaments and bracelets were invariably red, green and white, the Italian colours.[19]

One tomb in particular caught her attention as it had that of Jean-François Champollion, the Frenchman responsible for deciphering hieroglyphic writing, who stopped at Beni Hassan 21 years before Flaubert and Florence Nightingale.

Champollion had had scrupulous copies made of the tomb paintings in all their perfect, vivid modernity, perhaps remembering the story of an earlier Nile traveller. James Bruce had visited Egypt in the 1760s and returned home with images, from a tomb in Luxor, of a man playing a harp. Although his copies were faithful to the original, Bruce was mocked when he showed them at home. The great Dr Samuel Johnson, critic, compiler of the first English dictionary, and an authority on

North Africa, laughed loudest. Johnson had never been near the Nile, but that did not stop him commenting that Bruce's Egyptian scene owed more to an eighteenth-century Adam drawing room than to Ancient Thebes. He even went so far as to suggest that Bruce had not even travelled to Africa, but instead had taken a long holiday somewhere around the Mediterranean. Bruce never got over the accusation and died a bitter man.

The memory of this unhappiness seems to have hung over Champollion as he had the Beni Hassan paintings copied. Few people would have doubted his authority on Egyptian matters, but he knew how extraordinary these tomb paintings were and decided he would need 'the full complement of the 14 witnesses who saw them to convince people in Europe of the accuracy of our drawings'.[20]

Champollion was particularly fascinated by a series of images that showed foreigners being presented to a pharaoh's scribes. Here, he suggested, was a scene straight out of the Bible: Joseph of the coat of many colours, sold into slavery in Egypt and become the pharaoh's vizier, receiving his brothers. The tomb, Champollion believed, was certainly of the right date, and all the evidence seemed to suggest that this scene was related to the Bible story with which they were all familiar. Might this be Joseph's tomb? Or that of one of his brothers or someone else connected to the story?

Champollion's speculation sparked heated debate in Europe, as he knew it would. The possibility that real-life representations of biblical characters might have survived was of great importance in an age when Christianity was still so widely practised and yet was challenged on every side by new scientific theories.

The British scholar Sir John Gardner Wilkinson recognised the importance of the tomb, if Champollion's suggestion could be verified. 'Should this ever prove to be the case, they [the paintings] will be looked upon with unbounded interest, and be justly deemed the most curious painting on the Egyptian monuments.'[21] But he for one did not 'see sufficient reason for supposing them to represent that event'. Nightingale had her own opinion.

> To me it seems a matter of very little consequence to decide the question: whether or no . . . All that one wants to know is, that in this soil nearly 4000 or 5000 years ago men stood who felt and thought like us, who cared for their brothers, and mourned over their dead with an everlasting love and a preserving memory like us – that memorials of their love have remained while all remembrance of them has passed away – and while the sound of their names has died away into an hieroglyph, the sound of the beating of their hearts still echoes from under those dim lotus-leaved rocky chambers . . . The stone does find a voice, and the sand of the desert tongues, wherewith to speak to us.[22]

In the early afternoon, she and the Bracebridges, Paolo, Trautwein and the rest of the entourage, made their way from the 'holes' back down towards the river, and their *dahabiya* drifted slowly across to meet them. 'So ends our Beni Hassan day,' she wrote as the boat moved ever more slowly upstream, 'the first of many wonders, but none more curious.'[23] Prophetic words – and wrong.

Eight days after seeing the tombs at Beni Hassan, they rode up to the less famous caves of Lycopolis, above Asyut. 'There is nothing in them so interesting as in Beni Hassan,' she wrote home.[24] But that did not stop her spending the morning crawling into tombs and caches that had once been sacred to

Anubis, the jackal-headed god. They found parts of mummified jackals. Later, the caves had been used by early Christian hermits, the two different periods of history, the pharaonic and Christian, overlaying each other here as they did so often in Egypt. As Florence stood on the slope, looking down on to the chaos of Asyut below, thinking of the glory of Ancient Egypt, she decided that:

[I]t is good for British pride to think, here was a nation more powerful than we are, and almost as civilised, 4000 years ago, – for 2000 years already they have been a nation of slaves, – in 2000 years where shall we be? – shall we be like them?

It is good for Christian pride, too, to be called 'dog' in the street, pointed at, spat at, as we are here. No one looks at us with respect, hardly with curiosity, – we are too low. They take our money and have done with us.[25]

She might have been right about British pride and the downfall of nations, but she was wrong when she wrote that Egyptians thought nothing of her, that they had no curiosity. When Gustave Flaubert reached Asyut, months later, he and Du Camp also climbed up to the Lycopolis caves. While there, as he described in his journal, 'our guide takes us by the hand and leads us with an air of mystery to show us the imprint, in the sand, of a little boot – a woman's boot. It belonged to an Englishwoman who had passed there a few days ago.'[26] Du Camp added that the guide – 'poor fool!' – believed he would see this gracious female from the north when she sailed back down the Nile.

Was this another of those serendipitous moments when Nightingale and Flaubert came physically close to each other?

*

'You know what a dream is?' Nightingale asked her parents. It is 'a strange phantasmagoria' of thoughts and experiences linked in some deep, subconscious way.

> And such is Egypt, grand old solid Egypt, fuller of facts (facts graven on stone, and the very stones facts themselves) than any other country in the world, but fuller also of thought and more really spiritual than [the Holy Land] . . . And the Nile is the stream of Time; shall we call it a god or an emblem of eternity, or rather of the perpetual succession of events amid which we live? Glide up it and the world rolls back; rest at anchor, and time and events glide downwards past you on their course.[27]

It was a fitting introduction to Luxor, home to 'those awful spectres of dead Time and Space'.[28]

Would they stop at Luxor on the way south? She had woken one night with a nightmare that they were obliged to turn around and float back to Cairo without seeing it. Early on the morning of New Year's Eve, the wind was fair. More anxiety. But around midday, the wind dropped, the river was suddenly calm, the valley widened and the hills rolled back. 'The colonnades at Luxor and Karnak came in sight, the Ramesseum and the matchless pair. Thebes 4:00 p.m., 48 hours from Qena. There she lay, the glorious corpse of the spirit which had gone out and animated the world.'[29] And there they stopped.

If you have visited Luxor, or if you have any idea of how it looks today, at this point you need to clear your mind. You must try to imagine it without the hotels and shops and all the other clutter of a century and a half of rampant tourist development. You must undo the work of all those Egyptologists who have toiled under the sun and through winter winds to expose and restore the grand monuments of the past. Luxor today is a large city that lives off tourism. In the winter of 1849 it was no more than a scattering of houses dwarfed by ancient ruins. Most of what is now city was then either farmland or flood plain.

On the east bank, the modern city-side, the 3,500-year-old Luxor Temple was still mostly unexcavated. A route had been cleared into a part of the temple and one entered, as in ancient times, through the gate of the *pylon*, the massive outer mud-brick wall. The south side of the temple and the sanctuary were still buried in sand and silt almost up to the capitals of their mighty pillars. The colonnade, one of the temple's most striking features today, was only partly covered by silt.

Now that the temple and surrounding area has been excavated, the rebuilt tomb of Luxor's 'patron saint', the fourteenth-century Iraqi scholar Youssef Abu'l Hajjaj, gives an idea of the different ground levels on the site: it is perched on top of the ancient structure. A clutter of buildings had been built near the holy man's remains, among them the so-called 'French House', where the adventurer Giovanni Belzoni lived while arranging for the shipping of the great bust of Ramses II, 'Ozymandias', to the British Museum. A pencil sketch by Edward Lear, who visited in 1867, shows many other mud houses around it, all of them since demolished.

A mile and a half north of Luxor, the Temple of Karnak, the largest temple complex on earth and home to the great state god Amun-Ra, had been partially cleared by 1849, but was mostly grazing land for local herders. Across the river, several villages dotted the east-facing slopes of the looming Theban Hills, which still kept the secrets of the fabulous tombs and massed mummy pits. But whereas today you come to a city and look for the ruins, wondering as you peer through the haze across the river whether you are looking at a temple *pylon* or an apartment building, in 1849 you would have come to a scene of devastation and first looked for your letters from home.

The *reis* tied up the *Parthenope* under the colonnade of Luxor Temple. The sun was low over the Theban Hills, the afternoon light soft as a caress. Practicalities attended to, Nightingale ran up the bank to see the temple before dark. She started at the north end, away from the houses, where the obelisk that Flaubert had seen on a barge in Rouen harbour had originally stood. Its twin looked as ' fresh and unbroken as the day it was cut'. She walked past the colossi, past the colonnade of lotus columns. 'The Holy Places,' she wrote home, 'are all blocked up, choked with huts and sand; but the cartouches, when you *can* see them, are all so fresh and sharp that even our inexperienced eyes could read the legends of the Kings'.[30]

But in spite of her excitement at the fulfilment of her wish to live long enough to see this magical place, what struck her now was not the monument itself so much as the mud huts all around: some were no more than thin-thatched shelters, a few were more solid, mud-brick, palm-roofed houses. Flaubert's line that this 'was a great place for contrasts' was nowhere truer than here. Nightingale was horrified. 'I never before saw any of my fellow creatures degraded (thieves, bad men, women and children), but I longed to have intercourse with them, to stay with them, and make plans for them; but here, one gathered one's clothes about one, and felt as if one had trodden in a nest of reptiles.'[31]

This failure of compassion needed an explanation and Nightingale very quickly provided one. 'It is not the bodily misery which shocks one,' she wrote, trying to reason against her outburst, 'I have seen greater than that in London.' In contrast to the poor back home, the people who lived in huts around Luxor Temple raised calves, turkeys, hens, goats and camels. Their corn was excellent, their bread of the whitest, finest flour and as well baked as anything back home. She could have dealt with the physical misery, could have found some way to improve things. What upset her so much was what she thought of as this place's 'moral degradation, a voluntary debasement'.[32] How, she asked again, could people who had achieved such greatness have fallen so low? 'The contrast could not be more terrible than the savages of the present in the temples of the past at Luxor.'[33]

But time moved on, even here. Night fell, a new year approached.

'Yes, my dear people,' she wrote home for a second time that day, 'I think your imagination has hardly followed me through the place where I have been spending the last night of the old year. Did you listen to it passing away and think of me? Where do you think I heard it sigh out its soul? In the dim unearthly colonnades of Karnak, which stood and watched it, motionless, silent, and awful, as they had done for thousands of years.'[34]

Along with the rest of the party, Nightingale had ridden a donkey from the *dahabiya*, with one man helping her keep balance in the saddle, another leading the animal over the sand and rock. There was no moon and they rode in silence through the darkness until they came to a stand of palms. Beyond it stood 'a ghostly avenue [of] gigantic sitting sphinxes, with their faces toward us'[35] and a *pylon*, one of a series of massive sloped walls that guarded the sanctity of the temple complex. They seemed to reach to heaven and yet also provided a hint of the grandeur of the earth beyond them.

Scrambling over 'hills and valleys made of ruins', for the temple had not yet been cleared, they came to the forest of pillars, the most extraordinary hall of this, the most extraordinary religious complex. After the clutter of huts and animals in Luxor, here there was space, grandeur and silence:

they were completely alone. They sat beneath the stars, surrounded by massive, hewn stones. Dogs howling some way off made Nightingale think of 'the spirits of the old *Efreet* Egyptians let loose'[36]. When she looked at the forest of columns towering above her and blocking her way, each one unimaginably huge and carved with gods and kings and animal spirits, it was hard not to believe in the greatness of the people who had inhabited this sacred place. She and Mr Bracebridge climbed on to the roof of one of the buildings, but even from a height, it was too dark to see much. And anyway, by now she was exhausted. 'Thebes takes so much out of one. I fell asleep on my ass, riding home a mile and a half from Karnak. It was no use trying to think or to feel anything. I only managed to stick on.'

The following morning there was time for a little thought, to write another letter home before breakfast and to spend more than an hour back in Luxor Temple. There was not much of a wind, certainly not enough to warrant rushing off – the captain would not have insisted on it. But they had been invited to dine on another English boat that afternoon and they wished to be off. Preferring to be becalmed than bored, they set sail for the south as soon as possible, with Nightingale up on the poop. Seen from there, 'less disturbed by the mud huts',[37] the temple was beautiful. She watched it slide away as if waking from a dream, one of those strange phantasmagoria she had been trying to understand, the world rolling back as they glided up the 'stream of Time'.

8

Hunting the Bee

'I dance like a bee . . . I am not a woman, I am a world.
My clothes have only to fall, and you will discover on me
a succession of mysteries' – The Queen of Sheba in
Gustave Flaubert's *The Temptation of Saint Anthony*

When Gustave Flaubert and Maxime Du Camp reached
Luxor, at around 4.30 in the afternoon of Monday 4 March, the
wind was up and their *reis*, Ibrahim Fergali, wanted to seize the
moment and sail past the ruins.

The *cange* was smaller and faster than the *Parthenope*. Du
Camp described it as being around 40 feet long, painted blue,
with a cabin and salon for himself and a small cabin for his
servant, Sassetti. He made no mention of Flaubert. The
twelve-man crew and the *dragoman* ate, cooked and slept up
front on the lower deck.

Captain Fergali was a self-contained twenty-five-year-old,
the sort of man who rarely spoke, ate apart and was always

alert. He charted each shift of the river, watched every manoeuvre of the boat. In spite of the simplicity of his blue robe and white turban, Du Camp detected a certain grandeur about the man that was in no way diminished when he saw him, somewhere around Beni Hassan, rolling around the deck, howling and in tears, having just had a tooth pulled. In the normal course of events their captain had a naturally commanding way: as they came up to Luxor, for instance, one of the consular agents called out that there were letters waiting for the Frenchmen and the captain steered over to the bank to collect them, but forbade his passengers to land. He knew that if he let them off in Luxor he would have trouble getting them back on board. The mail was duly brought to the boat and the *cange* carried on south.

Travelling on the Nile was 'an important undertaking' in 1849. By the time Du Camp wrote those words, reminiscing in 1893, the journey along the Egyptian stretch of the river had become nothing more than an excursion. In a description that will be familiar to anyone who has cruised the Nile in our own time, Du Camp explained that:

> Steamboats ascend the Nile and stop at convenient stages. There are on board a guide to give information, a cook to provide meals, and a doctor to make up prescriptions. Everything is prepared and regulated. Breakfast at a certain hour, a time to admire, a time to dine, a time to sleep. The prices are quite reasonable . . . but all initiative ceases, and upon a journey initiative is an element which should not be left out.

He went on, almost incredulously, to mention the Winter Palace Hotel, which had opened seven years earlier, in 1886:

At Luxor, so it seems, there is an English hotel built near the ruins. Furnished apartments, mock-turtle soup and pale ale are provided, where I ate only hard-boiled eggs and drank sparkling water without inconvenience. I suppose that this is the progress of civilisation and of the business spirit which I admire, but which I am glad to say did not exist in my time.[1]

The reference to hard-boiled eggs is slightly disingenuous. As we have already seen, the list of items they brought from France or bought in Cairo was extensive and even included a large *tricolore* which hung from the mast of the *cange*.

They had been on the river for almost four weeks and had reached Luxor when Du Camp sensed that Flaubert was unhappy with the journey. He found his friend listless and bored, and suspected he was dissatisfied with the reality of the long dreamed-of Orient. Flaubert's spirits seemed to have sunk so low that at one point Du Camp suggested he abandon the trip. 'If you wish to return to France, my servant can accompany you home.'[2]

'No,' Flaubert insisted, 'I have come, and I will carry out my intention. Choose our route and I will follow you; it is all the same to me which way we go.'

But Du Camp misunderstood his companion when he wrote that 'to him one temple seemed precisely like another, the mosques and the points of view exactly similar'. And he was wrong when he interpreted his friend's inactivity for boredom, and in thinking that 'could he [Flaubert] have lain on a divan and watched the scenery, the cities and the monuments pass before him like a panorama, he would have liked travelling'.[3] Flaubert loved to travel and, for all his indolence, while he lay on the divan appearing to be bored, he was taking in everything he could see and hear and smell, gulping down the colours, absorbing the sights and sounds, turning over the thoughts and feelings they provoked, living 'like a plant', as he had described to his mother from Cairo.

As they came to Luxor, the supine traveller climbed on to the top deck, as Nightingale had done. He cleaned his spyglass. He must also have had his notebook to hand, for in it he recorded a sequence of impressions:

> The seven columns, the obelisk, the French House – Some Arabs sitting at the water's edge near a British *cange*. – The guardian of the French House calls out that he has a letter for us, it is a card from Baron Anca. – We stop. – Among the people beside our boat, a black, wrapped like a mummy, all gristle, desiccated, with a dirty little *takieh* on the top of his head; – some women washing their feet in the water – a donkey comes to drink.[4]

As they moved on, the setting sun turned the Theban Hills indigo, the palms as black as ink, the sky burned blood red and the river turned the colour of burnished steel. Night came suddenly. Each shift, each colour change, each movement, was observed in minute detail by the plant-like writer. His eyes flickered, his body lay inert, his friend despaired. Two nights later, in what has become the most famous and most reviled of all Orientalist scenes, there was rather more activity displayed by both of them.

Thirty miles south of Luxor, a barrage now straddles the Nile at Esna, measuring out the flow of water to the farmers below and forcing pleasure cruisers to pass through a lock. No such barrier blocked the river in the winter of 1849 and Florence Nightingale, who had already stopped at Luxor, sailed past Esna on a fair breeze. Ibrahim Fergali, Flaubert's *reis*, had other ideas. Esna was a port and industrial town, a hub on the age-old caravan trail between the interior of Africa, the Egyptian oases in the Western Desert and the Mediterranean in the north, and he berthed the French boat there for a day and a night to lay in supplies and for his crew to bake bread. The opportunity was not lost on Flaubert and Du Camp. To them, the word Esna had just one association: not bread, but *almehs*.

The Arabic word *almeh* translates literally as 'learned woman' and was used to describe those who were expert, above all, in the art of narrative song. Edward Lane had written about them in the 1830s in his *An Account of the Manners and Customs of the Modern Egyptians*, a book Flaubert had recommended to his mother as something 'that should distract you'.[5] In the book, Lane described how these women were often invited to harem celebrations and occasionally to larger gatherings: 'I have heard the most celebrated '*Awalim* [the plural of *almeh*] in Cairo, and have been more charmed with their songs . . . than with any other music I have ever enjoyed.'[6]

Muhammad Ali Pasha had allowed *almehs* to perform openly in Cairo from 1832, but they had so outraged public opinion and the religious authorities that they had been exiled to the south, to Esna to be precise. Since then, the nomenclature had become confused and all sorts of public performers now went by the name of *almeh*. The women of Esna were no bluestockings. As Gardner Wilkinson explained in his *Hand-Book for Travellers in Egypt*: '[T]he learning of these "*learned women*" has long since ceased; their poetry has sunk into absurd songs; their dancing would degrade even the *motus Ionico* [the lascivious dances] of antiquity; and their title *Almeh* has been changed to the less respectable name of *Ghawázee*, or women of the Memlooks [*sic*].'[7]

Esna looked a dreary place from the river. The Nile had eroded the riverbank and taken with it some of the town's finer houses. Du Camp, who crossed the river to take his photograph, shows it as a steep bank littered with building debris, above which are two surviving clusters of houses, divided by a fat, 11th-century minaret. The town had a sleepy market that came to life when caravans arrived from Sudan, filling the stalls and caravanserai with slaves, camels, ivory, ostrich feathers, gum senna and piles of other exotic goods. But there was no caravan in town when the Frenchmen docked, just *almehs*, and they did not have to wait long to meet one.

Soon after the boat had tied up near a clump of palms, while the men were eating, a slender young woman came to talk to the *dragoman*. Her name was Bambeh. Her face, only partly hidden by a blue veil, was not particularly attractive, but her eyes were memorable, highlighted with antimony. More striking than the woman was the sheep that walked behind her: as tame as a pet dog, its wool was dyed red with henna, its mouth muzzled with a black velvet strap. Flaubert laughed out loud at the sight of it.

Bambeh had come to invite them to visit her mistress, the famous *almeh* Kuchuk Hanem. The Frenchmen accepted the invitation and said they would visit her later. First, they went to town.

Esna failed to impress them. Du Camp found the souks small, badly stocked and without atmosphere. Flaubert thought nothing matched up to the towns further north – mud-brick Esna was not as large as Qena, its souks not as important; there were fewer prostitutes, their clothes were less wonderful, their appearance less impressive. He bought ink at a *madrasa* and went to the temple. This, at least, was worth the detour.

Construction of Esna's temple had begun around the middle of the second century BCE. It was dedicated to ram-headed Khnum, the god credited with creating the first men on a potter's wheel, and to the goddesses Neith and Satet, both associated with the Nile. It had been used throughout the Roman period but was then abandoned and overwhelmed by the debris of centuries. At the beginning of the 1840s, when the ruler Muhammad Ali Pasha had passed through, it was still mostly buried. The pasha had ordered the portico, the first hall of the temple, to be cleared, and even today it remains some nine metres below street level. Whatever survives of the main halls and sanctuary of the temple is still buried under the town, beside the souk.

The French travellers saw the Roman-era portico, complaining about the long flight of palm-trunk steps cut into the mud. While they noted inscriptions made by some of Napoleon's troopers 50 years earlier – Louis Ficelin, Ladouceur, Lamour, Luneau, François Dardant – they failed to recognise the irony of Esna's ancient name. The Greeks had called it Latopolis, city of the *Lates niloticus* or Nile perch. This particular fish was said to have devoured the god Osiris' penis, after his brother Seth cut his body into 14 parts, and was therefore an appropriate place of exile for the country's courtesans and dancing girls. From the temple, Bambeh and her sheep led the two Frenchmen to the house of Kuchuk Hanem.

There are many discrepancies between the two men's descriptions of this visit. Du Camp himself wrote two accounts of his journey in Egypt, one, *Le Nil: Egypte et Nubie*, published in 1853, in which Flaubert does not appear at all, and another in his 1890s memoirs, which does at least admit that his friend accompanied him along the Nile. Neither is entirely reliable. In the latter, for instance, there is no mention of *almehs*.

In the former, Du Camp records that the sun had already set behind the western hills when they reached the woman's house. He thought she was Syrian, the former mistress of

Abbas Pasha, the ruler, although Abbas, he had been told, preferred young men. He found her walking down the stairs into the courtyard of her house looking . . .

> . . . like an apparition. With the last rays of sun wrapping her in light, dressed in a simple gauze blouse the colour of Madeira brown and large, white, cotton pantaloons with pink stripes, her naked feet in *babouches*, shoulders covered by the blue silk tassel from her *tarbush*, her neck bound by three necklaces of big beads, her arms encircled with shiny bracelets, her ears decorated with trapezoid rings laden with gold balls, her hair plaited and tied with a black ribbon, white, firm, happy, full of youth and life, she was superb.[8]

Several other women and a couple of musicians arrived and raki (Arak) was served in champagne glasses left by an English tourist. At one point, the older musician stood up, put the bottle to his lips and emptied it, after which the men played, the women danced, the Frenchmen observed, night fell, a few lamps were lit, and an old woman arrived to dance with a skill that none of the younger ones had shown. 'As you can imagine,' Du Camp wrote, 'I was happy, but not satisfied.'[9]

He had come to the *almehs* expressly to see the Bee, a legendary dance that was said to drive men wild with desire. He did see it: Kuchuk Hanem danced for him. But instead of being consumed by lust, he recorded that it left him feeling tired, so he returned to the boat and they set sail around four in the morning.

When Flaubert read Du Camp's account, in 1853, he was unimpressed, and bothered more by the omissions than the fabrications. 'There is nothing either in its basic understanding or in its facts,' he wrote to Louise Colet.[10] 'The details he observed best, and most characteristic in nature, he has forgotten. You, who have read my notes, will be struck by that. What a rapid decline!'

Flaubert's own accounts of the night – and, like Du Camp, he left two of them, one in his journal, written the following day, and another in a long letter to Louis Bouilhet, written a few days later – match each other, but differ in many ways from Du Camp's version. To Bouilhet, Flaubert wrote:

> She had just come from the bath. A large *tarbush* whose scattered tassel fell on her large shoulders, and which had on its peak a gold plaque with a green stone, covered the top of her head. The hair around her forehead was woven into thin plaits and fastened at the nape of her neck. Her lower half hidden by immense pink trousers, her naked torso covered in a violet gauze, she stood at the top of the stairs, the sun behind her in the deep blue of the surrounding sky. An imperial wench, busty, fleshy, with flaring nostrils, big eyes, fabulous knees, and who, when she danced, had rolls of flesh on her belly. She began by perfuming our hands with rosewater; her throat smelled of sweet turpentine; a triple gold necklace hung below.[II]

In his journal he noted, 'She asked if we would like some entertainment.' Du Camp decided he would like to 'amuse himself alone' with her, so she took him to a ground-floor room – 'on the left as you come into the courtyard'. Flaubert took his turn soon after, and then there was a different kind of entertainment.

Kuchuk Hanem had sent for musicians, and a boy and an old man arrived, the latter with his left eye covered with a rag, presumably a case of ophthalmia. They both played the *rebabah*, a fiddle with two horse-hair strings and a spike that rests on the ground. Flaubert was unimpressed with their music.

Nothing could be more discordant nor more disagreeable. The musicians carry on playing: one has to shout to make them stop.

Kuchuk Hanem and Bambeh begin to dance. Kuchuk's dance is brutal like being slapped. – She squeezes her neck tight in her jacket, in a way that pushes her two naked breasts together, rubbing each other. To dance, she ties, like a belt, a folded scarf of brown and gold stripe . . . She lifts herself sometimes on one foot, sometimes on the other, a wonderful thing; one foot on the ground, the other is raised in front of the shin, all in a tiny jump. I have seen this dance on old Greek vases.[12]

After the dance, they go for a walk and there is plenty of messing about – Kuchuk wears Flaubert's *tarbush* on her head and rides on their backs as they charge along the alleys – and then there is a calm moment in a cafe: '[H]uts, with sunshine coming through the branches and making bright spots on the mat where we are sitting. We drink coffee – Kuchuk's joy at seeing our two shaven heads and hearing Max say: *La illah Allah Mohammed rassoun* [sic] *Allah*. [*There is no God but God and Muhammad is His prophet* – the Muslim profession of faith.]'[13]

When Kuchuk returned home, the Frenchmen went back to the Temple of Khnum, and then dined. By the time they knocked on Kuchuk's door again, it was dark outside; three oil lamps had been lit in the upper room. The musicians were already there. The Frenchmen brought *raki*: glasses were quickly drunk.

At this point they were joined by another woman, known as Little Saphiah to distinguish her from Kuchuk's neighbour, Big Saphiah. Flaubert described her as 'a small woman with a large nose and eyes that are deep-set, lively, ferocious and sensual – her necklace of coins rattles like a cart – she comes in and kisses our hands'.

The musicians played. The women sat in a row on a divan, in the dim yellow light, and began to sing and beat their drums. Du Camp may have been transported but Flaubert thought it sounded like a funeral dirge, and anyway at this point he had other things on his mind. He went down to the little room, on the left as you come into the courtyard, first with Little Saphiah – 'very corrupt, restless, pleasing herself, a little tigress' – then a ferocious one with Kuchuk, her necklace between his teeth, 'her cunt like rolls of velvet'. This was the moment in the evening when Du Camp, who had also been enjoying the women, declared himself 'happy but not satisfied'. There was one thing missing: they wanted Kuchuk to dance the Bee.

The origins of this dance, and of its legend, are lost in time, but no curious male visiting from Europe in the 1840s was likely to pass through Egypt without at least hearing about the Bee, in the same way that one might also hear rumours in Alexandria of the tomb of Alexander the Great, or in Luxor of hidden chambers filled with gold. You knew it was there, but you also knew you may never get to see it. This was especially so of a public dance in Egypt, not least because the official punishment for flaunting the pasha's banning order was severe: 50 lashes for a first offence and years of hard labour for repeat offenders. It was for that reason that La Triestina, the *madame* who had accommodated the Frenchmen in Cairo, had been so reluctant to have music played in her house. In Esna, these things were more easily arranged: the two sailors, who had been allowed to watch the dancing until now, were sent out, the musicians were blindfolded, and Kuchuk Hanem prepared to dance.

The dance was supposed to be a dramatic mime of a woman being attacked by a bee. According to the Frenchman Louis Pascal, who saw it a dozen years after Flaubert:

> The plot is extremely simple. A young girl is out for a walk . . . a bee mistakes her for a flower and settles on her mouth . . . the young girl's fright as she tries to dislodge the audacious insect; the bee stops, then charges again . . . and so begins a relentless chase . . . the more the young girl tries to dislodge it, the more the bee sticks with her and tries to hide itself in the most charming places...[14]

That, at least, was what was supposed to happen. Flaubert had had no problem describing the arrival of the caravan from Mecca, the effect of a puff of wind in a Nile sail, the subtle colour shifts of an Egyptian sunset, or a thousand and one other things he had witnessed. But he failed to describe the Bee in any detail in his journal:

> Kuchuk undressed as she danced. When she was naked, she only kept a scarf, behind which she tried to hide, and then finished by throwing that away – *voilà*, that is the Bee.
>
> She danced it very briefly and doesn't like to dance it – Joseph, excited, red, clapping his hands: '*Là, en, nia, oh! en, nia, oh!*' Finally, when she had repeated her wonderful moves, the legs passing one in front of another, she flopped on to the divan, where her body continued to ripple, someone threw her her baggy pink and white trousers, which she pulled up to her neck, and the two musicians were unveiled.[15]

When he sat down to write to Louis Bouilhet a couple of days later and went over his notes, Flaubert admitted that he had failed to capture the scene in words. 'I am going to spare you any description of the dance; it wouldn't work; it would take gestures to make you understand, and even then I doubt it would work.'[16] When writing to his mother, propriety excused him from any need for detail. This was not the sort of thing one shared with one's mother in 1849. Instead he told her that the dance 'was one of the most marvellous things it is possible to see. That alone is worth the journey.'[17]

Du Camp insisted that 'there was neither bee nor young girl stung'.[18] But then this was the man who claimed that he had had no travelling companion and had left after the performance. Flaubert, carried away by the moment, tells a different story. When it was time to go, he announced that he would like to stay the night. Kuchuk was afraid that the foreigners would attract thieves to her house, but Flaubert was used to getting his way: the Frenchmen had swords, extra guards were summoned, and while Du Camp settled on a divan in the upper room, Flaubert and Kuchuk returned to the room off the courtyard. He recalled:

We lay on her palm-frond bed, a wick burning in a lamp, of ancient design, hanging from the wall. In the next room, the guards talked in low voices with the servant, a black girl from Abyssinia whose arms were scarred from the plague. Her little dog slept on my silk jacket.

She was tired after dancing, and she was cold. I covered her in my fur robe, and she fell asleep with her fingers passed through mine. But I didn't close my eyes: I spent the night in infinitely intense reverie – that was why I stayed – watching this beautiful creature sleep, snoring with her head on my arm (my index finger had slipped under her necklace). I thought of my nights in the brothel in Paris – of a whole series of other memories – and of her, of her dance, of her voice that sang songs that had neither meaning nor a distinguishable word to me. This went on all night. At three in the morning I got up and went to piss in the street, the stars shining. The sky was clear and very distant. She woke up, went to fetch a charcoal brazier and crouched around it for an hour, warming herself, then came back to bed and slept again.[19]

There was more sex, more waterpipes, and then, at seven in the morning, the crew carried Flaubert's things back to the boat. In his journal, he noted that he had 'very calmly' said goodbye to Kuchuk Hanem. To Louis Bouilhet, two days later, he added that 'we said many tender things to each other. Towards the end there was something sad and loving in the way we embraced'.[20] From Kuchuk's house, he followed farmers and water buffalo across the cotton fields, where he went hunting. Later that morning he and Du Camp were back in Esna. They made a third visit to the temple, went to a *khan* where a tailor had made Flaubert some gaiters, bought a belt and a freshly caught gazelle from some Bedouin, and collected bread from Bambeh, whom Flaubert thought looked exhausted. They sailed just before midday.

Most published editions of Flaubert's travel notes include one more thought that occurred to him as he lay beside Kuchuk Hanem in Esna. 'How soothing it would be to one's pride,' he wrote, 'if, on leaving, one could be sure of being remembered, and that she thought of you more often than the others, that you would stay in her heart.'[21] These words were not written – and also perhaps not thought – that night nor the following morning, back on the boat. They were not even written in Egypt because they are not in the manuscript of

Flaubert's travel notes. Instead, they were added in the first months after his return to France, back at his desk in Croisset, when he rewrote his notes. As an afterthought, it is a significant one.

It is tempting to see Flaubert's night with Kuchuk Hanem as just another moment of debauch. There had been others before Esna, among them a fifteen-year-old girl at Asyut who had shown him all her jewellery: 'excessive avidity' he had noted in his journal. But for him, if not for Du Camp, the time with Kuchuk Hanem was different. Why did he want to spend the night at her house in Esna, knowing that she would have preferred it if he had left? Why, as he lay dreaming his dreams of other nights, going over many stories, among them that of Judith and Holofernes, the night becoming cold, the dancer snoring and coughing by turns, the bugs climbing the wall, did he think of her with such tenderness?

The critic Edward Said suggested that Flaubert experienced a moment of frightening self-discovery in Esna. It occurred because Egypt forced him to fall back on his own resources. And it did that, Said suggested, because it did not respond – as Kuchuk Hanem did not respond – in the way he expected. It left him feeling powerless.[22] So powerless that he felt compelled to stay in the house, in the hope that this might change things?

The letter Flaubert wrote Louis Bouilhet, six days after leaving Esna, bears out Said's suggestion. He was sufficiently pleased with his outing to write that 'at Esna in one day I came five times and sucked three. I say it without hesitation or circumlocution. And let me add that I enjoyed it.'[23] But he also admitted to feeling 'very empty, very flat, very sterile'. Or powerless, as Said saw it.

There was also perhaps a touch of post-coital sadness – what the French call *le petit mort*, the little death. Flaubert was exhausted and he had his guard down. But there is more to this interlude, something not Orientalist but something we should perhaps call Nilotist. Florence Nightingale had described it as a 'mysterious feeling [that] creeps over you as if it were the passage to some other world'.[24] Another world in which one might be another person. This process was at work on Flaubert as he responded to these shifting sensibilities. He had already recognised that the land around him had changed – beyond Luxor, he wrote, there is a new palette of colours as both people and landscape become darker. Now, instinctively, he was registering the changes in himself. He continued questioning his intentions. 'What am I going to do when I get home,' he asked in this same letter to Bouilhet, 'will I publish, will I not publish? What will I write? [A]nd even, will I write? The *Saint Anthony* business was a serious blow, I cannot deny.'[25]

He had tried writing since that night in France when his friends had told him to burn three years' work. First he had revived the idea of his long talked about Oriental tale, but that had not worked out. Then he had spent two days chewing over a story he had read in Herodotus, where the Pharaoh Mycerinus, builder of one of the pyramids at Giza, sleeps with his daughter. 'The first days on board I began to write a little, but thank God I very quickly recognised the ineptitude of such behaviour. Just now it is best to be an eye.'[26]

When he was twenty-one, he had written about 'women, their brown skin, their fiery look, who speak to me in the language of *houris*'.[27] Now, at twenty-eight, he had experienced things he had previously only been able to imagine. This was one of the shifts urged on him by Du Camp and Bouilhet that October night back in Croisset when he had read them the manuscript of *Saint Anthony*. By the time he left Esna, the transformation of style, from Chateaubriand to Balzac, from Romantic to Realist, was underway. But it was far from achieved and, to Du Camp's consternation, when the *cange* sailed out of Esna just before midday, Flaubert resumed his place on the divan, plant-like, 'an eye', ready to resume watching the world go by.

9

Grace and Truth

'Whence comes Thou, so marvellously dowered
As ne'er other stream on earth beside?
Where are thy founts of being, thus empowered
To form a nation by their annual tide?
The charts are silent; history guesses wide;
Adventure from thy quest returns ashamed;
And each new age, in its especial pride,
Believes that it shall be as that one named,
In which to all mankind thy birth-place was proclaimed' –
Richard Monckton Milnes, *The Burden of Egypt*

The *Parthenope* took five days to sail the narrowing channel of water from Luxor to Aswan. As the wind held, the captain stopped on only two occasions and briefly at that. At seven o'clock on the morning after they left Luxor, the party reached a place called Armant, where they snatched half an hour ashore to visit the remains of a Ptolemaic temple. The rest of that day,

143

and of each of the five days that followed, Florence Nightingale devoted to words.

She spent her mornings reading. After leaving Armant, she read aloud to Selina Bracebridge from Wilkinson's *Manners and Customs of the Ancient Egyptians*. Then she read to Charles Bracebridge from the German scholar Carl Lepsius' account of his recent excavations in Egypt. After that, she wrote a long letter home and some brief notes to herself. At 3 p.m. they dined on deck, and then the rest of the day was given over to further reading: that first day she chose some of the *Arabian Nights* and, after supper, the work of Epicurus, which she continued until midnight. Some time soon after that, they ran aground and had to wait on the sandbank until morning before they were pulled off.

Five days of calm, of writing and reading. After Lepsius, she tried to make sense of Baron Bunsen's history of the Egyptian dynasties. Five days of fair winds and rising temperatures: they were experiencing 'the hottest weather we have had'.[1] It must have been hard for a woman who had confessed that she was no '*dahabieh* bird' to be cooped up on the boat, with only the odd short walk ashore for relief. But this period of enforced confinement attests to the closeness of her relationship with the Bracebridges. Later in life, Florence was to write that Selina was more than a mother to her. It sounds like an exaggeration, the sort of thing one says on hearing of a death – which was indeed when she said it – but it also happened to be true. The five days sailing to Aswan were calm and happy, words that Nightingale had not used about her life at home for many years. Then they approached the gateway to another world.

'The Nile closes up,' she wrote to her mother, 'the country alters all at once to black granite, sticking out of the river in a hundred little islands, hemming it in with cliffs on both sides, striped with sand drifts, but projecting out of them the blacker and the more frowning."² They had reached Aswan.

Ancient Egyptians were less concerned with where the Nile started than with whether it would continue to flow. The most important question for a country that had almost no rainfall was how high the river would rise when it was in flood each summer. To help things along, the Ancient Egyptians bowed their heads to a god called Hapy, a pot-bellied hermaphrodite often depicted with a lotus or papyrus on his head. The only clue to their belief in the river's origins is an image that shows the Nile flowing out of a cave beneath the rapids just south of Aswan. This seems strange because they knew that it was not literally true; they could see that the river came from far beyond the cataracts. They had almost certainly travelled as far south as the present-day city of Khartoum, at the junction of the Blue and White Niles, and may have gone farther up the Blue Nile. But there was a logic to the idea that the Nile rose out of the cataracts; these rapids were a crossing point, the end of Egypt, the start of something else.

Aswan was the frontier of Egypt in the winter of 1849, as it had been in antiquity. It was the southernmost point of the homeland; beyond lay the conquered land. There were both geological and cultural reasons for this. The geological reason was immediately obvious as the black granite that Nightingale had described jutted out of the water and turned the river into a series of rapids that made navigation impossible. The only way of getting above the cataract was to have your boat pulled over it, and that could only be done if the river were high enough. The river rose in the summer, so the later one travelled in the winter, the harder the crossing. The man who decided whether or not one could mount the rapids was known as the Sheikh of the Cataract; his men would pull the boat, and it was his responsibility if things went wrong. So as soon as the *Parthenope* reached Aswan, word was sent to the venerable sheikh, inviting him to visit.

They did not have to wait long. Nightingale and the Bracebridges went for a walk on Elephantine, the main island at Aswan and site of the ancient frontier town. When they returned to the boat, they found what she called 'the Kings of the East, the three Magi, sitting on our divan, talking to Paolo, with each an arm passed round his neck'.[3] The sheikh had brought his two elder sons, 'the Bigs', to look over the boat and decide whether they could pull it over the rapids. 'The two "Bigs" startled us at first,' she wrote, 'and crushed our hopes about the boat.' Perhaps they had also come to take the measure of these foreigners, to see if there was room to negotiate a good price. Nightingale does not record the conversation, only that after this initial setback – and, no doubt, the foreigners' protests – the sheikh and his sons 'soon came to' and promised to take them up the cataracts.[4] The travellers were told to be ready to leave the following morning.

The Frenchmen had had better weather: they had taken just two days to sail from Esna to the 'black chocolate' rocks of Aswan. 'To the right, pillars of sand, naked, with nothing on them but the blue of the sky, raw, sharp. The air very profound, the light falling straight down, it's a negro landscape.'[5] Du Camp wrote of Flaubert in Aswan that, 'I am not sure he did not regret the fields of Sotteville [in Normandy] nor long for the Seine on the banks of the Nile.'[6] But there is nothing in Flaubert's notes to suggest homesickness.

That first day they met the governor of Aswan, who raised both hands to his turban to salute the *firman*, the official paper they had from the pasha in Cairo. The governor of Wadi Halfa, the town of the second cataract, deep into Nubia, was also there, 'a big obese blond man, wearing several robes'. Then, in a shop nearby, they met an *almeh*, Azizeh, a tall, slender woman in a red and gold robe, her black skin so dark it was almost green. She suggested that they might like her to dance for them.

She took them to a mud-brick hut in a part of Aswan away from the river and mostly in ruins. The hut was so low, the woman could only just stand upright. Azizeh swapped her red and gold robe for a thin cotton dress. 'She stands on one foot,' Flaubert recorded, his eye as sharp in this strange place as it had been in the more familiar landscape of a Parisian salon, 'lifts the other, the knee making a right angle, then brings it down firmly.' Like Nightingale, he recognised that he had come to a crossing place. 'This is no longer Egypt,' he continued, thinking of the glistening black girl with her belt of coloured beads and necklace of gold coins, 'it is black, African, savage. It is as wild as the other [Kuchuk Hanem] was calm.'[7]

The cataract above Aswan has been deprived of most of its water by two large dams and is now reduced to a string of pools and rutted channels. You glimpse it as you drive over the wall of the first dam, built by British engineers at the start of the twentieth century. To your left is a broad stretch of water on which Philae Temple now floats, and to your right the channel, the cataract, a straggle of houses and a string of electricity pylons. There were no dams in the mid-nineteenth century, so when Nightingale approached, even in relatively low water, it was an impressive sight, a series of whirlpools, waterfalls and eddies punctuated by stretches where the river was calm and flat.

The *Parthenope* had been prepared for rough water. Everything that could have been taken off the deck had been stored in the cabins. The pantry, larder and whatever remained exposed had been piled up and lashed down, to make space for the crew and the other men who were to pull them up the mighty river.

The Sheikh of the Cataract had come early in the morning, this time bringing all four of his sons as well as 'their children and grandchildren'. They set sail with a fair wind at nine in the morning and moved through the glittering narrow passage between Aswan and the rounded granite of Elephantine Island. A mile upstream, they came to the first of the rapids.

Sir John Gardner Wilkinson makes only a passing mention of the ascent of the cataracts in his *Hand-Book*. 'Now that the passage has been widened,' he explained, 'and the people have had so much experience, there is little fear of accidents.'[8] Fear was the least of Nightingale's emotions during the four and a half hours it took to pull the boat over the rocks and up through the fast-flowing water.

'In Europe,' she reasoned, searching for an explanation of what was to come, 'intellectual developments are quite enough to preserve life, and accordingly we see instinct undeveloped. In America, the wild Indian tracks his way through a trackless forest, by an instinct to us quite as miraculous as clairvoyance, or anything we are pleased to call impossible; and in Egypt the wild Nubian rides on the wave, and treads upon the foam, quite as securely as the Indian in his forest.'[9]

Du Camp in his turn described the 100 or so men who pulled his vessel up the cataract as having neither the gentleness of the Egyptian *fellah*, nor the softness of the Nubians. 'They are a breed apart, living among the rocks and fighting against the river.'[10] Flaubert, who thought there were 150 of them, described naked men in the river, riding palm trunks like horses, paddling with their hands. When they jumped up on to the boat, the water flowed off their bodies as it did off bronze statues in a fountain. The men pulling the *Parthenope* were presumably instructed to cover themselves in the presence of ladies. Or maybe not: was this what Nightingale was referring to when she noted in her diary that she saw 'Arabs in their glory'?[11]

The river was first disturbed by a series of eddies and, a little higher up, by a mass of bubbling foam. The sheikh's men were ready for whatever was to come; she called them the 'gods of the winds and the whirlpool'. Two ropes were thrown from the boat and pulled by men among the rocks and in the water.

When a sunken rock came in view, twenty eyes had already seen it, and a dozen men had thrown themselves out upon it, and were pushing the boat off by main force, their feet only against the rock, their backs against the boat; or had plunged upon an opposite bank and, throwing themselves upon their backs, were pulling the ropes towards them. On they sprang, from rock to rock, like chamois: I did not see one false step upon the shiny, slippery Syenite [pink Aswan granite]; one expected them to be dashed to pieces every moment. So the boat surmounted the First Rapid.[12]

The other rapids were passed with as much skill and no little drama. Ropes snapped, others were thrown, foot by foot the boat was hauled south until it came up on to still water – the upper river – and the passengers offered an abundance of salaams to the sheikh and his helpers for bringing them safely through such an adventure. Florence thought going up the cataract was 'one of the most delightful moments of my life'. Then, as always when she made such a definite statement, she tried to understand why. 'The inward excitement of European life is so great, its outward excitement so small, that a violent external call upon our senses and instincts to us is luxury and peace: the sense of power over the elements, of danger successfully overcome, is . . . one of the keenest delights and reliefs.'[13]

There was another thrill awaiting them above the cataract. They had hoped to visit the Island of Philae, but the wind picked up when they came on to the upper river and they did not stop. As they passed what Nightingale referred to as the Holy Isle, its temple dedicated to the great mother-goddess Isis, they saw camels and asses on the banks, and horses with scarlet trappings. Four great boats crossed the river in front of them, carrying worshippers and offerings. Up on the island, she saw a long procession of people in bright robes moving towards the ancient temple. She thought of the goddess Isis and her murdered husband. 'It was the worship of Osiris [Isis's husband] restored. We had come up stairs into the old world of 4000 years ago.'[14]

What she had seen was an Egyptian official on his way to take up a post in Sudan, stopping to visit the island. But whatever the reality, to her it had seemed like a dream. This vision of a past that had somehow survived, of an ancient worship still maintained, stayed with her for the ten long, hot days they spent on the *dahabiya* as the winds pushed them into the tropics.

They had left Cairo hoping to reach the second cataract at Wadi Halfa. But when the *Parthenope* tied up beneath the two colossal temples at Abu Simbel, at around 9.30 on the morning of 15 January 1849, 40 miles north of Wadi Halfa and some 925 miles by boat from Alexandria, she wrote that they had reached:

'[T]he last and greatest point of our voyage – greatest it is in all respects – I can fancy nothing greater. All that I have imagined has fallen short of Abu Simbel and thank God that we have come here. I can conceive nothing in Thebes to equal this, and am well satisfied to turn back now.'[15]

*

The two temples Ramses II constructed at Abu Simbel in the twelfth century BCE are among the most dramatic religious edifices in the world. On the side of what was an isolated hill on the west bank of the Nile, masons shaped the rock into colossal statues of the pharaoh and his family. Behind them, they cut chambers that run some 200 feet back into the hillside. The two rock-cut temples stand a few hundred feet apart from each other and were still pristine in 1813 when the Swiss traveller Jean Louis Burckhardt identified them on his way into Sudan, their entrances completely covered with sand. Giovanni Belzoni followed Burckhardt in 1817 and spent a fortnight with several other European travellers clearing the sand away. Since then, others too had taken up their spades and, although the façades had not been cleared, it was at least possible to visit the temples.

Du Camp took some of his best photographs here. One, taken from the east bank, shows the two temples, the *cange* docked below them, dwarfed by the colossal structures, and the chute of sand that still covered much of the great façade. Another photograph shows a member of the crew – is that Sassetti? – in white leggings, baggy white trousers, white cummerbund and dark *tarbush*, sitting on top of the crown on the northernmost of the four statues of Ramses, which is covered up to its lips in sand. The human being appears to be no larger than the stone pharaoh's nose.

Today, most people see Abu Simbel by flying across the desert to spend a few minutes in each of the temples before flying back north. Nightingale would not have understood the point of seeing them that way; she thought that even a couple of days here was not long enough. But Flaubert appears to have been suffering from what we would now call 'temple fatigue' when his *cange* reached Abu Simbel. His notes at the temples are full of the usual Flaubertian contrasts: he found the heads of the colossi handsome but their feet ugly; the temple inspired thoughts of the Pharaoh Mycerinus out for a chariot ride with a priest, but also of farms in his native Normandy 'in summer, when everyone is in the fields, towards three o'clock in the afternoon'.[16] Then, suddenly, there is a change of tone, a frank confession. 'Egyptian temples bore me profoundly,' he wrote in his journal. 'Are they going to become like churches in Brittany, like waterfalls in the Pyrenees? O necessity! [T]o do what one is expected to do.'[17]

Nightingale had no such problem. Thrilled by everything she saw in the temples, she was struck by two things in particular. She was impressed by their scale and grandeur, and she enjoyed the fact that she and the Bracebridges had the place to themselves, that there were no crowds of locals watching their every move, calling out *khawaga khawaga* (foreigner) and *baksheesh!* No foreigners either to torment them with invitations to long, tedious dinners and inane chatter.

She had spent a week on the way to Abu Simbel doggedly deconstructing and reconstructing her friend Baron Bunsen's dull account of Ancient Egypt. When they rounded a headland and the colossi came into sight off the starboard side of the boat, she was ready to escape. As soon as they tied up, she and Selina Bracebridge hurried to visit the small temple. Did Nightingale know, as she scrambled up the rocky slope, that something extraordinary was about to happen to her?

She had come to Egypt for respite from the endless struggle with family and friends over her belief that she had been put on earth to do something more useful than becoming a society matron. She had also come away to let time and distance heal the pain caused by the end of her relationship with Richard Monckton Milnes. She had written that not a day would go by without her thinking of him, and she hoped, as she had written to her mother before leaving England, that she would be reconciled to her situation by her return.

Unlike Flaubert, who had filled pages of his journal and of letters home with thoughts about his own dilemma, Nightingale had been silent about her personal struggle since arriving in Egypt. There had been a moment on New Year's Eve, after they had just sailed from Luxor, when she spent a solitary hour in her cabin: 'Washing and *dreaming*' as she noted in her diary. This was not the sort of dreaming you did when you went to sleep, but a form of daydreaming, and she thought of it as somehow wrong. But in the 14 days of the year to date she was so absorbed by all that she saw, and also so exhausted by it, there was no further time for dreaming. Abu Simbel was about to change all that.

'I never thought I should have made a friend and a home for life of an Egyptian temple,'[18] she wrote to her parents after visiting the temple complex. It had been a revelation, the only place she had seen in her travels that she could compare to St Peter's in Rome, and she was as surprised by her reaction as she was by the grandeur of the place. A liberal, a Unitarian, very much a Christian, she had not expected to find common ground with the gods of these ancient pagans, but that is what happened. In the cool depths of the rock-cut Great Temple, she responded to its atmosphere of peace and sanctity. In the shadows of an ancient cult she 'felt more *at home*, perhaps, than in any other place of worship'[19] she had yet been in.

The smaller temple at Abu Simbel was dedicated to Hathor, the cow-headed goddess; Nightingale translated her name as the habitation of Horus, of god. Hathor, she wrote home from Abu Simbel, is 'the "nurse, who fills heaven and earth with her beneficent acts"'.[20] She also understood Hathor to be the goddess of joy, 'the lady of the dance and mirth, a sort of joy like that of children playing at daisy chains'. God and nurse, dance and mirth. These were the elements Nightingale wished to unite in her own life. There was something inevitable about her 'love' for this place.

The temple, which echoed the design of the stone-built structures she had seen in Luxor, was divided into three halls. As she walked into the hillside, the light dimming, the huge columns looming above her, each topped with the head of the joyful, nursing goddess, the walls covered with enormous images of the great pharaoh who had commissioned this work so far beyond the frontiers of his kingdom, Nightingale noticed that Ramses had had his wife depicted as prominently as himself – something many a nineteenth-century wife might marvel at and envy. She was even more impressed with an image that seemed to show the great Ramses being crowned with both good and evil. 'What a deep philosophy! [W]hat theory of the world has ever gone farther than this? The evil is not the opposer of the good, but its *collaborateur* – the left hand of God, as the good is His right. I don't think I ever saw anything which affected me much more than this.'[21] She believed that early Christians appreciated the necessary existence of evil in the same way as early Egyptians. 'The Romans, who were a more literal people, and we their descendants, never understood this, and have set our faces against evil.'[22]

From the smaller temple, they scrambled and slid their way across an avalanche of sand to the four, seated figures guarding the front of the great temple. She did not see anything beautiful in the images, neither in their features nor their proportions, but she did find they held an unexpected spiritual grandeur.

Some of the sand that the tomb-raider Belzoni and his friends had cleared from the entrance of the Great Temple, 32 years earlier, had now blown back and a massive drift covered the entrance. This was not enough to reach the knees of the colossi or to block the entrance completely, but it did mean they had to slide through a three-foot gap at the top of the doorway. Crawling through on all fours amused Nightingale: 'I am not sure that the effect is not increased by it.'[23]

From the top of a 20-foot chute of sand, up towards the ceiling, she slid down to 'the bowels of the earth'. In the twilight, she could only clearly make out the rows of massive standing statues of Ramses, his arms crossed with the crook and flail. 'No light irritates your eyes, no sound annoys your ear, no breath of wind sets your teeth on edge.' This place of shadows was the home of beetles, bats and perhaps snakes, and the domain of the god Osiris in his role as lord of Amenti, judge of the dead, carer of the souls of the departed, the columns of the first hall carved into his image. Beyond, in the inner sanctuary, illuminated by a faint glow of daylight, sat what she understood to be 'the creative powers of the eternal mind', the creator gods Khnum, Amun, Ptah and Ra. It was intensely hot. 'Before them stood an altar, the first and last we shall see – the real old altar upon which stood the sacred ark.'[24]

'We shall never enjoy another place like Abu Simbel; the absolute solitude of it – the absence of a present, of any of one's fellow-creatures who contrast the past with that horrible Egyptian present. You look abroad and see no tokens of habitation.'[25] To be sure, she climbed back up the sand drift and out into the air, then scrambled to the top of the hill into which the temples had been cut.

I sighed for a walk in the Alps, the tropical Alps, and I walked round the valley and to the next mountain, and took a long last look south into Abyssinia . . . I saw nothing, met nothing, that had life, or *had had* life, but the whitened bones of a poor camel. And I reached the top of the next cliff. Oh, would I could describe that, my last real African view! [T]he golden sand, north, south, east, and west, except where the blue Nile flowed, strewn with bright purple granite stones, the black ridges of mountains, east and west, volcanic rocks, gigantic jet-black wigwam-looking hills.[26]

Nightingale had written of the joy of being free to walk to the temples by herself, without the *dragoman* Paolo or one of the crew coming along to make sure she was safe. But if they were not walking alongside her, they were at least watching her. So when Mr Bracebridge saw her climb to the top of the hill, he sent one of the Nubian sailors to attend on her. Instead of following her, however, he climbed to the top of the hill and lay face down in the sand where he went to sleep. When she spotted him, she thought he had had an apoplectic stroke and hurried to his aid, waking him. 'He carried me down the next sand avalanche like a child. They help you so beautifully, these Nubians, that your feet hardly seem to touch the ground.'[27]

She went back to the *dahabiya* to collect her friends, some candles and more of the crew, and they all slid down the sand pile into the Great Temple. It was as extraordinary and transformative an experience as Alice falling into Wonderland. By candlelight, she now saw that the walls were entirely covered with engravings. The images carved on to them had lost some of their original colour, but were otherwise intact: some showed Ramses making offerings to the gods; in others he defeated his enemies. 'It seems to me as if I had never seen sculpture before,' she wrote of that moment, 'as if the Elgin marbles were tame beside them! [A]s if I had now begun to live in heroic times.'[28]

Heroic times indeed: the carved images inspired her. One series, showing Ramses at prayer, 'taught me more than all the sermons I ever read'[29] about the relationship between the human and divine. Then she went as far as possible into the hillside and sat in the inner sanctuary. 'In Abu Simbel,' she mused, 'you first know what solitude is. In England, the utmost solitude you can obtain is surrounded by human beings; but there in the depths of the rock, in eternal darkness, where no sound ever reaches, solitude is no longer a name, it is a presence.'[30] The carvings inspired her even more than the solitude.

'I never understood the Bible till I came to Egypt,'[31] she wrote on 17 January. In the images of the vulture-goddess, her outstretched wings wrapped around the pharaoh, she found echoes of a line from the *Psalms*: 'He shall cover thee with his feathers, and under his wings shalt thou trust.'[32] Elsewhere in the Great Temple, she found an inscription describing Osiris as being 'full of grace and truth'. This reminded her that St John wrote in his gospel, 'We have seen his glory, glory as of the only Son from the Father, full of grace and truth.'[33] These parallels moved her more than anything else she had seen, or heard, or thought, on her journey along the Nile – and they stayed with her. Almost 40 years later, she remembered that in Egypt she had found a foretaste of the Christian religion.

When the sun set and the stars in the sky matched those on the temple ceiling, she and the Bracebridges climbed back to the top of the sand chute. Sitting up by the lintel, she watched the crew light a fire on the altar in the temple's holy place. Shadows played on the carved images. The figures on the walls began to move, swaying in the flickering light as though the old prophecy about them coming to life were true. Then she turned away, uncomfortable about lighting the fire. 'I felt as if the temple was profaned, and the solitude of the "Unutterable God" broken in upon – and I was glad when the blaze and glare were over.'[34]

The next morning Nightingale and Selina Bracebridge were

ready at first light to scramble back up the sandbank until they were almost level with the waists of the colossi. The air was very cold, the sand warm, and Nightingale calmer and happier than she had been for a long time. When the sun rose, the rock above them turned gold and the nearest statue came to life. 'One colossus gave a radiant smile as his own glorious sun reached him; he was bathed in living light, yes, really living, for it made him live while the other, still grey, shadowy and stern as a ghost, was unreached by the "Revealer of Life".'

They watched as sunlight went ahead of them and performed the same miracle on the Osiris statues inside the temple. 'One spot of golden light on the third Osiris spread and spread till it lighted up the cheek of the second and first. They smiled in their solemn beauty, but did not speak.'[35]

Beyond Abu Simbel, Sir John Gardner Wilkinson's *Hand-Book* advised travellers, 'there is nothing but the Second Cataract . . . less interesting than that of Assouán',[36] but that had not deterred Flaubert. *Reis* Ibrahim had taken the fast, light *cange* as far as Wadi Halfa and, if Maxime Du Camp is to be believed, Flaubert was extremely glad to have been there. If Du Camp is to be believed . . .

In *Le Nil: Egypte et Nubie*, the first of his accounts of their excursion to the south and the one in which he omitted all mention of Flaubert, Du Camp describes reaching Gebel Abusir, a mountain that rose above Wadi Halfa, formerly part of the frontier of Upper Nubia. 'I wanted to climb it,' he wrote, 'to contemplate the views from the summit.'[37] It was a remote and challenging place, where vultures perched close to the water and a crocodile basked in the sun. It was also hot – up in the high 30s – and the wind had dropped. The Frenchmen had long ago abandoned European-style clothing. They had their heads shaved every couple of days, let their

beards grow long, and wore only shorts and a long white shirt
or *gallabiya.*

The rock-strewn mountain was steep, it took three hours to
get to the top and back, but the effort was worthwhile for the
view from the summit was extensive and beautiful, including
the rocks of the cataract and a vast desert horizon. Flaubert
recorded in his journal:

> The back of the mountain resembled the back of the
> head of the Sphinx – a beautiful sandy ravine between
> the rocks – the second cataract, of which we can only
> see a part from here, seems flatter than the first – it is a
> succession of little lakes surrounded by black rocks and
> very shiny, like charcoal – here and there, between the
> water and the black granite, there are some thin green
> lines, these are plants which have pushed up between
> the rocks – the Abusir summit is covered with the
> names of travellers: all modern, few French, almost all
> English – some must have taken three days to carve.
> Belzoni 1816.[38]

Nowhere in these notes, or in the letters written from
Nubia, does Flaubert mention anything about his ideas for his
next novel. But in his memoirs, written in the 1890s, Du Camp
claimed that this was where they had conversations about
Madame Bovary, with the water murmuring gently around the
cange and the Southern Cross shining bright overhead.

> 'I am obsessed by it,' he would say to me. Amid African
> landscapes he dreamed of Normandy. On the borders of
> Lower Nubia, on the summit of Gebel Abusir, which
> overlooked the Second Cataract, as we were watching the
> Nile dash itself against the sharp black granite rocks, he

gave a cry, 'I have found it! Eureka! Eureka! I will call her Emma Bovary!' And he repeated it several times; he savoured the name Bovary, pronouncing the *o* very short.[39]

Critics have doubted the accuracy of Du Camp's recollection for the very good reason that Flaubert had not yet heard the story of Madame Delamare, the unfortunate young woman who was to be the model for Emma Bovary. There are other equally compelling reasons to doubt Du Camp: Flaubert makes no mention of *Bovary* in his journal for that day or for months afterwards. But that does not necessarily mean that Du Camp's recollection is false.

Flaubert may not have heard Madame Delamare's story when he climbed to the top of Gebel Abusir, but he had been turning over the idea of writing a novel about French provincial life for at least a dozen years. The name Bovary may even have been suggested to him by that of the manager of the Hotel du Nil, a certain Monsieur Bouvaret. So perhaps he did have that eureka moment at the top of Gebel Abusir, although Flaubert was never as clear in his recollections of this as Du Camp seemed to be. Whatever the case, one thing is certain: Flaubert might have appeared uninterested and indolent during their Nile journey, but his mind was hard at work. He was unable to forget the conversation he had had with Du Camp and Bouilhet that night in Le Croisset.

From the top of the mountain, they ran down a dune to the riverbank, sinking up to their knees in sand.

The next morning, Du Camp left early to take photographs around Gebel Abusir. Flaubert joined him around nine o'clock and they spent the rest of the day there, the sand so hot that Flaubert was unable to go barefoot as he had wanted.

'Return to Wadi Halfa in the dinghy, with Maxime,' he wrote in his journal, 'we are rocked by the wind and the waves, night falls – the waves hit the bow of our dinghy . . . The moon rises. In the position I was in, it shone on my right leg and the part of my white sock showing between my trousers and shoe.'[40] Flaubert's translator and biographer Francis Steegmuller called this 'one of the purest and most concentrated pieces of mature Flaubertian writing that we have before the great novels'.[41] The passage works by presenting the larger scene, the power of nature (the wind and waves), then the effect of that power (the boat rocks, the waves hit the bow), and finally the close-up, forcing us to look dispassionately at a single, unremarkable object, his sock, lit up by the moon. Aficionados of the Romantic style would not have understood why Flaubert focussed on the mundane and not on the way the moonlight glistened on the young oarsman's sweating brown skin or on the heaving chests of the foreign adventurers.

Back at the *cange*, they found that the masts had been taken down, the deck rearranged and a dozen 18-foot oars hung over the gunwales. There would be no more sailing. From here, they would float back down to Cairo, sped along by the crew at the oars.

At Abu Simbel, the *Parthenope*'s yardarm also was taken down, the big sails tied up, and the *dahabiya* turned to the north. When they left, at nine o'clock on a hot March morning, Nightingale had both tears and sand in her eyes. She felt sorry, tired and hungry. Perhaps more sorry than anything else, and not just because she thought Abu Simbel was the highlight of their voyage. Until this moment, whatever else she had been doing, she had been moving away from England and from the confrontation with her family. Stepping away from it and embracing the novelties of Egypt had brought instant relief.

Now that they had turned back, each day spent on the Nile, each site she left, each mile she floated downstream, would bring her closer to home and to the moment when she would have to resolve her dilemma.

To the Holy Isle

'The struggle between God and the devil is perpetually visible before one's thoughts, for the earth seems the abode of the devil; the heavens, of God; and you do not wonder at the Orientals being the mystical people they have become, nor at the Europeans, where all beauty is of the earth and the thoughts turn to the earth, becoming a practical, active people' – Florence Nightingale, 11 December 1849

It was late in the season, the Nile was low, temperatures high, and Nightingale spent much of the first couple of days after leaving Abu Simbel in her cabin, writing detailed accounts of her recent experiences. She had acquired some chameleons and was amused by their changing colours and moods. They were useful as well as diverting, for they ate the flies in her cabin. She could hear the crew up towards the prow, singing as they pulled at the oars, rowing her back towards the cataract, Aswan, the north.

But although she was left to herself and her thoughts, she still had certain obligations. One morning, for instance, was devoted to organising the notes Mr Bracebridge had made about Ramses' great temple. She stayed on board and enjoyed the solitude when the Bracebridges went up the steep hill to visit the ruins of Ibrim's medieval citadel. And she was still in no mood for sights or temples or people the following day when they stopped at the little ruined ancient temple of Wadi as-Sabua, which she dismissed as 'a humbug'.[1]

Something in her was changing, almost chameleon-like, as she was drawn into the dramas of the ancient past. 'Egypt is beginning to speak a language to me,' she had written home from Abu Simbel, 'even in the ugliest symbols of her gods.'[2] A couple of months of travelling in the country, a couple of weeks amongst the grand temples of the south, had fired her enthusiasm. Her reaction to the message of Abu Simbel, almost more than to its spectacular form, was proof of that. So what was Egypt saying? 'I find there such pleasant talk – philosophy for the curious, comfort for the weary, amusement for the innocent.'[3] The more she saw of Ancient Egypt and read about its theology and philosophy, the more she enjoyed making parallels between the Christianity she had been raised in and the religion that had been practised along the Nile.

She wasn't interested in visiting everything; even on such a leisurely journey, there was simply too much to see. Nor did she enjoy all of the temples she did visit. After the 'humbug' of Wadi as-Sabua, the early Roman temple at Kalabsha, the largest in Nubia, was dismissed as 'vulgar'. The small temple her 'dear' Ramses the Great built at Derr made so little impression that, when it came to writing home, she remembered absolutely nothing about the place. But she had found plenty of philosophy for the curious at Abu Simbel and she was about to find even more at their next stop, the small temple at Dakka.

Du Camp had little to say about Dakka Temple and the photograph he took there reflects his lack of interest in the place, for it shows nothing more than the façade, the two thick lotus-flower columns at the entrance framed by the squat mass of the cut-stone walls. Flaubert added a long account of some inscriptions, but even that lacks his usual flair and was in stark contrast to the way he wrote about something that happened soon after leaving the temple. On their way back to the boat, some Nubian men approached them with an offer to sell some unusual souvenirs: the hair – and hair ornaments – of their wives. The thing the Frenchmen had not considered was that the hair was still attached to the women's heads! When the deal was done, a shaving blade was brought out. 'This must have been devastating for these poor women, who appear to prize their hair greatly,' Flaubert wrote with sympathy, relieved not to be doing the shaving himself. 'The women being shorn weep, but their husbands, who do the shearing, make ten piastres a head.'[4] This was twice what the Frenchmen had paid for sex at Beni Souef and was roughly a week's pay for a boatman. It must have been an attractive price because word spread quickly and before they had settled back on their *cange*, another man arrived with his wife and a knife. As they pulled away from the riverbank, with more hair in the bag, Flaubert saw the women's shaved and greased heads shining in the morning sun 'like newly-tarred boats'.[5]

Nightingale thought Dakka Temple was as ugly as the others they had just passed. But what she knew, which the Frenchmen appear not to have done, was that it was dedicated to Thoth, the ibis-headed god of wisdom, and that Ancient Greeks had linked Thoth – and this particular temple – to Hermes Trimegistus. Hermes the 'thrice greatest' was the author of a large body of esoteric texts known as the *Corpus Hermeticum* or the *Hermetica*. Flaubert had read some of these as background for *The Temptation of Saint Anthony*; the *Hermetica* was part of 'the wilderness of books' in which Du Camp said his friend had become lost.

Nightingale viewed Hermes as a being who embodied nothing less than the intelligence of the universe. The Hermetic texts reflected the diversity of that intelligence and were a potent cocktail of Platonic and Stoic philosophy, Ancient Egyptian theology and ideas borrowed from Judaism and other religions of the region. They also concerned themselves with alchemy and magic. This ought to have earned them the damnation of the early Christian Church, but some Christian scholars believed that the Hermetic prophesies prefigured the coming of the Christ. So in spite of the passages on esoteric and occult 'sciences', they earned praise from key figures, among them St Augustine. 'This Hermes,' he wrote in *The City of God*, 'says much of God according to the truth.'[6] With such praise came acceptance.

The wonders of the *Hermetica* are matched by the story of their survival. They had passed easily from Ancient Egypt to Greece and, like many other texts, arrived in Byzantium, Constantine's 'new' Rome and the centre of eastern Christianity. Then in 1460, after Constantinople had fallen to the Ottoman Turks, a copy of the *Hermetica* made its way west, from Macedonia to Italy. It arrived at the Platonic Academy in Florence. The Academy had been created by the Florentine ruler, Cosimo de Medici, to build on the achievements of the Academy of Ancient Athens, closed for almost 1,000 years. The new academy's leading scholar, Marsilio Ficino, was just beginning a translation of Plato when the Hermes manuscript arrived. It is a sign of the esteem in which the *Hermetica* was held that Ficino's patron ordered him to put everything else aside and to translate it immediately.

Interest in his translation was so great that it went through

16 printings in 40 years and was translated into several other European languages. But with its suggestion that Christianity was part of a universal religion and its enthusiasm for magic, the *Hermetica* could be a dangerous work to have to hand. One of Marsilio Ficino's colleagues, the philosopher Giordano Bruno, was burned as a heretic for appearing to champion the Ancient Egyptian occult as expressed in the writings of Hermes.

The texts themselves then came under closer scrutiny. The claim that Hermes Trismegistus had composed the work in remotest antiquity was discredited in 1614, when the scholar Isaac Casaubon presented convincing evidence that the texts were written no earlier than the Christian era, and not by one man, but by several Greeks living in Egypt. Still, the old myth lived on. In 1652 the Jesuit scholar Athanasius Kircher, who had devoted much of his life to Ancient Egyptian studies, credited Hermes Trismegistus with creating hieroglyphs and called him 'the prince and parent of all Egyptian theology' and 'the first who . . . asserted that God is One and Good'.[7]

By the mid-nineteenth century, most scholars had been won round to the theory that the *Hermetica* had been written not by a god but by a group of Greeks in the Roman era. Curiously, Sir John Gardner Wilkinson, Nightingale's main 'guide' to Egypt, was not one of them. He still believed Hermes was a single author who had lived in early antiquity. Even more curiously, Nightingale seemed convinced by Wilkinson's argument and admitted to having a sense of 'ungovernable romance' about the man. So when the *Parthenope* tied up below ugly Dakka Temple, she believed she was about to step into the workplace of 'the inventor of hieroglyphs, of medicine, theology, mathematics'.[8]

She ascribed the temple's ugliness – 'everything shabby, still and rigid' -to the fact that it was built 'late', around 300 BCE.

Poor architecture, clumsy decoration and ruined remains were not enough to alter her feelings towards the place. Not even the noisy crowd of Nubians who followed her up from the *Parthenope* – 'hooting native jackals', she called them – could spoil her mood. She settled on a stone at the entrance to the temple and began to study the inner walls.

It didn't take long to find one of the images she had come to see: she interpreted a solar disc, an asp and a pair of protective wings as a representation of the Holy Trinity, which she believed Hermes had been the first to recognise. 'In that symbol we have the Holy Trinity complete: the eternity, the Word, the Spirit.'[9] 'He [God],' she wrote, quoting Hermes/ Thoth, whom she now called 'the only Father "who is *truly* Good . . .", "the fountain of all things", "He made himself shine forth" (here is our "glory of God"), the self-ruling God".'[10] She noted that this ancient divinity was called 'God of Gods', the same phrase Christians use to refer to their Almighty.

The idea of the early philosopher and the details of his *Hermetica*, of which she had only a partial understanding, ignited her passion: 'Here perhaps he wrote his 42 books, the sacred books of the Egyptians (how like our sacred books) which were carried in procession . . . O, call it holy ground, the ground where first they trod, who won for us freedom and under- standing to worship God in spirit and in truth! [A]nd let them all be holy to us, the Egyptian Trismegistos [*sic*], the Persian Zoroaster, the Jewish Moses.'[11] Nightingale worked herself into such a passion that she took off her shoes, insisting to the Bracebridges that one should go barefoot on such sacred soil – although perhaps not the whole way back to the boat.

There were consequences to the conversation she was having with Egypt, consequences to the talking she had been doing: it had reminded her that the same God who had created the world and inspired Hermes Trimesgistus had a mission for her; He had called her to serve Him. Twelve years after that first call, she was still bound by social constraints and apparently no nearer being able to act. In the face of such disappointment, of the frustration of her plan to take up nursing, she did what so many young women of her age did, what she herself had done on New Year's Eve at Karnak: she gave in to the temptation to dream.

It is impossible to know exactly what Nightingale meant when she wrote about *dreaming*, but it was clear that she did not view it as the best use of her time. In *Cassandra*, a vitriolic novel she wrote the year after she returned from Egypt, drawn from her own experience and considering the plight of young women, one of her characters confesses that, 'I lived for over seven years dreaming always, never accomplishing – too much ashamed of my dreams, which I thought were "romantic", to tell them where I knew that they would be laughed out, if not considered wrong. So I lived, till my heart was broken. I am now an old woman at thirty.'[12] This echoes something else she wrote that year, 1851: '[M]y daydreams were all of hospitals and I visited them whenever I could. I never communicated it to anyone – it would have been laughed at – but I thought God had called me to serve Him in that way.'[13]

This dreaming was exactly the sort of idle thought that Flaubert captured so precisely in *Madame Bovary* and that led his heroine to her downfall. When he wrote, of Emma Bovary, that 'her thoughts, like dancing girls on some flowery carpet, leapt from dream to dream, from sorrow to sorrow',[14] he could have been describing Nightingale.

Unable to act, she found herself dreaming and fought against it because, if she dreamed, she would never act. Dreams could not be shared because they would be considered wrong, or romantic, and be mocked. Nightingale's biographer Cecil Woodham-Smith, writing in 1950, described it this way:

She fell into trances in which hours were blotted out; she lost sense of time and place against her will. In daily life she moved like an automaton, could not remember what had been said or even where she had been. Agonies of guilt and self-reproach were intensified by the conviction that her worst fears were being realised and that she was going insane . . . She would have killed herself if she had not thought it mortal sin.[15]

There was more internal drama at the village of Gerf Husein, ten miles north of Dakka. The sun had set before they began the walk up to the small rock-cut Temple of Ptah. She described the scene to her parents:

> In the solemn twilight we entered the awful cave of Ptah, the God of Fire, the Creator. The Sheikh of the village, with his descendants, walked before us, carrying great serpents of fire to light up the rude magnificence of this terrible place. The serpents were thick twisted coils of palm fibre set on fire; but they looked like Moses' serpent set up in the wilderness; and twisted and flamed before this fire shrine, this God of the Hidden Fire, who has his dwelling in the thick darkness.[16]

But there were so many villagers in the cave and their lights flickered so much that she saw nothing. Nevertheless, the memory of the torch-lit visit and the thought of the fire god remained with her. That evening she wrote in her blue diary, 'O heavenly fire, purify me, free me from this slavery.'[17]

Two days after leaving Ptah's purifying cave, the *Parthenope* brought them to Philae, one of the places Nightingale had most looked forward to visiting. It did not disappoint.

She had always known that Philae would be special, but she

had not understood why. Wilkinson had written that Philae 'is no less interesting from the subjects contained in its sacred buildings than for the general effect of the ruins'.[18] He even went as far as to call the island and its surrounding rocks beautiful.

When they had sailed south – only two weeks earlier, but how long ago it seemed now – Nightingale had glimpsed some of that beauty in the procession of people moving towards the temple. Now there was no imagining: she was sitting on deck, the *dahabiya* was moving fast in the stream, there was moonlight all around and Philae Island had just appeared on a broad stretch of water. She had spent time on the boat preparing herself for this moment. She had read Wilkinson's description of it and the myths of Isis and Osiris in his *Manners and Customs of the Ancient Egyptians*, and her preparation paid off handsomely.

More than the beauty of the place, she had come to Philae to understand the connections between the pagan religion and her own. The temple at Dakka and the writings of Hermes, who had recognised the Holy Trinity, had been preparatory steps towards this. Philae was the next, the bigger step. The gods to which it was sacred, Isis and Osiris and their son Horus, in some way prefigured the Christian idea of God, the Virgin Mary and the son Jesus.

She went out as soon as the boat was secured and walked to the forecourt of the Temple of Isis. 'I thought I could see *Him*,' she confided to her blue diary, '*His* shadow in the moonlight.'[19] A couple of days later, she followed up this thought in a letter home. 'The myths of Osiris are so typical of our Saviour that it seemed to me as if I were coming to a place where He had lived, like going to Jerusalem, and when I saw a shadow in the moonlight in the temple court, I thought, "[P]erhaps I shall see Him: now He is here."'[20]

Philae Temple sits on a small reach of the Nile between the old and new Aswan dams, the island on which it originally stood now lost beneath the water. In the 1960s, when the Aswan High Dam was built and water levels rose, the temple was moved block by block to higher ground on nearby Agilkia Island, which was reshaped to look like its original setting . The move might have been the lesser of two evils – the alternative was to let the temple be submerged – but while it saved the temple structure, it irrevocably compromised the site's sacred geography. The full significance of the original site lay not just in the temple being on Philae, but in its relation to another small temple on nearby Biga Island.

The story of Biga lies at the heart of late Egyptian mythology. There are many different versions, but one of the simplest tells how, in the early days, long before history, the Egyptians were blessed with a good king called Osiris. At his birth, a celestial voice announced that the Lord of All was coming. He was one of the four children of Geb, the earth, and Nout, the sky. Osiris married his sister, Isis, while his brother Seth married their other sister, Nephthys. Osiris and Isis ruled along the Nile valley, Seth and Nephthys out in the desert wastes.

The Nile people flourished. Osiris taught them how to live in society and worship the gods, how to organise themselves to make the most of the Nile flood and to farm the fertile land it left behind. His loving wife taught them social skills and how to bake bread. As Egypt became peaceful and wealthy, Seth became increasingly jealous. Eventually he decided to act. He invited his brother to a feast in Upper Egypt and commissioned a chest that would fit him exactly. After eating, Seth proposed that they play a game to see who could fit inside the chest. Osiris lay down inside it and won, but before he could climb out, Seth locked the lid and threw it into the Nile.

The chest – and the good king – floated down the Nile. The good wife Isis wailed and wept, her tears causing the Nile to flood. She then went looking for her husband, following the chest down to the great sea, the Mediterranean, to the shore of Lebanon, near Byblos. A tamarisk tree had grown around it. The King of Byblos had had this tree – with Osiris inside – cut down and used as a pillar for his palace. When Isis eventually recovered the body, she hid it in the Nile delta. But Seth hunted it down and cut it into 14 pieces, which he scattered along the length of the river. Isis again went looking for her husband and found all but one of the pieces, his penis. This was said to have been eaten by three different fish, *lepidotus*, *phagrus* and *oxyrynchus* (none of which are eaten in Egypt today).

Isis reconstructed her husband like a jigsaw and wrapped the pieces in linen. She then created a phallus and, in a consummate act of magic, turned herself into a bird, hovered over the body and conceived a child, Horus, the son who would later avenge his father by killing Seth. The parts of Osiris' body were then buried in different sites, from the cataract to the Nile delta, and temples or shrines were eventually built over all of them, from Biga in the south to Abydos in the middle and Busiris in the north.

As well as promoting beneficial social values and providing a precedent for the divine nature of kingship, the cult of Osiris offered the hope of resurrection, of an afterlife. By satisfying this fundamental longing, the god's cult became widespread. Pharaohs and lesser mortals chose to be buried wrapped in linen bandages in imitation of the god of the underworld, who would be their judge and, they hoped, protector.

The southernmost centre of the cult was on Biga Island; his grieving wife was worshipped on its neighbour, Philae. Until the Temple of Isis was moved in the 1960s, one could look through the arch built by the Roman Emperor Hadrian and see Biga framed by its stones. Carved into that frame were scenes from the life, death and victorious afterlife of Osiris.

Various mysteries evolved around the worship of Osiris and soon only the initiates were allowed on to Biga – Wilkinson quotes the Greek philosopher Plutarch, in Egypt in the first century CE, who wrote that, '[T]he island near Philae, it is said, is usually untrodden and unapproached by any man, not even birds come down on it; but at one appointed time the priests cross over and sacrifice there to the dead god, laying garlands on the tomb.'[21] In late antiquity, when Isis was worshipped around the Mediterranean, from Rome to Delos, Philae became the centre of her cult. The temple was only officially closed in 550 CE, long after most other pagan sites had been converted to Christian worship or left to the ravages of desert sand and Nile silt. But even after the temple was closed, the cult continued: there are tenth-century records of villagers returning to Philae to honour the goddess, and stories that this practice continues into our own time. The cult's survival is easy to understand: like the Virgin with the baby Jesus on her lap, the loyal wife Isis and the infant Horus represent that most fundamental human urge, the maternal instinct.

Well preserved, in a beautiful setting, wrapped in myth and romance, Philae was rich ground for studying comparative rites and philosophies. No wonder Nightingale waxed lyrical. No matter that wherever she went after Philae or what she did in her life, she recognised that this place would have the power 'to make sad moments joyful – to people solitary moments – to make us young again when we are old'.[22]

They had reached Philae on the evening of 22 January and they stayed five days, longer than they had spent anywhere since leaving Cairo. The natural beauty of the place was not lost on Nightingale: 'The position of the island, high above the water (the Greeks called it *abaton*), the calm, shadowy *lake* around (which the Nile becomes there), the "Golden Mountains" (the Hemaceutae), which hem it in, the stillness, the tufts of wild palms, which grow out of the cliffs of the rocks all around the island, the solitude – for all its Arab inhabitants have deserted it – there *can* be nothing like Philae in the world!'[23]

Flaubert had other feelings towards the Holy Isle. By the time he and Du Camp arrived there with their attendants and crew, they had been travelling in Egypt for almost five months. Du Camp had become increasingly devoted to his mission to photograph the monuments they visited. Although he could not have known it, he had just taken some of his finest images. 'I am now returning to Cairo,' he wrote to his friend, the author Théophile Gautier while still south of the cataracts, 'pausing and resting wherever I may find anything worth studying . . . I take photographic impressions of each ruin, of each monument, and of any scenery I may think interesting. I take the ground-plan of every temple and rubbings of all the most interesting bas-reliefs. Add to that notes as complete as possible, and you will understand the slowness of my movements.'[24]

In the face of all this industry, and bored with what he had called the 'necessity' of visiting temples, Flaubert became increasingly withdrawn. He must have remembered the words he had written five years earlier to his 'dear and tender' Alfred le Poittevin: 'Don't travel with anyone else! Anyone!'[25] The situation was not helped by Du Camp's continuing failure to understand his companion's 'plant-like' behaviour. Only many years later did he recognise that Flaubert was like Balzac, someone who 'appeared to be observing nothing, and yet he remembered everything'.[26]

As soon as they landed, they pitched tents on the east side of the little island, near the kiosk built by the Emperor Trajan. It was five o'clock and they were seven miles from Aswan, but Flaubert was desperate for news from home. He had not heard from his mother for more than two months and he was worried. So although he knew that he would have to return in the dark, he and Joseph rode donkeys along the sand and dirt track, past the cataracts and quarries where ancient masons had cut granite for statues, to reach Aswan, only to be disappointed.

Du Camp had had news from France – even Sassetti had letters – but there was nothing for Flaubert in Aswan. The following day, he wrote home to say that they were safely back from Nubia and 'in good shape, if one can say that, having had no news at all for two long months from the one we hold most dear. Yesterday evening we reached Philae at night-fall. I immediately set out for Aswan on a donkey with Joseph, in the hope of having a packet of letters: nothing . . . The sky was beautiful last night, the stars shone, the Arabs sang on their camels. It was a real Oriental night where the blue sky disappears in a profusion of stars. But I was sad at heart.'[27] What he did not tell his mother, for fear of frightening her, was that they had had to be armed to the teeth for the ride back to Philae. The boy who ran in front of them, carrying the lantern so they could see the way, confirmed that several people had been attacked along the path by hyenas.

Du Camp was more impressed by the landscapes at Philae than by the temple. It felt good to be off the boat. They slept on land and swam in the river each morning and night. When not taking photographs, the Chevalier of the Légion d'Honneur liked to smoke a waterpipe and drink coffee, watching the water shift and the light play on the green palms, the bare black rock and yellow sand. At the end of the day he climbed to the temple's roof to watch the sunset over the river, the cataracts, palms, rocks and desert. He thought he was 'the happiest fellow alive'.[28]

On their second day on the island, they were surprised by the arrival of two more Frenchmen, a Dr Willemain and Paul Mouriez, a historian working on a four-volume history of Muhammad Ali Pasha. They had previously met both gentlemen in the north. On the third day Flaubert returned the compliment, shooting the rapids in a small boat with a priest on the gunwale, who prayed incessantly. 'We arrive in Aswan at midday,' he wrote in his journal, 'me dying of hunger. Lunch of fried fish and dates in a café. What a good lunch! Shave. Visit the boat of these gentlemen [Mouriez and Willemain] – Mouriez is in the *broc* [brothel]. Visit these women.'[29] Dogs bark, children cry, Willemain puts his arms around a blonde girl, Mouriez sweats with another. But while the others get on with their women, Flaubert has a problem: he cannot perform. 'Je ne puis.'

No news from home, a rare failure at the brothel, red clouds, a hot wind and anxiety over his literary future: Flaubert returned to Philae even more indolent and upset than he had left it. And matters only grew worse. Three days later he complained that he had not left the island. 'I am bored. What is it, O Lord, this permanent lassitude that I drag around with me everywhere! It has followed me on my travels! And I have brought it home! Deianira's tunic was no more stuck to Hercules' back than boredom is to my life! It eats into it more slowly, that's all.'[30] He was also irritated that the heads, hands and feet of many of the temple's figures had been hammered out. But he did find some things to admire: the 'charming' image of Isis suckling Horus, the embalming of Osiris, Isis mourning. 'Best of all is the famous inscription, "A page of history should not be defaced" and the response "A page of history cannot be erased".'[31]

There was one detail of his time at Philae that Flaubert omitted from his letters and journal, but which Du Camp included in his *Literary Recollections*. While Du Camp was off photographing monuments, Flaubert sat in the relative cool of the Temple of Isis reading *Gerfaut*, a novel by the French writer Charles de Bonnet, which Flaubert had bought in Cairo. De Bonnet was a disciple of Balzac and *Gerfaut* was considered his finest work. Here was another sign of Flaubert moving towards a new style of writing. *Gerfaut* may also have helped with the storyline of *Madame Bovary* because, in similar fashion, it tells the story of a married woman with romantic inclinations who falls in love with another man.

For several days Nightingale made no entries in her red 'public' diary, but there is one for each day in the private blue one. At sunrise on the first morning, she 'discovered the chamber of Osiris'.[32] This was where she chose to spend most of her Philae days, staying away from the rest of the temple, perhaps because, as she wrote home, 'everything in Philae is *ugly*',[33] built at a time when Egypt was ruled by Greeks and Romans and when temple artists lacked the delicacy and refinement of the era of her beloved Ramses II. 'The Puritans – I mean the Persians – have destroyed every vestige of the old part.'[34] As at Dakka, she treasured Isis' Temple not for its structure or decoration, but for the divine presence she felt reigning over it. She thought that the island itself was holy, though its spirit was fading: 'like the last leaping up of the light in the socket which shows the dying face you loved'.[35]

She approached the temple by a long colonnade, which sheltered cloisters and, in shadowy gloom, various store rooms and antechambers. The main entrance was framed by the soaring towers of the *pylon*: she passed a long inscription, beautifully carved but graffito nonetheless, which recorded the passage in 1799 of the Napoleonic army under General Desaix, chasing rogue Mamluks into Nubia. The doorway to the inner temple lay beyond another open courtyard, its dark pillared halls leading to the innermost and most holy sanctuary. Here the goddess's pedestal remained, although her granite shrine had already been taken to the Louvre. To the left of the sanctuary lay more side chambers and, beyond them, a Nilometer that had long recorded the miraculous rise of the Nile waters each summer following the fall of Isis' tears. Hadrian's gateway to the Island of Biga stood nearby, as did the last-known carved hieroglyph. But none of this fired Nightingale's imagination as much as the upper chamber, where the resurrection of Osiris was celebrated.

'Hours and hours I sat there wondering,' she remembered after they had left for the north, 'to find almost all our Christian ideas among these old Egyptians.'[36] The upper floor of the temple has been closed to visitors for some years because of safety concerns. Were it open, one would be able to follow in Nightingale's and Flaubert's footsteps up the dark staircase that leads to the roof, then walk through the gloom, hands reaching out for balance or support, fingers brushing over the carved processions of gods and kings and priests. The roof's outer chamber is decorated with images of women mourning – one of them caught Flaubert's eye long enough for him to note a 'woman wailing on her knees, desperately lamenting with her arms; the artist's observation here breaks through the ritual of conventional form'.[37] Inscriptions on the walls of the inner chamber tell the story of Osiris' end, of Isis' search along the Nile for the 14 parts of his corpse, of the immaculate conception of the divine son, and the glorious resurrection into the afterlife. No wonder it all seemed so familiar to the Christian traveller.

Nightingale wrote a detailed description of this room for her sister, but at the same time warned her that, however many pages she filled, she could never describe the whole thing. She had read somewhere that there was one lotus plant carved for each year of the god's life. But how many years had that been? 'I *felt* over every sculpture in that much-defaced dark chamber, with my hands, that what escaped the eye might not fail the touch.' When she reached the end, she was unsure if there had been 28 or 30. 'The last two,' she admitted, 'might be defects in the wall.'[38] But what mattered more than simple arithmetic was the detail that both Osiris and Jesus lived to be about thirty and that Nightingale was then approaching her own thirtieth birthday.

She filled pages with comparisons between the stories of Osiris and Jesus. First she wondered whether there had been a man, Osiris, as she believed there had been a man, Jesus. Then she wondered whether Osiris was an earlier incarnation of the same divine urge that had created Jesus. 'He may have come twice as well as once,' she wrote in justification of this premise. 'The one is not more difficult to believe than the other.'[39] She then extrapolated what she believed was a universal truth – that humans prefer their gods to suffer than to sit in pomp and glory. She went further and visited the Osiris story, as she viewed Jesus' life, as proof that one needed to suffer in order to achieve goodness. And while she thought all this through, how could she not have been thinking of her own struggle, her own calling, and of the suffering it had already caused? 'We want a God,' she wrote towards the end of this, one of her longest letters, 'who will tell us what He is like and what His will is like, now: His present will and what ours is to be, what our connection is with Him, our intercourse and what His qualities, that we may explain by them the puzzles we see every day.'[40]

But it was not all gods and devotion, as it had been in Abu Simbel. Philae was not crowded with Egyptians or Nubians, but there were several Europeans. On their first morning on the island, while they were out at sunrise, Nightingale and the Bracebridges were surprised to discover that an English couple had already installed themselves in the temple. But they were not of the same type as Milord Northampton, travelling ahead of them, whom Nightingale had cursed for pushing up the price of boats, food and anything else they might want. This was John Frederick Lewis, the Orientalist painter, and his wife.

Lewis had settled in Cairo in 1842, setting himself up in the local style, far from the European influences of the Ezbekiya. He had learned some Arabic, acquired Egyptian servants and perhaps also a harem. He had, in other words, 'gone native'. The novelist William Thackeray, who had known Lewis in London and saw him in Cairo in October 1844, described him:

> . . . in a long yellow gown, with a long beard, somewhat tinged with grey, with his head shaved, and wearing on it first a white wadded cotton night-cap, second a red *tarboosh* . . . When he goes abroad he rides a grey horse with red housings [trappings], and has two servants to walk beside him. He wears a very handsome grave costume of dark blue, consisting of an embroidered jacket and gaiters, and a pair of trousers, which would make a set of dresses for an English family. His beard curls nobly over his chest, his Damascus scimitar on his thigh. His red cap gives him a venerable and Bey-like appearance.[41]

Lewis's native household had been transformed two years before the meeting on Philae, when he had married Marian Harper. He was forty-two, she the twenty-year-old niece of a British judge. One of his old friends wrote with alarm that Lewis 'promises to lead a domestic life . . . is going to keep a carriage, and spares not floos [money], that his house is to be a terrestrial Paradise, and every thing delightful.'⁴² Everything, it seemed, was still delightful.

Lewis had left Cairo in October to paint or sketch the monuments along the Nile, which was what he was doing in front of Philae Temple at sunrise on 23 January 1850, when Nightingale and her friends arrived. It would not have taken them long to discover that they had mutual friends in Cairo, among them Consul Murray and Dr Abbott, the antiquities collector.

'He is making a series of drawings of the temple,' Nightingale wrote of Lewis, 'and is a picture himself; he always wears the Turkish dress – a blue *gubbeh*, white kaftan, red turban, and a long white beard; his wife, a nice little woman, young and pretty, always sits by him.'⁴³ That afternoon, the Lewises walked over to the *Parthenope* to dine and, a few days later, they returned the compliment, inviting the travellers to Lewis's 'princely tent' for what Nightingale described as a Nubian *dîner-en-ville*.

It was an impromptu affair – they had to take their own chairs and carpets – but the less like a society dinner it was, the more Nightingale was going to enjoy it. The Lewises were camped downstream, so around moonrise they climbed into their *felucca*, the little sailing boat they towed behind the *dahabiya*, and floated down on the current, threading through the rocky defiles. They landed on a sandy beach, walked through a palm garden, past some sleeping camels, and were announced to Mr and Mrs Lewis by their servant, who had two chairs on his back and a carpet wrapped round his head.

Mr Lewis came out, like a rather fine gentleman as he is, and expanded himself in compliments. He had got a young Englishman to meet us – he was so happy – we were so kind, etc.; and Mrs Lewis's Cairene woman, trowsered [*sic*] and veiled, stood like an Oriental slave while we took off some of our blankets. The tent was, however, bitterly cold; our *dahabieh* is more comfortable . . . The dinner was very much like a London dinner: Mr Lewis was fine and courteous; Mr Sutton was stupid and silent; Mrs Lewis was nice and *naïve*.[44]

Conversation turned to the fire that had just ravaged Lewis's house in Cairo. 'The pasha next door wanted the ground for his garden, and sent a slave *to burn it*, the method of purchase in Egypt.'[45] Lewis then showed them some of the work he had done in the south. Nightingale thought 'his figures are beautiful, his buildings commonplace',[46] which was perceptive and not unlike the comments his paintings later attracted from art critics when he displayed them in London.

'After having drunk as much coffee as we could, we walked down to the beach, in preparation for going home – Mr Lewis shuffling first, in Turkish slippers, and losing one among the sand; his Nubians following with our chairs and carpet.' They had a quick sail back to the *dahabiya*, but Nightingale still complained. 'These late hours destroy one's health,' she wrote. 'We were not home till nine o'clock.'[47]

The Lewises and their style of entertaining appealed to Nightingale's non-conformist nature. She shrank in horror from the 'ruck' of English people at Aswan. Consul Murray was there, but so too were Lord Northampton and his party, who 'had devoured everything like locusts, even all the rice and milk'.[48] Nightingale and the Bracebridges left calling cards for them and then fled. 'This animal,' she wrote home by way of explanation, 'it is impossible to tame; it can never be domesticated, but remains in its savage state in spite of all kindness (and constraint) that can be lavished upon it.'[49]

But the Lewises were different, and the day after their dinner, Mrs Lewis took Nightingale and her friends to meet some villagers she knew on Biga Island. Unexpectedly, given her passion for Osiris, Nightingale makes no mention of the temple there, perhaps because, however large the sacred sanctuary had been in antiquity, almost nothing of it had survived.

Biga Island was then occupied by one extended family: 'the original grandfather and his posterity'. Nightingale warmed to a four-year old girl called Zehnab, who wore nothing but a little row of beads around her neck and another around her waist. Zehnab's mother was only sixteen, but already a widow. Her aunt, of ten, had just married and proudly showed them her house, which Nightingale thought was better than the 'holes' she had seen elsewhere. It was small – you could not stand up in it – but furnished with a mud bench, which served as both chair and bed, and a water jar.

Up until this moment, Nightingale had been challenged by the condition in which Egyptians lived. Like most Europeans visiting Egypt at that time, she had never before seen such poverty and was shocked by it. In some places she showed sympathy. In others, she could see no solution than that the wretched villagers should kill themselves rather than continue living in such deprivation. But the visit to Biga with Marian Lewis changed all that: Nightingale now decided that these people were not so 'rubbishy'. The girl's hut, at least, was well swept, and there was a separate space for the chickens. Instead of finding the islanders beyond help, she now devised a plan for Zehnab. 'I tried to persuade Mrs Lewis to take her and educate her, and send her back to educate the island.'[50]

At this point, Zehnab's aunt asked for Mrs Lewis's wedding ring, and to distract her the young Englishwoman began talking about her wedding. 'They listened with great attention to her story of our marriage ceremony. Then they asked if her husband beat her and were astonished to hear that he did not! Next how much he had "given for her" – as in Egypt the husband gives the dowry, not the father – and when she said thirty shillings, they said, "it was very cheap".' Nightingale did not record Mrs Lewis's response to this conversation. Her own thoughts on marriage were unequivocal: she likened it to prostitution. In marriage as in prostitution, she argued, women sold themselves for money, position or a home. But perhaps she also spared a thought here for Richard Monckton Milnes.

Nightingale gave a brief sketch of this conversation in her 'public' diary, but in her private one admitted that, however wonderful she found Philae, she 'spoiled it all by dreaming. Disappointed with myself and the effect of Egypt on me.'[51] She and Flaubert were so different in so many ways and were having such diverse experiences, but they did have this in common: both of them were depressed as they reached the end of their stay in the remote, desolate, upper land beyond the cataracts.

There were two more visitors before the *Parthenope* left Philae. Late on their last afternoon on the island, a Sunday, Anthony Harris and his daughter Selima arrived. Florence and the Bracebridges had met Harris in Cairo when he had shown them his collection of antiquities – she had been fascinated by the story of his papyrus. She had found Harris 'very learned and very queer' and had liked his daughter very much, 'the child of an Abyssinian woman . . . a really sensible nice girl – black'.[52] Harris, 'a great hieroglyphist', offered to walk them around the Temple of Isis one last time.

But while he went off with the Bracebridges to decipher texts and explain images on the walls, spinning the latest theories and showing them the place that priests in late antiquity identified as the tomb of Osiris, Nightingale went off by herself. She was in no mood for what she called 'the claptrap of the place'. Philae was too rare and sacred a space to concoct stories around. She had loved Abu Simbel for its solitude, but she adored Philae for other reasons. 'Philae is cheerful, living, sunny, compared with Abu Simbel, and yet the roar of the cataracts is not like life; it is like eternity, and everything in Philae seems like another world.'[53] But she had another reason for not wanting to follow Harris through the temple courts: she had already said her farewell to the place.

Early that morning, she had visited the temple alone, walking through the outer courts, feeling her way up the worn stone steps and then going directly to the Osiris chamber where she knelt down, as she had done so often in other places on other Sundays. But instead of closing her eyes, she began to scratch at 'the sacred dust' to dig a hole. In it she buried the crucifix she had brought with her from home. As she did so, she imagined that she was binding Jesus and Osiris in the ground as she had done in her thoughts. She then filled in the hole and, having thoroughly covered her traces, spent a while in prayer, savouring this unique moment of spiritual clarity.

The Harrises returned to the *dahabiya* for tea. After they had gone and the moon had risen, Nightingale went for a last, silent walk around the island and then spent the rest of the night with her head leaning out of her cabin window, 'learning every line of the temple under the palms by heart'.[54] In the morning they left for the north.

II

Daydreams and Old Dust

'Well, dearest people, here is your daughter really in Thebes, though I can scarcely believe it. How beautiful it is, after the extreme ugliness of Egypt and even of our beloved Nubia! How pleasant it is to find oneself in beautiful country once more, in this glorious plain, all surrounded by those violet-coloured hills with rich fields bordering the blue Nile and groves of palm trees and acacias and tamarisks overshadowing the ruins of a world' – Florence Nightingale in Luxor

'Ah! the sky is so beautiful here, what stars, what nights! We have seen nothing of Thebes, but it ought to be magnificent. We are going to stay a fortnight, I imagine, because it is *immense*, and as we want to see it carefully, we will take our time' –Gustave Flaubert in Luxor

How does history shape our thoughts? How can a journey change our lives? These two questions occurred and recurred to Florence Nightingale and Gustave Flaubert as they made their way along the Nile. They had visited most of the same sites from Alexandria to Abu Simbel and had sailed or rowed along the same stretch of river, but they had been travelling in very different ways and had enjoyed very different journeys. While Flaubert had thought it best to be passive, like 'an eye' or a plant, Nightingale had wanted to free her soul, to let it fly. Things are never quite so clear-cut, but in some fundamental way Flaubert had been making a sensual journey and Nightingale a spiritual one. Now they were approaching Luxor, El-Uksor, 'the palaces' of the Arabs, Homer's hundred-gated Thebes, the place Ancient Egyptians called Waset. They had done no more than glimpse it on their way upriver. This time, they intended to see it thoroughly. It would defy their expectations and provoke a similar response in both of them: it was going to dazzle them. But first, they had to get there along the 125 miles of gently flowing waterway from Aswan.

The *cange* and *dahabiya* had each taken five days to sail up-stream from Luxor to Aswan and, with the yardarms stowed and the crews pulling at oars, the passengers had expected the return to be as quick or perhaps quicker. They were wrong. A contrary wind turned the Nile into a foaming sea, while sand storms hid the electric green countryside behind a dull ochre veil. It took Nightingale almost a week, Flaubert nine days, to reach the ancient capital. But between the storms, there were moments of blissful calm.

The river between Aswan and Luxor is now the focus of Nile tourism and several hundred floating hotels ply the water between the two, stopping for quick visits, photo-opportunities, brief shopping forays at the temples of Kom Ombo and Edfu. Most boats nowadays hurry past the quarries and temple at Silsileh, the tombs and chapel at El Kab, the Coptic monasteries and other sites that travellers in an earlier, slower age insisted on seeing. Our travellers saw it all and were calmed by the experience, their demons held at bay. For several days, their letters and notebooks were curiously devoid of self-doubt and angst; there is hardly a mention of God, of higher callings or literary longings. Flaubert captured the spirit of ease that hung over this interlude when he wrote in a letter to his mother of the wonderful life they were living.

> The trip to Nubia is over, and the end of our stay in Egypt is coming . . . Now we are going slowly down, by oar, on this great river up which we went with our two white sails. We stop at all the ruins. – The boat is tied up and we go ashore, there is always some temple buried to its shoulders in the sand, partially visible, like an old dug-up skeleton. – Gods with heads of crocodiles and ibises are painted on walls white with the droppings of birds of prey, which nest between the stones. We walk around the columns. – With our palm sticks and our daydreams, we stir up this old dust. We see the incredibly blue sky through holes in the temple walls. The high Nile snakes through the middle of the desert with a fringe of green on each bank. *That's Egypt for you.*[1]

Daydreams and old dust were a magical combination. The sheep were black and the naked boys, lithe as monkeys, had cat's eyes and ivory teeth. Women dressed in rags collected goat dung and brought chickens for the foreigners to buy. And over all this, over Flaubert and Du Camp in their *cange*, over Nightingale and the *Parthenope*, the brilliant sun shone and made everything glitter with what Flaubert called 'the butterfly colours of an immense costume ball'. Then there was another shift in perspective: 30 miles before Luxor, bad weather forced both boats to tie up at Esna.

Esna was – and still is – a town known for its woven fabrics, and it didn't take Nightingale long to spot the local industry. 'We were astonished,' she wrote home, 'to see blue linen dycing and hanging across the streets, so that the passengers had to lift it up as they went along; shops, and a marketplace; and, passing into the bazaar, we saw – oh, what a moment! a bale of Manchester goods! Here we burst into tears – no, we *ought* to have done so, but didn't: no emotion did the Manchester mark produce on my mercantile soul.'[2] But how could it have done? It was Sunday, the Sabbath. She teasingly imagined Manchester on a Sunday, the shops and factories all shut, the God-fearing population with their heads full of matters divine.

The town was also graced with a palace and, as Nightingale and the Bracebridges had not stopped here on their way upriver, they took a short walk from the centre of town to see the sight. The palace garden was planted with mint. The palace's flat roof shook underfoot when they stood on it, but was worth the risk for the grand view it gave over the countryside. The rooms, however, were disappointing, some having a little furniture, most of them none. The exception was the bedroom. Here there was a gilded sarsenet French bed with some 'dirty' blue fabric on it. 'The guide showed Mr B. *what it was for* and how to use it! As we had, of course, never seen a bed before!'[3]

The governor, who was absent when Nightingale visited, was back in residence when Flaubert reached Esna for the second time, and the Frenchman watched him leave the centre of town one night. As the governor rode across the fields to his palace, two of his escort carried torches of burning resin, which threw shadows against the mud walls and left a trail of embers on the ground behind. But the Frenchman's thoughts were elsewhere: a few hours after the *cange* docked at Esna, Bambeh came to greet them.

She came without her pet sheep, which had died, and with a

bandana over her right eye, which had festered. The Frenchmen sat her down and treated her with ointment from their medical chest. But whatever else had changed, the offer she carried had not and the friends followed her through the warren of Esna's dirt streets to the mud-brick house of Kuchuk Hanem.

'The house, the courtyard, the ruined staircase, it was all there,' Flaubert wrote in his journal with all the breathless eagerness of a romantic lover, 'but she was not there, she, high up, with her naked midriff, lit by the sun.'[4] This time there was no sun either; the sky was overcast and the air heavy. Flaubert climbed the crumbling steps to the first-floor room. Kuchuk wasn't there, but he could hear her voice, so he waited.

> She arrives, without *tarbush*, without necklace – her short tresses falling all over the place – bare-headed; also her head is very small above the temples – she seems tired, and to have been ill – she ties up her hair in a kerchief – she sends someone to fetch her necklaces and ear-rings which she keeps with a *sharif* in town, along with her money – she keeps nothing at home for fear that it might be stolen – we exchange pleasantries and compliments – she has often thought of us – she thinks of us as her children and has not met such amiable foreigners.[5]

Unlike their previous visit, this time there was dancing first, sex later. The old musician arrived with a colleague and a couple of women, one of them a dance teacher. Flaubert, who was the only one to record the moment, thought that her movements were 'close to the ancient dance'.[6] Kuchuk rose to the challenge and danced like an Egyptian, flicking her neck and putting one foot in front of the other. Then she took him downstairs.

The Abyssinian servant had been there before them and

sprinkled water on the ground to cool the bedroom. 'I only screwed her once,' Flaubert wrote later to Louis Bouilhet – so there was no repetition of the extravagant exertions of his previous visit. When the deed was done, while she slept close to him, he lay awake, taking in the scene. She had glued two labels on the wall as decoration. One was of Fame throwing crowns, the other was covered with Arabic script. 'I looked at her for a long time to fix her image in my head.'[7]

When he left her, she was perfuming her breasts with rosewater. He promised to return the following day to say goodbye. Out in the courtyard, some thug introduced himself as her *ruffiano*, her pimp, and held out his hand. Flaubert paid and left.

Back in the bazaar, he spent the afternoon in a cafe watching the world go by and feeling infinitely sad about Kuchuk Hanem because he had decided that he would not see her again.

Once the decision was made, he was crushed by the realisation that she would be lost to him as inevitably as night follows day. He had tried so hard to remember her, had spent hours on the previous occasion studying her face while she slept, memorising her body, her hair. He had scrutinised her movements as she danced, as she sprawled on the divan, as she squatted over the brazier in the cold and over his body in the heat of those passionate encounters. But nothing he could do – nothing he could write – could prevent the memory of her fading, little by little, as the taste of something exquisite fades on the tongue. 'I savoured the bitterness of it all,' he confided to Bouilhet. 'That's the point; I felt it in my entrails.'[8]

A funeral procession passed the cafe and he watched men from the bazaar leave their stalls to help carry the dead man on his way to the cemetery. It was a suitable prelude to his arrival in the great dead city of Luxor.

*

'The traveller who wishes merely to *say he has seen* Thebes, may get through it all in three days,' John Gardner Wilkinson wrote in his *Hand-Book*, but neither of our travellers was the sort to want such a thing. They had been hurried past Luxor on their way upriver, making the most of the winds. Now, on their return, they wanted to see everything, and to take their time over it. In the end, Flaubert and Du Camp spent two weeks in Luxor, Nightingale was there for three, and all of them devoted at least three days to Karnak Temple. It was not enough. 'To come to Thebes for a fortnight,' Nightingale complained to her parents, 'is what going to Rome for a fortnight would be.'⁹ Possible but not satisfactory.

Luxor was a day away from Esna by boat in 1849, but a world away in time. Esna's spinners and dyers were busy, its caravanserai filled in the travelling season with traders from Sudan and buyers from Cairo. Business was conducted in its bazaar, children attended its schools, and its dancers were kept busy. Luxor, on the other hand, was as quiet as a grave. A grave that still echoed with the memory of a time more than 3,000 years earlier when it had been the biggest, the liveliest, the most important city along the Nile, the capital of Ancient Egypt in an age when Amun was the universal god and a pharaoh's word was law across the Near East. In a city that had been embellished over thousands of years and then left to decline for thousands more, time assumed a different dimension.

In the winter of 1849, there were three separate districts to the ancient city, separated by the river as well as by large swathes of farmland and desert. Luxor village, on the east bank, was built in and around the part-buried colonnade of Luxor Temple and had two parts to it, the 'old town' and a modern part, beyond the outer wall. The second district, Karnak, was the mostly abandoned ruin of a religious complex that included the sprawling ruins of the temple of the god Amun-Ra. The third, Thebes, over on the west bank, was the abode of death and included funerary temples, the valley tombs of kings, queens and nobles, and several mud-brick villages scattered across the slopes of the Theban Hills.

The *Parthenope* tied up at Luxor around midday on 4 February 1850 and Nightingale and the Bracebridges immediately walked up to the village to find the local governor. The 'lord-lieutenant', as she called him, emerged from his mud-brick house in a coat 'like a red flamingo'. Among his many duties was the responsibility for looking after travellers' letters, so he immediately ducked back inside to look for their post. While they waited, two things occurred which revealed something of the nature of Luxor. First, a woman walked past with a fish on her head that was almost as big as she was. They stopped her to admire her catch and ended by buying it for dinner. Then they noticed a chain nailed to a post outside the governor's house and fed through a hole in the door. When Mr Bracebridge pulled the chain, he found 'it was fastened to the neck of a prisoner inside, who smiled; and Mr B. smiled, to show that they were very glad to see one another. The prisoner had four friends to chat with him, who were seated on the ground round him'.[10] Before their acquaintanceship could develop further, the governor reappeared.

Gardner Wilkinson strongly recommended saving the best till last. 'To enable the mind freely to contemplate the beauties of the ruins of this city, it is obvious that Karnak, from being the most splendid, should be the last visited by the stranger.'[11] But our travellers had already spent New Year's Eve at Karnak on their way upriver and they returned there now to read their letters in the shade of the temple's generous columns.

The following day, when they began their study of the ruins in earnest, they heeded Wilkinson's advice. With the *Parthenope* tied up near the temple on the east bank, they crossed over to the west, a journey they repeated each day for more than a week, as Nightingale described:

> Do you want to know how we pass our days, dear people? We rise up early in the morning, and are breakfasted perhaps by eight o'clock. Then we cross the water in the 'sandal', which is a small 'dingee', to western Thebes; the asses rush into the water to meet us, or the crew carry us ashore; we mount the asses, and with a great multitude – for in Egypt every attendant has his ass, and every ass his attendant – we repair (preceded by a tall man with a spear, his wild turban coming undone in the wind), like a small army, to a tomb; the tomb instantly fills – we suffocate for two or three hours, the guides having, besides, lighted fires and torches therein. When nature can sustain no more, we rush out, and *goollehs*, bread and dates are laid upon a stone. Those who have strength then begin again, till dark; those who have not, lie on stones in the valley.[12]

At sunset, the process was repeated: the asses and their attendants, the gentle return to the river past goats, water buffaloes, women and children. Then the slow glide back across the river. 'And home we come to the little fleet of European boats moored under the colonnades of Luxor, which really from the river are almost beautiful.'[13]

This interlude must have sounded calm and dreamy to her family back home, which was what she intended, and for the first few days that was exactly how she felt. She was fascinated and soothed by the beauty of what she called this 'great plain of death' and by the fact that they were staying put for a while. She could see nothing unpleasant about the deathbed of Thebes – even the villagers, dressed in rags, covered in dust and dirt, were spared her damnation, perhaps because they refrained from begging.

On these first days, she was full of energy and enthusiasm, and equally full of opinions on everything she saw. 'I am only writing my real and individual impressions,' she reminded her family, and then proceeded to break with convention. The two enormous statues of Pharaoh Amenhetep II, which she called the colossi of Memnon, were considered wonders by the ancients and often called the most accomplished of Theban sculptures by nineteenth-century visitors, but Nightingale was unimpressed. She thought the colossi of Ramses II at Abu Simbel were superior both in style and size. The thing she liked about the Theban colossi was the moral they seemed to impart; she likened them to Shakespeare's *King Lear*: 'as if the lightning of heaven had rested upon them, and made them the awful ruins you see; as if Amenophis had been the author of some fearful secret crime, and this was the vengeance of God'.[14]

That afternoon, she and Mr Bracebridge crawled on hands and knees into a newly opened tomb cut into the hillside. The paintings in the tombs she had seen so far had been blackened by soot from the torches that guides lit for visiting foreigners. This tomb was as fresh as if it had been painted last week: 'the white ground with gilding and colours looks like the most beautiful porcelain'.[15] But what really caught her eye and fired her imagination that first afternoon was the little fourteenth-century BCE temple of Pharaoh Seti I.

This temple now sits a couple of miles from the Nile, the river having changed course over the past century and a half. In 1850, it flowed close to the temple's *pylon* and outer walls. A large old sycamore tree that stood nearby on the riverbank was so prominent a marker, even on this plain full of landmarks, that it appears on maps from the period. Wilkinson's *Hand-Book* recommended mooring your boat 'under the sycamore tree', and this was where the *Parthenope*'s dinghy was tied up. The Bracebridges approached Seti's temple with their customary diligence, but Nightingale was already tired out by a day of sightseeing. So while her friends walked through the courts into the inner sanctuary, she sat on the stump of a column at the front the temple and, as Flaubert had put it, became an eye. She watched the play of light on the landscape as the sun dipped low over the Theban Hills. She was happy.

When Flaubert finally visited this small temple, he noted nothing more than its name. Du Camp thought it barely worthy of mention, even though he stopped long enough to photograph the façade. The image he captured is a bleak one. Taken facing due west, it shows the temple portico supported by eight remaining columns, the foreground and background filled with sand and limestone. It is curious then that Nightingale thought that she had never seen 'so beautiful, so poetic a scene'.[16] The topographical explanation is that the photograph was taken facing west while the beauty of the scene lay all to the east. Ahead of her – and behind Du Camp when he took his photograph – stood a grove of palms and acacias; beyond them, the river. Across the water and up the mud bank opposite, she could see the Temple of Luxor. Behind this, the violet-tinted mountains were fringed with gold. The view reminded her of something out of the *Book of Revelations*, which may be another reason why she found the place so full of poetry and beauty.

'In that sunset light all signs of decay disappeared, and in the stillness of that evening hour, with no sound but that of the flocks and herds going home, I felt like a Theban maiden sitting there in the colonnade of that solitary temple, where she had come for the evening benediction.'[17] She decided that this ancient 'Theban maiden' would have thought and felt much the same as she, Florence Nightingale did, sitting there. Marvelling at the attributes of the 'Unknown God', Nightingale 'felt quite friendly with her'.[18]

The following day she went to the Valley of the Kings and, although she was impressed by what she thought was the entrance to Hades and the parallel world inhabited by the dead, decided that it was 'quite enough' to see three tombs.[19] Here, the red public diary and the letters she wrote home diverge from the little blue pocket diary she kept for her own eyes. But then they need to, for they have different tales to tell.

Take the day she visited Medinat Habu, the west-bank mortuary temple of the twelfth-century BCE Pharaoh Ramses III, in whose reign, she knew, 'art and power suddenly declined'.[20] Her letter makes the connection between 'freedom and art, between purity of morals and religion, and a high state of national prosperity'.[21] In the public diary she noted: 'Great court with the coronation. "Elegant columns", height one foot more than circumference.'[22] But in her private diary she mentions being 'very poorly' in the temple and noted that she 'could only sit about'.[23]

Two days later, the public diary records their turkey parading up and down beside the *dahabiya*, scaring off wild dogs. The private diary explains how she knew this: a 'sore throat prevented me from going out, but also from doing anything'.[24] So she stayed on the *Parthenope* and read about Moses in Sinai in Harriet Martineau's *Eastern Life*.

For the next couple of days there are no entries at all in the public diary. The private one explains what had happened.

10 *February*
In bed, but made some use of my day as a pause in this spiritual and intellectual whirlwind.

11 *February*

Did not go out, but the demon of dreaming had possession of my weakened head all the morning.[25]

This would have turned into another crisis if she had been at home in England. But she was in Luxor with Selina Bracebridge, who understood her thoughts and dreams as well as anyone and who, as Nightingale had written a couple of years earlier, 'does not look upon one as a fanciful spoiled child'.[26] In this 'deathbed of a nation' and with this atmosphere of understanding, things settled again as they had in Abu Simbel and Philae. Nightingale regained her health and some sense of emotional balance. The dreaming stopped and she felt well enough to go out. Once again, they crossed the river to spend days visiting the sights. Keeping busy seemed to help.

Now that she was well again, they received visits from passengers on some of the fleet of 17 boats tied up by Luxor Temple. She described to her parents how:

After dinner when we are all hung up by the tails, like the chameleons, pretending to be dead, and waiting for half-past seven, or at latest eight, to bury us, lo! a dreadful plash of oars, or Paolo puts in his head, with an abominable grin at our mute misery, and says, 'The Hungarian count!' or 'The German professor!' and so on. Mr B. immediately retires to his own room, whence he is generally heard to snore. Σ [Selina] and I unwillingly, but nobly, sacrifice ourselves to our duty, sit up (in the brown Holland dressing gowns we are sure to have on, having been much too tired to dress) and talk.[27]

One night, a Captain Murray (no relation to Consul Murray, who was also in Luxor at the time) persuaded them to dine on his boat. Another night, they invited both Murrays to join them for dinner. 'As soon as our guests were gone,' she admitted to her parents, 'sometimes before, we went to bed. Don't think us grown quite savage and uncivilised.' Then she made one of the clearest statements of the way in which Egypt was imposing itself on her. 'It is very hard to be all day by the deathbed of the greatest of your race, and to come home and talk about quails or London.'[28]

But not everyone was as sensitive to the glory of the place. Nightingale found that most visitors had very little interest in the ruins, or, as she put it, could not care whether Ramses lived before or after George IV. She approved of Mr Feetham, a British businessman who seemed to have a great desire to learn, and of a German doctor who was teaching himself hieroglyphs. The party travelling with Lord Northampton was at least interested in the art, and she 'quite loved' Lady Marian Alford, his lordship's daughter, who was about the same age as herself, for being passionate about that. But even then, the only questions the Northampton party asked about the tombs or temples was, 'Is there anything to draw?'[29] Not even Captain Murray was spared criticism. One day he found Nightingale at Karnak, in one of the outer courts before the main hall. He chattered a moment, looked at the inscriptions, made some clever remark and disappeared. *'That was the only time he ever went (or had been) to Karnak.'*[30]

'What do people come to Egypt for?' she concluded, with more than a touch of exasperation. 'I cannot think.'

Nightingale was not alone in wondering why people went to Egypt, nor in questioning the effect the place had on them. She had clearly recognised the life-changing nature of the experience for herself. In the days after leaving Luxor, Flaubert did so too. 'I don't know if the sight of ruins inspires great thoughts,' he wrote to Louis Bouilhet. 'But I wonder where this profound disgust comes from that I now have at the idea of becoming famous and being talked about.'[31]

He had arrived in Luxor weighed down with lethargy and *tristesse*, but this malaise vanished in the face of the immense ruins. In Nubia he had been disgusted by the temples, or at least by the necessity of constantly visiting them because one felt one *must*. He was not interested in that sort of social obligation. He wanted to see things for the pure pleasure or fascination of it, and that sense of pleasure and fascination was something he had lost while in Nubia. Luxor – and the Valley of the Kings and Karnak Temple in particular – restored his sense of wonder. He thought Karnak was 'by far the finest place we have seen on this trip' and recognised that he could have stayed a long time 'in a state of perpetual astonishment'.[32]

'Imagine an entire valley cut into a mountain,' he wrote of the Valley of the Kings, 'where there is no more vegetation than on a marble table and, on both sides, some quarries; these are the tombs. You descend into each one by a flight of steps, one after the other, which seem as though they would never end. Then you reach large rooms, painted all over, even the ceiling. You travel there – I mean that literally.'[33]

The Frenchmen spent a week on the west bank, first sleeping out near the colossi, where they were devoured by mosquitoes, then inside one of the chambers of Ramses III's Temple of Medinat Habu, and finally inside the entrance to Tomb 18 in the Valley of the Kings, belonging to Ramses X. The sky was so clear, the stars hung in semi-circles 'as if they were half of diamond necklaces', he noted in his journal, 'which here and there were missing a few stones'. Then he thought about what he had written, about the image he had just used, and added, 'Sad misery of language! To compare stars to diamonds.'[34] He still had some way to go before resisting the old Romantic temptations.

Flaubert was almost always more interested in people than in monuments, and in Egypt there were almost always people to meet, even out on the edge of the desert, at the entrance to the Valley of the Kings.

There is . . . an old Greek who trades in antiquities. He lives there as though in a tower, in the middle of the mountain, in a house full of mummies, all alone, and far from humans. Some old withered corpses propped up against the wall grimace from a corner of the tower, his ground floor is stuffed with coffins, and the room where he received us had a shutter made from a piece of wood that once covered a citizen from the time of Sesostris. He came to visit us in the morning, as we were camped at the foot of one of the colossi of Memnon. He wore a white turban, a white Nubian shirt and a white cotton umbrella. This old son of Lemnos carried in his left hand his pipe and a white-wood baton he had carved himself, tipped with metal, which helped him walk over the rocks. His feet were naked in his slippers.'[35]

Du Camp went further and noted that the Greek, called Rosa, had been employed for a long time as overseer of excavations by Monsieur Drovetti, the former French consul. Over the years, Rosa had become used to living in this remote place. Now, he bought things from villagers and sold them to foreigners. 'For 20 years he didn't leave his mountain,' Du Camp wrote, 'old, without a wife, without children, he stayed, praying to God and sometimes coming down to the boats to offer foreigners some rarities from ancient Egypt.'[36] The idea of buying something obviously appealed to Flaubert, who had wanted to return home with a mummy, but the export of antiquities had recently been banned and both the risk and the cost were now too high.

Their sense of wonder at seeing Thebes, the Valley of the Kings and 'Sieur Rosa's treasure-trove of a house, paled beside their reaction to Karnak. For once it was Du Camp who captured their astonishment at entering the temple when he wrote that:

> I have crossed Italy from Venice to Paestum, I have seen the last little village of Greece; every day for a month I wore down the hard paths of the Acropolis of Athens, I have pitched my tent at Baalbek, I have slept at Ephesus, at Sardis, at Milet [*sic*]; I have walked along the empty streets of Rhodes; I have seen many ruins in many countries, but never, ever, have I seen anything to compare to Karnak.[37]

They camped inside the temple in what they called the King's chamber, a massive pink granite chamber built in the fourth century BCE by Alexander the Great's half-brother, Philip Arrhidaeus. This was a shrine, the home of the most powerful god in the region and the centrepoint of the Egyptian empire. Each night, for many centuries, the high priest shut the gilded doors of this sanctuary so that the great god Amun could sleep in darkness.

As if their own imaginations were not enough to people the vast empty spaces between the soaring columns and to animate the images that now surrounded them, their local guide, Temsah, whose name translates as Crocodile, told them all sorts of wonderful stories about djinns and other spirits that inhabited the abandoned temple.

The Frenchmen slept not far from the sacred lake where the priests of Amun had drawn water for their ablutions. They observed, in its mirror-like surface, the movement of the stars across the clear night sky. To add to the wonder of such a place, Temsah mentioned that when the Persians came and sacked Karnak in 656 BCE, the priests of Amun took the gold and silver from the storerooms and threw it in the lake. All of it, from sacred images of the gods to the bowls in which their divine meals were served each day. And now, Temsah added, speaking very softly, every night, a golden boat was seen crossing the water, guided by women of silver and followed by a blue fish. Many people had tried to reach the boat, but it always disappeared in a puff of smoke before they could do so. If he had needed any further inducement, this story alone would have been enough to persuade Du Camp to bathe in the lake's stagnant water.

These stories of wonder combined with the extraordinary grandeur of the ruins gave Karnak a unique power. Flaubert talked of glimpsing the life of giants there. Other visitors found the life of the Bible.

One of the temple's most resonant biblical connections could be seen on a doorway between the first and second *pylons*, where the tenth-century BCE Pharaoh Sheshonk had commissioned an inscription to celebrate his victory over Reheboam, King of Judah. This Reheboam was none other than the son and heir of King Solomon and his defeat was sufficiently momentous to be recorded in the Bible: 'In the fifth year of King Reheboam, Shishank [*sic*], King of Egypt came up against Jerusalem; he took away the treasures of the house of the Lord and the treasures of the King's house; he took away everything. He also took away all the shields of gold which Solomon had made.'[38]

Here, then, was one of those links to the Bible that so excited European Christians; something that Nightingale might have been expected to have relished. She clearly enjoyed the opportunity to flaunt her progress at learning hieroglyphs: 'There could be no doubt of it, I could read the letters on his cartouche quite plain, IOUDA MELEK, King of Judah.'[39] But this was not what she had come for. 'Oh, I was so sick of it – people seemed to think it a holy pilgrimage, like a visit to Jerusalem, to go and look at it. I suppose I have been there 50 times with different people, and we don't know anything which makes Rehoboam [sic] so very interesting to us. But people seemed to think that Rehoboam was the only thing that was true'[40] in Karnak. She knew otherwise.

She called Karnak 'the history of a race, the greatest race perhaps that ever existed – a race of giants, who illustrated themselves in their successive generations in this temple palace.' She thought Karnak was a political, ethical and religious manifestation of the 'Unknown God', and called it 'the residence of his vice-gerents, the kings – the sanctuary of his wise men, the priests – the place of Justice'.[41] She considered that, 'St Peter's [in Rome] and Karnak are the only two worthy expressions of "Him that is ineffable" which I have ever seen – yet how different: Karnak, like the thoughtful metaphysical Egyptian faith; St Peter's, like the fervent Roman Catholic. In Karnak you think; in St Peter's you feel.'[42]

She mocked the temple decoration in her public diary, suggesting that the lists of gifts made by pharaohs were there so that 'the god might not take the gold for gold plated goods nor have the trouble of counting them'.[43] But she told another tale in the private diary. 'Karnak,' she wrote, clearly distressed, 'and where was I? All the while that I was on the *propylon* and half the afternoon, dreaming. Karnak itself cannot save me now, it has no voice for me.'[44]

The voice she needed was finally found on the other side of the river.

*

The funerary Temple of Seti I at Gurna is a small and relatively unspectacular structure. It has none of the grandeur of Karnak, nor is it as well preserved as the Temple of Medinat Habu; it lacks the romance of the Ramesseum and the drama of Hatshepsut's Temple. Yet because it was near the sycamore tree landing on the west bank, because the small boat they used to ferry themselves across from the *Parthenope* tied up there, they saw this temple each time they went to the necropolis. It became a refuge, somewhere one could rest under the colonnade while waiting for the boat to arrive or the others to come down from the hillside. Nightingale had been there on her first afternoon and it was here she came on 22 February, her last full day in Luxor. 'Long morning by myself at old Qurna [*sic*],' she wrote. 'Sat on steps of portico, moving with the shadow of the sun and looking at that (to me) priceless view.'[45]

She told her parents she had spent an evening and a morning at 'that exquisite little temple of Qurna [*sic*], and each time more in love with it'. She gave them an idea of what she had done while she was there: 'moving with the shadow of the columns, as it turned with the sun, and looking out upon that matchless view under the different lights; the distance, to the west over the green cornfields – then the palm garden – then the eastern hills on the other side of the river – then more palms . . . '[46] She explained how she felt about the peace of the place, about water being pulled from the canal, a woman carrying a vase on her head, about sunsets and birdsong. But there was one crucial detail she omitted both from the letters home and from the public diary, something that happened that day in Seti's temple, which she confided only to the private diary: 'God spoke to me again.'[47]

As with the original calling in England almost 13 years earlier, we cannot know what was said nor how it was heard. There are no other notes, no mention of it in the letters and no elaboration in the private diary. Just that one entry. After the revelation in the sanctuary at Abu Simbel and the solemn moment of burying her crucifix in the Osiris chamber at Philae, weeks of passionate longing had culminated in a visitation and a renewal of Florence Nightingale's calling.

Settling the Question

'All day drifted down,
Wind quite contrary;
Dined in my dressing-gown
And sculled when it was airy;
Smoked a new pipe-tick,
Which almost made me sick' – Mansfield Parkyns, 1842

'I wish I were a poet, I could have made such a pretty picture out of it' – Florence Nightingale in Asyut, 9 March 1850

Neither Miss Nightingale nor Monsieur Flaubert, nor indeed any other passenger on the Nile at that time, had any great expectations of the return journey to Cairo. They had read about places such as Luxor, Abu Simbel and Philae in advance, had copied maps of towns and temples and carefully planned their visits. But the voyage from Luxor back to the capital was expected to be nothing more than a necessary interlude.

The Bracebridge party now knew better than to ask how long it would take to paddle down from Luxor to Cairo because they had learned that the Nile had its moods. They had missed the ancient temples at Dendera and Abydos on the way south and Nightingale hoped to revisit the tombs at Beni Hassan on the way back. But they all knew the best lay behind them; none of what was to come could compare with what they had seen in Luxor, which Flaubert too recognised as 'the high point of our entire trip'.[1]

But travel is about more than seeing the long-anticipated sights; often it is just as much about seizing pleasures or surviving unexpected problems. A river never runs straight. Alongside the anticipated joys, there are always delays, diversions and setbacks. As Nightingale's party was about to discover.

It started well enough. The *Parthenope* pulled away from the Theban sycamore tree and out into the stream at four o'clock on the clear, sunny afternoon of 23 February 1850. The crew sang as they pulled at the oars, partly to keep themselves amused and partly to strike up a rhythm. The *reis* looked on in his silent, authoritative way, and Florence Nightingale scanned the west bank in the hope of catching a last glimpse of the landmarks of the dead city. She had not expected to become so familiar with, so passionate about, Thebes. She had thought that Philae would forever be the most special place to her. But not even Philae, her crucifix buried in the sand of its Osiris chamber, meant as much to her as Seti's Temple in Gurna. How could it match up to the place where God had spoken to her? With the late-afternoon sun already low over the Theban Hills, the temples and tombs thrown into sharp relief by the slanting light, she scanned the landscape and its monuments for the last time.

As well as the memories, she was taking away some physical reminders of her stay among the tombs and temples. In her cabin, surrounded by cases and tin boxes, ribbons, papers and books, she had placed some ancient figurines. They carried a hoe in one hand and a bag of seed in the other, and their arms were crossed over their chests in imitation of Osiris. As she had bought them in the Valley of the Kings, perhaps she had had dealings with the same elderly Greek, 'Sieur Rosa, who had so fascinated Flaubert and Du Camp. Nightingale was going home with one other notable antiquity, something she valued even more highly: an official seal of the time of Ramses the Great, which had the cartouche of her 'hero' carved on it. But more precious even than these objects was the time she had spent in Seti's Temple – the memory of it sharp and clear in her mind.

By daybreak the next day they were tied up 50 miles north at another of the Nile's junction towns. Qena stood at the shortest point between the valley and the Red Sea port of Quseir and, as a result, it was one of those places where travellers stopped in the hope of finding mail, news, supplies, and, in the case of the Frenchmen, the company of willing women.

The Bracebridges found Charles Murray, and the British consul had news. He had just been informed that Britain had declared war against Greece, a move that was expected to test the stability of diplomatic relations in the eastern Mediterranean. Murray was hurrying back to the capital to reassure the Egyptian pasha of Britain's intentions, as well as to report back to his masters in London.

As a passionate supporter of the Greek cause, who had been intending to stop in Athens on his way back to England with his wife and their friend, Mr Bracebridge discussed the situation with the consul before he hurried north.

*

Just before leaving Luxor, Flaubert paid a farewell visit to Karnak. 'I wanted to see our little chamber once more,' he wrote in his journal, 'and the stone where I slept under the stars. Karnak seemed more beautiful and grander than ever – Sadness at leaving stones! Why?'[2]

He had the couple of days' sailing to Qena to consider his response to Karnak, and returned to the theme in a letter he wrote from the boat. Describing their last day in Luxor for his mother, he explained that they had ridden around the ruins and then lingered at Karnak. 'It was with a heavy heart that we said goodbye to the place. What a strange thing! To be moved when leaving stones! And when you are moved by so many other things.'[3] For a man who thought he knew himself, such sadness was a mystery. But more significant than his response to the stones is his surprise at it. We may expect a romantic to be tempted by the melancholy of a long-lost city. Flaubert seems to have found the emotion strange, unexpected, even slightly embarrassing.

He had begun writing to his mother at one o'clock on a hot afternoon, intending to have finished by the evening, before they reached Qena. There had been no post for him in Luxor or Aswan and he knew that if there were none at the next stop then he would have no news from home before reaching Cairo. 'God bless the post office, and the people at the consulate! If only I knew that you were receiving my letters? I try to make my mailings as regular as possible, and I send express letters by horseback messenger if there is no other way. But with all that, I'm afraid that you often pass several postings without receiving my news.'[4] To this, Du Camp added a postscript, assuring Madame Flaubert that she 'will only have cause for self-congratulation about this long journey. It is fine and warm, usually from 33 to 37; the young man perspires profusely; his beard reaches his waist. He is dark as a mole and eats like a wolf. I am very sorry that you cannot see for yourself the way we travel; it is one long promenade.' In case he had not made his point, he closed by suggesting that she 'not worry in the least: write as often as you can . . . '[5]

It took longer to reach Qena than they had anticipated, but by the following morning the *cange* was tied up on the beach below town and the Frenchmen hurried off in search of their mail. 'What joy! [D]ear mother, my heart jumps with it,' Flaubert wrote in a hasty note after finding a packet of ten letters waiting for him, most of them from his mother, one from his devoted uncle François Parain, another from Louis Bouilhet. His relief was immediate and unrestrained. 'I kiss you till you suffocate. I see that you are well, that you are being sensible, and I love you a thousand times more for that.'[6]

Later, when the excitement had died down, they went back into town. They had some calls to make and shopping to do – they were planning an excursion across the eastern desert to the Red Sea and then back to the Nile and the *cange*. They visited Monsieur Ortalli, a doctor, and Monsieur Issa, a Greek grocer from Chios. Then Flaubert walked further down the road to the house of a woman he called Osnah Taouileh – Hasna the tall one. She was, he wrote, 'a beautiful whore who loved me a lot and who made signs that I had beautiful eyes'.[7] She also complained about his scratchy beard.

Mansfield Parkyns, Richard Monckton Milnes' university colleague and travelling companion, had discovered that Nile winds could be 'quite contrary'. Nightingale and the Bracebridges found them far worse than that. A choppy river rocked the *Parthenope*, high winds rattled the window panes and sand found its way into everything. For Nightingale, the storm outside her cabin window was matched by the one gathering inside her head.

They had left Qena at sunset on 25 February, having received news of the Greek war but otherwise at peace. The wind had picked up the following morning and blown against them all day, making progress very slow. Twenty-nine miles and 36 hours later, they were becalmed off a village called How. Here, they rode inland to visit a small Greco-Roman ruin.

Nightingale was charmed by the scenery, particularly by the acanthus and sycamore trees and the well-tended fields, which stretched for a mile inland. She was even more impressed by what came next. 'Without warning or apparent difference of level, or tongues of sand encroaching, but only divided by a sharp straight line, began desert, which reached to the foot of the square of mountains or rather cliffs.'[8] She stepped over this line from the fertile to the barren, from the lands of Osiris to the realm of Seth, and sat in the sand with Selina Bracebridge where they were immediately joined by elders from a nearby village; she thought the sheikh looked 'like a St Peter' with his crimson turban and white beard. 'But conceive our desperation when we found the tomb we came to see positively carried away bodily – the stones, the painted stones, gone to make a sugar factory at How, where Mr B. saw them.'[9]

The wind kept them within sight of the offensive factory all afternoon. Her diary entry for the following day reads: '*Nile*. North wind blew such a gale we could not get on.'[10] They were still unable to move the following day when a sandstorm hit. When they did finally move, it was with the crew out on the riverbank, pulling at ropes, towing the boat downstream. Their rate of progress then halved: it took them three days to cover 35 miles to the town of Girgeh, where Nightingale had enjoyed a morning walk and early coffee at the caravanserai on their way south.

She had not gone on an excursion with the Bracebridges on their first day at Qena, on the pretext that she wanted to stay 'home' and catch up with notes and letters. Afterwards she admitted that she had been unable to write, but could not explain why. Four days later, with the storm raging outside, she noted in her diary that God had called her again. This time, He reminded her of what her *madre*, Laure de Sainte Colombe, had said. Two years earlier, at the Convent of the Sacré Coeur in Rome, she had told Nightingale not to cut herself off from people. 'What does it matter even if we are with people who make us desperate?' her *madre* had asked then. 'So long as we are doing God's will, it doesn't matter at all.' And had finished by reminding Nightingale that she had been called to serve. To do that, she needed to surrender her will: 'He calls you to a very high degree of perfection. Take care, if you resist, you will be very guilty.'[11]

By the time they were halfway to Cairo, Mr Bracebridge and one of the crew were ill, Paolo had had a fall, and Nightingale had noted in her private diary that the boat was now 'a hospital'. That day they lay off Abydos, the pre-eminent centre for the cult of Osiris, the god she admired almost more than any other for his affinity with the Christian trinity. But it was 'too stormy to visit', she noted, almost with relief, consumed as she was by her own inner turmoil. She then made a despairing entry in her diary: 'Oh! [M]y *madre*, my *madre*. This was the time I made the retreat with you, which you said was more for me than for the children. Two years ago.'[12] The thought of it sapped her energy and her will. Two days later, still powerless in the face of her visions and the storm, she was unable to get up and stayed in bed all morning. 'God gave me the time . . . to "meditate" on my *madre*'s words.'[13]

When the storm finally passed and the wind dropped a little, they went into Girgeh. This time they went in search of candles to light their evenings. When they found none in the souk, Paolo had the idea of going to a church. 'We went to the Latin [Catholic] church, which, to judge from its size, must have a congregation, but the Latin father was gone, to Asyut. But with what joy I entered a Christian church again! – really my heart leaped within me! The mass-book was in Coptic and Arabic.'[14] While Nightingale studied the Mass, Paolo spoke to the clerk, a friend of his. Eight hours after their return to the *dahabiya*, the clerk came aboard with some candles for them. 'Pure wax with the honey in it they certainly were,' Nightingale wrote home, 'but unless appearances are *very* deceptive, they were stolen out of the church's store; and we are now burning the ecclesiastical candle.'[15]

The day after leaving Girgeh, Gustave Flaubert began a long letter to Louis Bouilhet. He had written to his confidant at each significant stage of the journey so far. There had been two letters from Cairo, full of posturing, studded with strange and grotesque stories, padded out with bragging and exaggeration – and perhaps also a fabrication about being masturbated in the *hammam*. There was a more thoughtful one as he left Aswan and crossed the Tropic of Cancer, describing his exploits with Kuchuk Hanem, complaining that he felt empty, flat and sterile, and shooting out some questions: 'What will I do when I get home, will I publish, will I not publish? What will I write? Will I write?'[16] Now, as he set out on the last leg of the journey back to Cairo, there were more questions.

He had had plenty of opportunity to sit at the bow of the *cange*, watch the river run past and consider what to do with his life. In this period of intense introspection, he recovered many forgotten memories. He felt he was on the cusp of something, but did not know what and could not know where it would lead him. That did not stop him from wondering what would happen next. 'Am I starting a new period,' he asked Bouilhet, 'or one of complete decadence? From the past, I dream my way forwards, and I see nothing there, nothing. I am without plans, without ideas, without projects and, what's worse, without the ambition to do anything.'[17] He could not see the point of making the effort. Every bright idea that cropped up in his head was knocked down again by 'the eternal what's the use?'

'You don't become gayer while travelling,'[18] he warned his friend back in Rouen, and then began to unburden himself with a great outpouring of thoughts and emotions. He doubted that he had the strength, the physical strength, to publish. And for what? For whom? The public is so stupid, he wrote, they read nothing, they know nothing, so why care what they think? Why bother to offer your work, your thoughts, your time to them? He thought it was better to write for himself and have the satisfaction of knowing that he had done something well. It was a different life from the one he was living now. No more plant-like absorbing, no more being an eye, observing all. 'When I return, I will resume and for a long time, I hope, my calm old life at my round table, between my fireplace and garden. I will continue to live like a bear, not caring about my country, about criticism or anything.'[19]

The thought of his study at Croisset tempted him as he sat in the shade on the boat, the Nile propelling him north, back towards home. It also brought back memories of the days and nights he had spent reading aloud *The Temptation of Saint Anthony*, just before leaving for Egypt; of the long silence when he had finished; of the awkwardness of Bouilhet and Du Camp and their verdict that he should throw three years' work in the fire and never mention it again. Those memories ate away at his resolve.

Du Camp was completely opposed to his idea of locking

himself away again and thought there was no need to refine his work or hone his talent further. His friend thought he should get himself into print as soon as possible, in any way he could. The two writers picked away at this conundrum – to publish, not to publish – throughout the long days aboard the *cange*. Whatever he might have said to Du Camp, Flaubert finally revealed himself in this same letter to Bouilhet. 'We take notes, we make journeys, misery, misery. We become scholars, archaeologists, historians, doctors, cobblers and people of taste . . . Where will all this lead us,' he wondered, 'what will we have done in ten years? For me, it seems that if I get the next book wrong, there will be nothing left but to throw myself into the water.' Outside the window of his cabin, the water was as choppy as an ocean, the storm gathering strength over the Nile.

Neither Paolo, the *reis*, nor any of the crew had ever seen such weather on the Nile. Their water world was suddenly unrecognisable to the voyagers on the *Parthenope* as strong winds transformed the languid river into a torrent, stirred up the desert sand, turned hot days cold, and at times made it impossible for the *dahabiya* to continue downriver. When they were able to move, they made little progress, caught between the need to avoid running aground on the sandbanks and to arrive at a safe mooring. When the wind was too strong, they tied up under a tall bank that gave some protection from the storm. But wherever they went and at whatever time of day or night, there was no escaping the wind. It whistled through the boat, rocked them from morning to night, and carried so much sand with it that it caked their eyes and hair, chafed inside their clothes and beds, and made their food gritty. Throughout all this, Nightingale struggled with her own personal demons, trying to reconcile the irreconcilable, hoping to find a way to answer the call while still meeting her family's expectations.

Two days after leaving Girgeh, they were forced to tie up near a hill that was called the Mountain of Sheikh Heridi. The hill was named after a Muslim holy man who was said to have been turned into a snake and had performed miracle cures on the righteous sick. This was perhaps a more modern representation of one of the oldest of Ancient Egyptian deities, the protecting serpent. Whatever the truth of the matter, country people – women in particular – visited the sheikh's old home in the hope of finding cures for their ills.

The storm pinned down the *Parthenope* beneath the sheikh's tomb for two nights and a day. Nightingale recorded nothing more extraordinary in her public diary than the fact that they were unable to move downriver and that they had walked to an Arab encampment of screens of Indian corn with a few jars, dogs and buffalos. But the private diary brings the momentous news: 'God called me in the morning and asked me, Would I do good for Him, for Him alone and without the reputation?'[20] It was the same internal debate about her true calling, the same demand that she submit herself to this other will and serve without 'reputation', without taking the credit for anything. This last point was of great importance to her, for she moved among people of repute and had seen how corrupting vanity could be. But, as before, she had no answer to the call. Like their boat pinned down beneath the magic mountain, she had no idea how she would ever find a way forward.

The wind dropped that night and at three in the morning they pulled away from the bank. 'Wobbled about all day', was how she recorded it. They sat down to dinner late in the afternoon, as usual, and then Nightingale returned to her cabin. Looking out at the sunset over the water, she 'thought much upon this question my *madre* said to me: Can you hesitate between the God of the whole earth and your little reputation?"[21] But it was not purely a matter of her reputation. Like Flaubert, she wondered whether she had the strength to achieve all she wanted; to do all she knew needed to be done.

Two weeks after leaving Luxor they had expected to be in Cairo but had only just reached Asyut, still 235 miles south of the capital. But given the weather and the illness on board, they were pleased to have made it this far. They were also happy for an excuse to go into town: Mustafa, their cook, had invited them to his house.

Nightingale had been shocked by what she had seen in Asyut on the way upriver. She had read accounts of African villages in the books of Mungo Park and James Bruce, 'but no description gives the idea of the debasement and misery'.[22] This time, however, there was no mention of savage life or animals, nor of going up above the town to the caves of Lycopolis that she had so enjoyed on her earlier visit. 'My noble mind was bent not upon tombs,' she wrote home – this was her first letter in ten days – 'but upon hareems [sic], upon Mustafa's (our cook's) "womans". I do not care a doit about seeing Abbas Pacha's hareem, one never gets further than the sweetmeats and the fine clothes; but I do want to see the common hareems. So, armed with needles and pins, we went to Mustafa's house, nominally to thank for some bread they had presented us with on our way up the river.'[23]

Mustafa had left the boat before them and spent the morning preparing himself and his home to receive the illustrious visitors. The house was large, but simple: the floor was of beaten earth, the walls of mud-brick, the roof supported by palm trunks, the windows unglazed but covered with mats. They were led upstairs to the main room, which had no furniture but did have a rug on the floor, where they were invited to sit. The kitchen was down off the courtyard – little more than a tent, equipped with a brazier, pots and pans, and one very old clasp knife.

'What a curious sight it was,' Nightingale wrote home, 'the incongruities! – [T]he principal lady, the married sister, dressed like an oriental queen, but without a shift or anything which could be washed, next to her skin . . . The second wife, in a blue shirt, stood on the threshold. The mother was baking downstairs; and two slaves peeped in at the door.'[24] Nightingale wore her usual black dress with its white lacy collar, but Mustafa's 'principal lady' was dressed to impress. She wore 'Cachemire [sic] trousers, of a delicate small pattern – a "yelek" [caftan] with hanging sleeves, of exquisite Brusa silk, crimson and white, trimmed with gold binding – a "tob" [a loose robe] with immense sleeves, of lilac silk – and over it (for the Arab never wears her gayest clothes outside) a purple gauze drapery embroidered with silver, and veil of the same colour, embroidered in silk.'[25] The meal was good, Mustafa's women were charming, and Mustafa himself beamed at the honour done to his house.

They were back on board the *dahabiya* by early afternoon when something extraordinary happened, another of those unexpected, fast-moving, far-reaching events that shaped Nightingale's life. She had sent Trautwein back to Mustafa's house on some errand, to deliver a gift perhaps or to collect more bread for the journey ahead of them, and while her maid was away, Nightingale spent half an hour alone in her cabin. It was 9 March, the Feast of St Françoise. Afloat on the Nile, tied up outside Asyut, the conversation she had begun in the grand temples of southern Egypt now reached its conclusion. She wrote in her private diary, in her usual spidery script, that she had 'settled the question with God'.[26]

Her struggles were not over, far from it: some of the worst were still to come. But there had never been anything like this before. For the first time in her life she had reached a conclusion. There would be no more talk of marriage or family, no more temptations or prevarications. She would submit her will. She would serve. She would nurse.

13

Cairo and Alexandria

'So farewell, dear, beautiful, noble, dead Egypt, the country which brought forth a race of giants, giants in war, art, science and philosophy. Farewell, without regret, without pain (except a merely personal sorrow), for there is nothing mournful in the remains of a country which, like its own old Nile, has overflowed and fertilised the world' – Florence Nightingale, Cairo, 25 March 1850

Nightingale might have settled the question with God, but things were far from resolved with man.

She had decided what she must do with her life from then on. She would strive to attain the very high degree of perfection that Laure de Sainte Colombe had challenged her to achieve in Rome. She would avoid being 'very guilty'. She would not care about her own reputation. A decision had been made. But she still had two very different and daunting struggles ahead of her. She must convince her family and friends that it was acceptable for a woman of her social position to devote herself to nursing; and she must find a way of fulfilling her calling, of making it happen.

Nowadays we look at this period of Florence Nightingale's life in the knowledge that she does win through. We already know she gets her way, trains as a nurse, runs a nursing home in London's Harley Street, is called upon to help the British Army in the Crimea and becomes the Lady with the Lamp. But *she* did not know any of this. What was more, if someone had told her of it, as she was rowed back to Cairo against the northerly winds, she would not have believed them. How could she? She knew what she wanted and had a sense of how this wish could be fulfilled. But she did not see how she would ever be allowed to do so, nor did she have the faintest idea that at least one of her struggles was about to reach its conclusion.

The voices continued to speak to her for as long as the storm raged along the Nile. They provoked her and she responded. Enclosed in her cabin, the wind howling through the slats of the shutters, she lost herself in introspection and longing. If she had been in England, she would have had to hide all this from her family. But there was less need for concealment on the boat. The Bracebridges understood that she was going through some sort of crisis, and even if they did not know or could not understand the exact nature of her struggle, they were at least sympathetic.

None of this found its way into her letters home, but she did leave clues in her private diary. The day after settling 'the question' and leaving Asyut, she sat in her cabin contemplating her *madre*'s words. The following day, as they struggled on to Tell al Amarna, she speculated on the thought that they could have spent an extra fortnight in Luxor, rather than being blown back up the Nile, but was aware that without being storm-tossed on the river, 'I might not have had this call from God.'[1]

Somewhere beyond Minya, late the next night, she stood looking out at the stars, the tall mast, the palms, the river: ' . . . (we were at anchor, they were all asleep, I could not go to bed) and tried to think only of *God's will* and that everything is desirable and undesirable only as He is in it or not in it, only as it brings us nearer or farther from Him. He is speaking to us often just when something we think untoward happens.'[2]

There was more good news: the dreaming had stopped. Three nights later, looking up at the stars, she wrote: 'God has delivered me from the great offence and the constant murderer of all my thoughts.'[3] Relief and happiness returned, just as they reached Memphis.

The guardian priests of Memphis had done their best to protect the city that had once rivalled Karnak for the position of the country's religious centre. They had maintained the cults of the gods, made sacrifices, kept themselves pure and encouraged the same of the pharaoh and his subjects. They had even gone so far as to refuse to allow Alexander the Great to be buried there, for they knew that wherever the great conqueror lay, there would be trouble. But trouble came anyway and this, one of the most ancient cities of Egypt, fell. Most of it had been built from mud and was simply washed away by the Nile flood. The temples and other stone buildings were later dismantled, their blocks used in the construction of the city of Cairo. There was little left for Nightingale to see.

She knew all that and had thought Memphis would be another of those places she would struggle to appreciate after the wonders of Luxor. But she was wrong. She found it poetic, melancholy and, above all, immensely beautiful. 'I have seen nothing like it except in my dreams,' she noted in surprise.

Why was this? Was she once again projecting her thoughts and feelings on to her surroundings? Or were her surroundings influencing the way she felt? When she was in turmoil, a storm had raged along the river. Now that she was happy, she saw that she was surrounded by beauty. 'A palm forest, the old palms springing out of the freshest grass, the ground covered with a little pink flower' – she tried but failed to press one to take home – 'and the most delicate little lilac dwarf iris. Here and there a glassy pool and a flock of goats and kids, the long sun-light streaks and shadows falling among the trees.' In the middle of this bucolic wonder lay a statue of 'her' Ramses: 'the most beautiful sculpture we have yet seen. I must even confess that there is nothing at Abu Simbel to compare with it.'[4]

'There he lies upon his face, as if he had just lain down weary. You speak low that you may not wake him to see the desolation of his land . . . It is the most beautiful tombstone for the grave of a nation I ever saw.'

That line, and the sentiment it expressed, was worthy of Flaubert in his most Romantic period, yet the Frenchman had reached Memphis armed not with poetry but with a rifle: he was out hunting. He stopped to smoke a pipe and drink coffee, killed some doves on the edge of the ditch in which this most beautiful statue of Ramses lay, and then headed back to the ancient burial grounds at Saqqara, hoping to find an ibis mummy. 'We go down into one of the pits,' he wrote of his adventure at Saqqara, 'a corridor in which you have to crawl on your stomach – you move over fine sand and pottery fragments – at the end the ibis pots are arranged head to toe like sugared bread at the grocer's.'[5]

Nightingale and the Bracebridges also rode from Memphis towards Saqqara, across this 'grave of a nation'. The land was pitted with burials like a battlefield scarred with bomb craters, and their asses' hooves turned over bones, linens once wrapped around mummies, and broken fragments of pots. When she looked up, she was in front of the pyramids at Giza and was distinctly unimpressed.

'Hardly anything can be imagined more vulgar, more uninteresting than a pyramid in itself, set up upon a tray, like a clipt yew in a public-house garden; it represents no idea; it appeals to no feeling; it tries to call forth no part of you, but the vulgarest part – astonishment at its size – at the expense.'[6] They rode towards the pyramids through fields of corn and dwarf iris, and in the shade of an avenue of tamarisk trees.

The first thing one did on reaching the pyramids at that time was to climb them. 'Σ [Selina] of course did not'. Nightingale of course did. A team of Egyptians went with her and Mr Bracebridge, pushing and pulling them up the large stones. 'The Arabs begin at the bottom with tying all your clothes in a knot behind. As by this time you have learnt that the Arabs always know best, you *laissez-faire*.'[7] But not even the view from the top of the best preserved of all the wonders of the Ancient World could impress her. She walked around, trying to summon a suitable response. 'The stones certainly were remarkably large, the view was remarkably large, the European names cut there were remarkably large. Here are *three* sentiments: which will you have?'

Coming down was more fun. It was faster, for one thing, and with her clothes wrapped tight around her and the drop from one ledge to another so long, she had nothing to do but to submit to the men around her. 'You embrace an Arab tight round the neck and fairly swing yourself down by him, being perfectly sure of his standing like a column. After all, it is not worse than polking [dancing] and looks singularly like it.'[8]

She was even less impressed by the inside of the pyramid and likened it to being a rat in a sewer. But coming out was more exciting. Because of the heat and the need to crawl around, she had gone in without shoes or bonnet or her many-layered dress. As she emerged, barefoot and bare-headed, in her flannel and brown Holland underclothes, she was mortified to discover three Turks from Constantinople and their harems settled by the entrance, waiting for their turn to go inside. Selina Bracebridge saved the moment. 'She had not been in, and, though she could not speak for laughing, she pounced upon me, wrapped me in a shawl, and stuck on my bonnet. The Turks *never moved a muscle*.'[9]

The following day, she was afraid to think of what she had written about the pyramids. 'I expect you will murder me,' she wrote to her parents. 'I could almost murder myself: all I can say for myself is, that I have faithfully rendered in blue ink what impressions the pyramid makes."[10] Remorse, then, but no contrition: she still held to her conviction that, after all she had seen in Egypt, the pyramids were uninteresting. She made one last effort to justify herself.

Egypt is like a vast library, the finest, the Alexandrian [L]ibrary of the world. You read, and look, and study; and read, and look, and study again. And if it is so interesting to me, you say, who can only read one word in a page, what must it be to him who can read two? At last you come to a huge folio, which, the librarian tells you, is the oldest and biggest book in the world. You run up the ladder and turn over one blank page after another: you soon get tired of that work.[11]

They slept on board the *Parthenope* for the first few nights in Cairo, moored first to the south, then across on the western bank at Giza, and finally tied up where they had started, near the pasha's palace on Roda Island. She went out to find a bulrush to take home as a reminder of the place where Moses had been found, but this time could find only roses.

Paolo, their *dragoman*, who had been too ill to escort them to Giza, was still unable to help them look for a house to rent when they reached Cairo. Not feeling capable of finding a house without him, Mr Bracebridge decided to take rooms in a hotel. Lord Northampton's party had taken all the rooms in their first choice of residence, so they opted for Monsieur Coulomb's Hotel d'Orient on the north side of Ezbekiya, where Flaubert and Du Camp had stayed before sailing for the south. Wilkinson called it the best hotel in town. William Thackeray thought it as large and comfortable as the best hotels in the South of France, and had been amused to find: 'England here in a French hotel kept by an Italian at the city of Grand Cairo in Africa.' It would be the perfect antidote to the months spent in cramped quarters on the boat. They returned to the *Parthenope* to pack and, while their bags were sent off to town and a hot wind blew off the desert, went to visit the ruins at Heliopolis.

Nightingale had looked forward to this moment in the way she had anticipated visiting Philae: Heliopolis was one of the oldest and most influential of all Egypt's centres of learning. It was the last significant sight she would have of Ancient Egypt and, although she knew from her guidebook that there was little left to see, in some ways she thought it would be the best. 'No soil,' she explained, 'not even Thebes, is so sacred as this.'[12]

They crossed cornfields to reach the little that remained of the ancient city, less even than at Memphis. 'The mounds are small. A gateway of Tuthmosis III, the king of the Exodus, has just been dug up by the Arabs.'[13] They found a garden of orange, lemon and almond trees, belonging to Selim Effendi, an Armenian with a nose that reminded Flaubert (who passed here a month or so later) of a bird of prey. The garden contained an obelisk from the Temple of the Sun. They had already seen its twin, the so-called 'Cleopatra's needle', soon after their arrival in Alexandria. Florence thought this obelisk was as beautiful as the ones in Karnak and wrote an idyllic description of the scene:

> Wild bees have settled all over the obelisk . . . and their pleasant hum filled the citron trees and cactuses, and the sweet smells floated on the air. How pleasant it was, how lovely. This obelisk stood before the temple where all the learning of the world was cherished! Here Moses sat, and Plato, the pair of truest gentlemen that ever breathed. But Moses was the greater man; for whereas Plato only formed a school, which formed the world, Moses went straight to work upon the world . . . the chisel as it were to the block, his delicate perceptions acting upon those miserable savages.[14]

Her parents would not have missed the obvious joy in this letter, if only because joy had been lacking from many of her earlier ones. There was an unmistakable lightness of touch. The words reveal a sense of her feeling at one with the world, or at least with this part of it. Perhaps her parents would have put this down to their daughter being back in Cairo, off the boat and out of the storm. Maybe they thought that she was happy to have returned to civilised society after the months of relative isolation in the south, and to have clean clothes and access to a *hammam*; relieved to be staying in a spacious room with a soft bed after the close confines of her cabin and the beaten cotton mattress of her divan on the *dahabiya*. There was some truth in this. 'Our first day in a respectable inn,' she wrote in her public diary, 'but we did not know how to sit or do long dinners or behave ourselves, but, in memory of our boat, tried to catch fleas and go to bed.'[15] In her private diary, she added that she 'enjoyed the luxury of having a room to myself for the first time', and wondered 'what use shall I make of it?' But there was a more powerful reason for this welling of happiness. Something remarkable and unexpected had just happened to her.

Three and a half years earlier, when her friend Baron Bunsen had first told her about the deaconesses' institution at Kaiserwerth and given her their yearbook, she had immediately recognised that this was 'my home, there are my brothers and sisters at work. There my heart is and there, I trust, will one day be my body.'[16] She now knew that the dream was going to come true: the Bracebridges had agreed to take her to Kaiserwerth on their way back to England.

It is not clear exactly how this had come about. Nightingale's biographers have suggested that the decision was taken much later, so late, according to the latest view, that 'there was no time to seek permission from the Nightingales for this change of plan'.[17] The diaries tell another story.

On 16 March, while still sleeping on board the *Parthenope*, she wrote in her public diary that she 'rode into Cairo for our letters and back, having good news at the pace of caliphs',[18] sedately, slowly. The public diary offers no clue as to what this 'good news' might have been, but it is there in the private one. 'As I sat in the large dull room [at François', the hotel Lord Northampton's group had filled] waiting for the letters, God told me what a privilege he had reserved for me, what a preparation for Kaiserwerth in choosing me to be with Mr B. during this time of his ill health.'[19] This is the first mention of Pastor Fliedner's institution in the surviving letters and diaries from Egypt. It is the first suggestion that she knew, as early as March 1850, that she would be able to visit Kaiserwerth. The

Bracebridges had watched her wrestle with her demons while the *dahabiya* was pummelled by the storms. Mr Bracebridge had been taken ill. Hence they had decided to stop off en route in Germany, at Pyrmont, for him to take a water cure. He would need to stay there for some weeks. From Pyrmont, it was just a day's ride to Kaiserwerth.

Flaubert, now a long way behind Nightingale, had hit even worse weather: he and Du Camp had lost a fortnight coming down from Luxor to Cairo in the *cange*. Nightingale had left the 'sweet *Parthenope*' wondering who would care for the boat the way she and her friends had: 'I dare say by this time she is full of fleas and hareems.'[20] Flaubert had had a similar moment as he finally walked up from the port at Boulak to Monsieur Bouvaret's Hotel du Nil. 'Cairo seemed empty and silent,' he noted, 'the impression you have . . . when you find yourself alone in a hotel, with nothing to do.'[21] He unpacked the canteen to pass the time. That night, he admitted to an 'enormous' longing for the journey. He missed the sound of the oars on water. 'Poor *cange*! [Y]es, poor *cange*, where are you now? [W]ho is walking on your boards?'

He wrote more about this in a letter to Louis Bouilhet, two days after his arrival. 'I left our poor boat with great sadness. Back at the hotel in Cairo, my head was buzzing, like at the end of a long coach ride. The city seemed empty and silent, although it was full of people and movement. The night I got back . . . I kept on hearing the sweet sound of the oars in the water, which for three months had set the rhythm for our long, dreamy journey.'[22]

He also heard plenty of chatter: his notebook is full of meetings. In the street, he came across Monsieur Brochier, the co-owner of the Hotel du Nil, and then found Consul Delaporte and the usual crowd at the consulate. He visited

Aimé Rochas, a French photographer, to buy some daguerreo-types, which seems strange, given that he had just travelled the Nile with a photographer. And then *Reis* Fergali and the crew of the *cange* hosted a dinner for their two clients at Boulak. One evening they enjoyed music at Ezbekiya with the engineer Lambert and an archaeologist named Batissier; another they had a long night drinking with the historian Paul Mouriez, whom they had met in Aswan, staying up until it was dawn. The cock was crowing, Flaubert's two candles having burned out; his back was slick with sweat, his eyes sore. 'In four hours I am leaving Cairo – Goodbye Egypt – *Allah!* As the Arabs say.'[23]

His sadness at leaving reminded him of how excited he had been on arrival. It also brought memories of the state he had been in before the Nile journey, of his pain at the failure of *Saint Anthony*. But the journey appears to have worked its magic. There had been a transformation in Flaubert too. Since returning to Cairo (and reading Bouilhet's letter) he had been in the grip of a new intellectual intensity. His mind was buzzing. 'The pot,' he announced joyously to his friend, 'has suddenly begun to boil, I have a burning desire to write.'[24]

On her way south, Nightingale had had little desire to socialise in Cairo, and this, at least, seemed unchanged on her return: three days after arriving at the Hotel d'Orient, she noted that, 'Cairo is overflowing with Franks [foreigners]; but we have hitherto refused all invitations, we were too tired.'[25] One day, Anthony Harris and his daughter called to see what the party had bought on their journey. On the Sunday – Palm Sunday – they went to church, but came away frustrated with the priest. 'How could a man preach such a sermon in the land of Moses!' Nightingale thundered.[26] Selina Bracebridge went to sleep, while Nightingale was disturbed by the fleas. Two or three people fainted. They all stayed 'home' for the remainder of the day.

Later, she regretted that they had 'idled' away their first week back in Cairo. They had originally intended to spend three weeks in the city, but Mr Bracebridge, who still preferred to make all decisions on these matters, had cut that down to two, presumably because he had news of developments in Greece. Whatever the reason, they suddenly found themselves with only a few days left in this 'rose of cities', and spent them in sightseeing and shopping. Nightingale went to buy presents at the goldsmiths and the silk merchants. She looked for stuffed birds for her cousin, Shore, the young man who would inherit the family fortune when her father died. She bought daguerreotypes from the dealer Schranz, in his little shop in the Coptic quarter, so she could show her parents and sister some of the sights she had visited. Afterwards, like so many people before and since, she worried that her presents seemed insignificant compared to the splendours she had seen. 'You have no idea how difficult it is to find anything in Cairo you like,' she wrote, defensively, 'unless you buy the house and window – that *would* be a present.'[27]

The diaries hold few surprises during this fortnight. Two days after Palm Sunday, she noted in her private diary that the storm had returned and while the *khamsin* blew, she spent time in her room reading her '*madre*'s words'. She did not go to church the following Friday – Good Friday – but stayed in her room and thought about Osiris and Jesus, her *madre* and herself. The day before her departure, she again stayed in the hotel, happy for 'God to have it all His own way. I like Him to do exactly as He likes, without even telling me the reason why.'[28]

There had been a round of dinners, including one hosted by Consul Murray to which their lordships Northampton and

Lincoln and their respective parties had been invited. There were repeat visits to the old city and others out into the desert. One day, as part of a large party that included the Northamptons and Lincolns and the consular officials, Nightingale went to see the sights along the main street of the old city, 'the most beautiful of all the streets of Cairo'.[29] She made repeat visits to the tombs of the sultans and the City of the Dead, a place that had filled her with despair when she had first visited it and where she now appreciated its beauty. Wherever she went, she entered mosques.

She had felt very uneasy visiting the mosque in Alexandria all those months ago. 'I knew so little about the Muhammadan religion,' she admitted, 'and it interested me so little.'[30] She had known as little about the religion of the Ancient Egyptians, although she had been more interested. But having been to the south and now visited the 'wonderful' mosques of Cairo, she wrote that 'when one goes into any church, be it the temple of Karnak, be it St Peter's, be it the Mosque El Azhar, be it St James's, one always feels, Here is the foot of Jacob's ladder, and angels are ascending and descending upon it – this is the gate of heaven.'[31] Few European visitors to Egypt in the mid-nineteenth century would have been so comfortable making these clear parallels between Christianity, Islam and the religion of the pagans, just as few Egyptians today would be happy comparing Amun and Allah. But the journey up the Nile had revealed many things to her, and one of them was that these different religions stood on common ground and spoke about similar things.

There was no steam-tug to pull the ferry to Alexandria, so horses were used to tow the barge instead. It still took a day and a night to move from the capital to the coast, a long journey that was eased by the company of congenial women. Madame Rosetti, the Tuscan consul's wife, was there, as she had been on the way from Alexandria to Cairo back in November. There was a nun, the Reverend Mother of the Good Shepherdesses, 'a German of high family', and also an old woman from Smyrna, 'her beautiful hair, at sixty years of age, dressed round a red *tarboosh*, with a blue gauze cockade . . . looking like the head wife of a pacha'.[32]

They reached the junction of the river and the Mahmoudieh Canal late at night: 'too late to bid adieu to our solemn Nile; who, indeed, had been all that day as ugly and as contrary as it was possible to be'.[33] Whatever the time, this was not the moment for farewells or nostalgia: they had to change boat. 'If anybody could have drawn that scene, how good it would have been,' Nightingale wrote home. The old Smyrniot storming off ahead, a Hungarian count carrying someone's little dog, 'helpless females' scared of walking the thin plank to the dark riverbank . . . she loved it all. 'A most wonderful night with a vast deal of livestock, human and (*not*) divine,' she wrote in her public diary, 'besides animals, in one small cabin.'[34]

In Alexandria, they checked back into the Hotel d'Europe, on the main square. The news from Greece was not good. Mr Bracebridge had booked their passage on a steamer to Corfu, where they would sit out quarantine and, from there, either move on to Athens or head for Trieste and northern Europe. The Corfu boat would leave in three days, which left just enough time to shop, wash, pack, pay last calls – Miss Harris was in town – and prepare for the time at sea.

Flaubert and Du Camp had a week to spend in Alexandria before their ship sailed. They were on their way to Beirut and from there to Turkey, Greece and Italy. Du Camp left no impressions from these days in either of the accounts he published. For Flaubert it was different: his 'pot' continued to boil and he shaped two stories.

The first, which he sent to his friend Frédéric Baudry, concerned the state of politics in Egypt: 'Abbas-Pacha has pigeons which wear diamond collars, collects dogs from around the world, has many young nubile boys and a magnificent mouthpiece on his waterpipe. I saw both, cute and piping, the first are dressed with redingotes [coats], straps that fix their trousers underneath their shoes, and cravats, it's pitiful – what's more, I thought these strange creatures were ugly. But the richly decorated mouthpiece excited my longing. His Highness serves terrible coffee.'[35]

The second was included in the last letter he wrote to Louis Bouilhet from Egypt, along with a guarantee of its authenticity. 'A young, beautiful woman (I saw her), married to an old man, couldn't have sex with her lover when she wanted. In the three months they had known each other, they had only managed to fuck three or four times because the poor girl was watched. The husband, old, jealous, ill, aggressive, was tight with his money, and annoyed her in every possible way . . . '[36]

At seven in the morning, a few days later, he and Du Camp boarded the *Alexandra* and prepared to leave, but a whirlwind delayed their departure. When they did finally set off it was without ceremony and without Flaubert on deck to witness it. 'The boat left while I was sleeping,' he wrote with some regret. 'I didn't see the land of Egypt disappear over the horizon – I did not say my last goodbyes . . . Will I return?'[37]

'Saturday was our day for leaving Egypt,' Nightingale wrote to her parents, 'our last day in the East; and really I think my most curious day – perhaps the most curious day of my life.'[38]

She was up early. The *Schild*, the steamer for Corfu and Trieste, was not due to leave until 4 p.m., but their bags had to be ready by 8 a.m., presumably so that they could clear customs. She was out early enough to pay a last visit to the St-

Vincent-de-Paul dispensary. The German nun who had travelled with her from Cairo was there, as was the head of the Sisters of Mercy from Australia, who had come to set up her own mission. Nightingale observed them with longing. 'There is a freemasonry . . . among the Orders,' she wrote home. 'They all go to one another's houses for hospitality; and whether they can speak one another's language or not, they are always sure to find help and sympathy.'[39] She craved both help and sympathy and would have stayed until it was time to board the ship, but she had an appointment with Madame Rosetti.

When she had visited the house of Mustafa, the cook from their *dahabiya*, she had said she had no desire to see the pasha's harem, complaining that 'one never gets further than the sweetmeats and the fine clothes'.[40] To her consternation, however, the Tuscan consul's wife had arranged just such a visit for herself and Selina Bracebridge. Engeli Hanem, the only wife of Said Pasha, son of Muhammad Ali Pasha and now heir to the throne, herself the future Queen of Egypt, would be happy to receive them. They rode asses to the palace and walked straight into a scene out of an Orientalist fantasy.

Two successive curtains (two successive gardens between) were lifted up to let us pass. Troops of beautiful white Circassians came to receive us; a black showed the way. Through marble halls, with fountains in the middle, we passed, till we reached the room where Engeli Hanum [*sic*] rose to receive us. Tall, and with a beautiful figure, unlike these Turkish women, she seemed to us the most lovely woman we had ever seen, with that soft melancholy eye, that exquisite mouth and complexion.[41]

The large marble hall contained a raised dais embroidered with the Turkish star and crescent, which served as the princess's large divan, and some seating for the guests. Nothing else. The princess was certainly splendid, wearing a fur-trimmed green robe and yellow trousers. Nightingale was in her travelling clothes and a little ashamed to be so plain in such grand surroundings and a royal presence. Perhaps she remembered her *débutante* appearances in London. But the princess was too well bred to appear to take any notice of what they were wearing.

'There we sat, without even the weather to talk of. Coffee came, of course, and pipes covered with diamonds.' But however luxurious, however sumptuous, Nightingale found the palace claustrophobic – even the windows on to the garden were covered with closely worked lattice screens. 'I would have died for her,' she concluded, 'but I could not have lived with her.'

When the princess said goodbye, she sent her compliments to Nightingale's husband. Had she not made the connection before, Nightingale would have been relieved at that moment not to be married, not to be trapped in a big, comfortable house with nothing to do but have children and entertain. The options she had had in her life to date, the choices she had made . . . everything was now as clear to her as an Egyptian night sky. 'If heaven and hell exist on this earth,' she wrote in her notebook and in a letter home, 'it is in the two worlds I saw on that one morning – the Dispensary and the Hareem.'[42] Flaubert, the doctor's son, would have chosen the harem. Nightingale knew that heaven for her existed in the dispensary.

The *Schild* sailed that afternoon.

14

Destiny

'I believe she has little or none of what is called charity
or philanthropy, she is ambitious – very, and would like
well enough to regenerate the world with a grand *coup de
main* or some fine institution' – Parthenope Nightingale
to Madame Mohl, 1853

'But are we men's equals, or are we not?' – Mary Taylor
in Charlotte Brontë's *Shirley*

'To live in Paris, to publish, to move, all that seems very
tiresome, seen from such a distance' – Gustave Flaubert
to Louis Bouilhet

Two twenty-something-year-old passengers board a ferry. He
climbs on to the top deck, she settles in down below. They
spend a day and a night being pulled towards the big city. On
arrival, they check into different hotels on the same square. In
the following months, they follow the same itinerary but on

different boats, in different company, and everything they see, they see through different eyes. Such coincidences happen all the time. But this story is different because these two people have spent many years struggling to fulfil what they believe to be their destinies. Both have been in despair and both are on the cusp of success beyond their dreams. Egypt has played a significant part in these developments.

Florence Nightingale and Gustave Flaubert followed the same itinerary, moored in some of the same places, stayed in the same hotel and saw the same sights. They even met some of the same people. And while Flaubert had been plant-like, Nightingale had expressed herself on paper, even writing a meditation on the spirits that inhabited the ancient holy places, an essay she called *A Vision of the Temples*, as strange and passionate as anything Flaubert included in *The Temptation of Saint Anthony*.

Nightingale had been quick to recognise the power of the surviving monuments along the Nile. Just four weeks after setting sail from Cairo, she wondered whether anything mattered beside the grandeur of Karnak. Sitting among its fallen columns and soaring halls that moonlit New Year's Eve, she had realised that Egypt was a place that could tempt you out of yourself, that could transform you. Some people found it impossible to go home and live life as they had once done after such an experience. She must have sensed, and hoped, that *she* would be one of them. She knew that the ancient ruins and the ideas they represented had inspired her in a profound way. Egypt had provided the space, the circumstances and the spiritual suggestions – found on the walls of tombs and temples – that had allowed her to attain clarity of thought about her role in the world and the purpose for which she had been born. It was there that she had 'settled the question with God'. Yet back in London, on the night of 20 August 1850, as she lay down in a room she knew well at the Burlington Hotel on Old Burlington Street, with what apprehension did she put her head on the pillow? 'How many revolutions of mind I have celebrated there?'[1] she wondered in her diary. With what trepidation did she board the Derbyshire-bound train at Euston Station at 8.30 the following morning? Seven hours later she walked unannounced through the front door of Lea Hurst and surprised her parents and sister in many ways.

She had left Egypt four months earlier and been away from home for almost ten. The possibility of getting to Kaiserwerth had hung over the end of the journey like a brilliant sunset over a storm at sea. There were moments when she thought she would never live to see the place: in Athens, for instance, she confided in her diary that she suffered 'the suspension of all my faculties. I could not write a letter. Could not read. Could not exert myself in any way.'[2] She had met an American missionary couple, the Hills, who had set up a school in Athens. Mrs Hill encouraged her to do what God suggested, not what she thought she should do. This provoked more introspection: 'I have read over all my history,' she wrote from Athens on 18 May, 'a history of miserable woe, mistake & blinding vanity, of seeking great things for myself.'[3]

The closer she came to Kaiserwerth, the more wracked she was by doubt and despair, and by self-criticism for wanting 'great things' for herself, for thinking of fame and her own reputation. After another sleepless night in Athens, she described herself as 'physically & morally ill & broken down, a slave'.[4] Even allowing for her love of melodrama when writing these private notes, it is clear she had hit a low point. Two weeks later, on the way to Prague, she spent a night of meditation during which she called 'upon God to save me. My soul spoke to His & I was comforted.'[5] After Prague, there was a miserable week in Berlin. 'I did not think it worth while to get up in the morning. What could I do but offend God?'[6] It was then that she looked back on the past few years and saw clearly the three paths she might have followed. 'I might have been a married woman, a literary woman, or a Hospital Sister.'[7] All three paths converged a week later.

When they reached Hamburg, she did what she had done in other cities along the way: she saw the obligatory sights and then devoted herself to visiting schools, hospices and caring institutions. She wrote entertaining letters home and kept her own thoughts private except from her diary. Then in Hamburg, on a day she visited the Ragged House, a home for destitute boys, she met Richard Monckton Milnes.

He was on his way to take the waters at Marienbad. They spent a happy day together and, when they parted, Nightingale declared herself 'well satisfied with our lark'. The reason for this change of tone is easy to find: in an echo from Shakespeare's *Richard III*, she confided in her diary that 'Richard was himself again'.[8] He may have been 'himself', but the meeting changed nothing between them, as she must have known it would not, and could not. He continued to Marienbad, Nightingale and the Bracebridges to Pyrmont. Once again, she vowed never to allow herself to be lured by the possibilities of such a relationship. She had settled the question with God. And anyway, the time for thoughts of marriage to Milnes was over because a few weeks later, on his return to London, he announced his engagement to another woman.

A couple of days later, Nightingale and the Bracebridges were installed at Pyrmont, where Mr B. prepared for his water cure and Nightingale waited for his permission to leave for Kaiserwerth. While she waited, she settled down to read *Shirley*, Charlotte Brontë's second novel, which tells the story of two very different women. One, the heroine of the title, is a wealthy, socially independent heiress; the other, Caroline, has lost her parents, has neither money nor social freedom, and is obliged to marry. *Shirley*'s publication, the week before Nightingale left England, had raised the profile of an ongoing debate about the role women could and should play in society. Change was coming. The attitudes and behaviour of a well-to-do wife were being examined in a way that would have been considered socially and morally unacceptable ten years earlier. 'I often wonder what I came into this world for,' Caroline asks herself, and then echoes Nightingale's plea: 'I long to have something absorbing and compulsory to fill my head and hands, and to occupy my thoughts.'9 Another of the novel's characters, Mary Taylor, is more confrontational when she asks, 'But are we men's equals, or are we not?'10

Nightingale knew she was at least men's equal and felt she had a role to play in this new movement, perhaps even more than one role, just as she recognised she might have led three very different lives. Her work as a nurse in the ten years that followed the Egyptian journey is well known. Her work as an author during this time is not. She had written a short fantasy, *A Vision of the Temples*, during and soon after the Egyptian journey and then began writing a novel, *Cassandra*, a scathing attack on the role of women in society. She revised it over many years, eventually attaching it to another work, the three-volume *Suggestions for Thought*, which she had privately printed in 1860. 'The ennui of existing was too great for me,' Cassandra, with whom Nightingale clearly identified, says in the novel. 'I, who could have done everything, now I can do nothing.'11

Nightingale had known this feeling herself on her way through Europe, but she had also visited a range of hospitals and schools run by well-to-do ladies and she knew that there was a way for her to be useful. From Berlin, she wrote home about the example set by Prussian women. 'I was struck with how much freer and fuller their life is than that of an Englishwoman. If an Englishwoman is not married and has no children, she has no profession, no career, no absorbing and compulsory vocation but a class in a Sunday School.'[12] In Germany, there were other options and Nightingale wrote about how women went out on their own during the day, wore what they wanted, took a basket to shop in the market, attended lectures, went to read in the library . . . even helped to run hospitals and schools. The head of an infant hospital had rooms 'exactly like my lady's drawing rooms in London', while the deaconesses at Berlin's New Model Hospital had rooms 'just like ours at Embley'.[13] And yet, as she knew when she wrote the letter, 'I shall meet with no *réponse* to this.'[14]

Nightingale reached Kaiserwerth on 31 July 1850. 'I could hardly believe I was there – with the feeling with which a pilgrim first looks on the Kedron [the river that runs between Jerusalem and the Mount of Olives], I saw the Rhine – dearer to me than the Nile.'[15] She had been chaperoned thus far by Trautwein, but the following morning sent her maid back to Pyrmont and presented herself at the Institution unaccompanied. She was welcomed by its founder, the Evangelical pastor Theodor Fliedner, and moved into a room in the grounds. 'The courage which falls into my shoes in a London drawing room rises on an occasion like this. I felt so sure it was God's work.'[16] With that question solved, another one needed answering: what would her parents say when they heard she had been to the Institution?

The Bracebridges had not mentioned Kaiserwerth in their letters to the Nightingales, a fact that would later be viewed as treachery. Florence had not hidden it – she had written from Berlin, in the middle of July, that the air at Pyrmont would not agree with her or Selina Bracebridge and that they might leave Mr B. there and 'go to Kaiserwerth, where we may stay a week or ten days, if you don't object, and where he will catch us up'.[17] There had been no reply, but then she knew there would not be. She had delayed mentioning Kaiserwerth until she was certain there was not time for her parents to write forbidding it. Since then, nothing.

Before leaving England the previous year, she had written that she hoped to be more of a comfort to her family when she returned. She had thought the Egyptian trip would provide an opportunity to stretch her mind and organise her thoughts. 'In that solemn slow progress up the Nile,' she had written the evening before leaving England the previous November, 'I think I shall have time to gather [my life] together (among the ruins of a sleeping nation) and order it better.'[18] She had not counted on the many temptations – to thought and to action – that the journey would present.

At 3 p.m. on 21 August 1850, with her mind both more ordered and more determined than ever, she walked up the lane she knew so well and into Lea Hurst. Parthenope and her parents were sitting in the drawing room. They were expecting Dr Richard Fowler and his wife to visit from Salisbury Infirmary. They were not expecting Florence. She walked in unannounced with an owl in her pocket. She had bought and tamed the bird in Athens, and given it the name of the city's protecting deity. Athena was easily assimilated by her family. Florence was not.

Louis Bouilhet had told Flaubert to, 'Forget work! Enjoy yourself! See all you can!'[19] He fulfilled two of his friend's injunctions. From Alexandria, he and Du Camp had travelled at leisure and with poetry through the Holy Land, Syria, Turkey and Greece, ending at the port of Patras, where they looked out on to Byron's deathplace at Missolonghi.

The journey north from Naples was equally leisurely and

graced with poetry, but tinged also with sadness at the imminent end of the journey: they would part in Rome where Flaubert had arranged to meet his mother. No more palms, deserts or waterpipes. No more temptations. No stones that could seduce them without their knowing how, or women seducing them in languages they could not speak. In Rome, Flaubert recorded one last such encounter in his journal. He had been to the Pyramid of Cestius and the Church of St Helena and had just entered the Basilica of St Paul Outside the Walls when he saw a young woman in a red dress. She was helping an older one. Something about her forced Flaubert to go closer. For a moment the urge was irresistible and he wrote that he wanted to throw himself down in front of her, kiss the hem of her robe and beg for her hand in marriage. Then she walked on.

This was the last personal entry in a journal that he had studded with intimacies. There were other changes, too. The long beard 'that I washed in the Nile, had been blown by the desert wind and that had been so long perfumed by tobacco smoke'[20] was shaved off. He swapped his red *tarbush* for a European hat, his *galabiya* for jacket and trousers. Even his romantic adventures seemed to be at an end. By the time he returned to their hotel in Rome, the woman in the red dress from the basilica was consigned to the past, 'her features already fading from my memory'.[21] The one romance he had devoted himself to and consummated, with Kuchuk Hanem, had become nothing more than a fantasy to him now. He acknowledged this while still in Rome, when he wrote to Bouilhet that 'she is no longer in Esna, my poor Kuchuk, she has gone back to Cairo! But that's not important, for me, she will always be in Esna, as I saw her there.'[22] The sadness here comes mostly from the passing of a young man's dreams. He had replaced his long-held fantasies of the Orient, those fancies he and Du Camp and Bouilhet had nurtured for years, with more personal memories.

The friends parted company in Rome. Flaubert was determined to return to his old life in his study at Croisset, turning over thoughts while stretched out on his white bearskin. Du Camp intended to write, publish, edit, frequent salons and make a name for himself. In this, as in so much else, they disagreed. The disagreement became increasingly rancorous, until Flaubert settled the matter by pointing out that they were 'no longer travelling along the same road'.[23]

Falling out with Du Camp did nothing to help him discover what he should do next. He was determined to return to Croisset, and Louise Colet was determined that he should return to her. He did both, after a fashion. But more than anything, as when he returned to Cairo, he longed to write: that pot was still boiling.

When the pens and ink and paper had been arranged, when the novelty of returning home had worn off a little, what would he write about? What was his subject? Where was his story? While still travelling, he had confessed to Bouilhet that, 'speaking literarily, I don't know where I am . . . I meditate very little, daydream occasionally. My kind of observation is preponderantly moral. I should never have suspected this side of Travel.'[24] In Constantinople, as the end of the journey came more clearly into view, he had outlined three possible subjects for his next book: *One Night of Don Juan*, *Anubis*, the story of 'the woman who wants to be screwed by the God'; and his Flemish novel about 'the young girl who dies a virgin and a mystic'.[25] Bouilhet, he now discovered, had another idea for him.

Du Camp was later to claim that Bouilhet suggested the idea for Flaubert's next novel while they were sitting in the garden at Croisset before they left for Egypt, after the disastrous reading of *The Temptation of Saint Anthony*. To this he also added an account of the moment in Nubia, looking down over the

Second Cataract, when his friend had shouted that, 'I'm going to call her Emma Bovary!' But it seems that Flaubert only turned his mind to his next novel when he had been back in Croisset for a while, and after he had rewritten his travel notes: 'finished copying these notes Saturday night, on the stroke of midnight, 19 July 1851, at Croisset'.[26]

It is impossible to be sure when exactly Bouilhet told the story that became part – perhaps the most identifiable part – of the inspiration that went into imagining *Madame Bovary*. But it seems to have been some time between July 1851 when Flaubert reoccupied his study, left untouched since his departure, and Friday 20 September. That was the evening when he addressed a sheet of paper to Louise Colet '*Ma chère amie*', and announced, 'Last night I began my novel.'[27]

Perhaps the most compelling reason to doubt Du Camp's claim that Bouilhet told Flaubert the story before they left for Egypt is that it relates to something that happened while the travellers were on the Nile. When they were away, Bouilhet went to visit Madame Flaubert in Croisset, as he had promised he would do, and found there an old lady. Bouilhet, who had known the woman's son, asked after him. Mention of his name brought tears to her eyes and she muttered something about the tragedies that had overtaken him.

Flaubert had also known the son, one Eugène Delamare, for he had studied medicine in Rouen under Dr Flaubert. Delamare had neither the brilliance nor the funds to complete his studies and so had left Rouen as an *officier de santé*, a medical officer, rather than a fully fledged doctor. He set himself up in a village outside Rouen and married an older woman, who did not live long.

Delamare's second wife was a young farmer's daughter, a convent-educated girl of seventeen or eighteen with a heightened sense of romance and extravagant tastes. Delamare was no match for this strong-willed girl, just as his dull, country life was no match for her fantasies. The black and yellow striped curtains she hung in her drawing room embarrassed her mother-in-law, and the neighbours gossiped about her pretensions, her good looks, her way of dressing and her high-handed way with her servant. Her husband, a hard-working simple man, more trusted than admired, shared none of her tastes but was so besotted with her that he indulged her and obeyed her every whim.

With a sense of the inevitability of these things, Flaubert heard how she took lovers, ran up debts, neglected their young daughter and made her husband miserable. Nine years into their marriage, with scandal and debts about to overtake her, she poisoned herself. The husband, as unwilling to face life without her as he had been unable to face the realities of life with her, followed soon after. The mother, whom Bouilhet had met at Madame Flaubert's house, was left to care for the little girl, the two of them living in poverty.

The Delamares' lives and deaths were tragedies of small-town provincial France. It took Flaubert a while to recognise that this could be the subject for his next book, that out of these small lives he might fashion the literary thunderclap he craved. It took even longer to set aside *Don Juan*, for which he had written a synopsis and detailed notes, and *Anubis*, which had not progressed so far. It took longer still for his Flemish novel of the young woman who dies a mystic virgin to give way to the wanton wife of the dull Norman medic – to Madame Emma Bovary.

But the transition was finally underway. 'The colours I am working with,' he wrote to Colet a month later, 'are so new to me that I keep staring at them in astonishment.' They were not just new, but also in perfect contrast to the colours of the Nile. He wanted 'to write . . . a book about nothing, a book dependent on nothing external, which would be held together by the internal strength of its style, just as the earth, suspended in the void, depends on nothing external for its support; a book which would have almost no subject'.[28] A book, in other words, which was as unlike *The Temptation of Saint Anthony* as Balzac was from Chateaubriand. 'We must live for our vocation, climb up our ivory tower, and there . . . . dwell alone with our dreams.'[29] Egypt had convinced him of this and made him capable of it.

Yet there were times when he had to come down from the tower and one of them occurred at the end of September 1851. Just a week after telling Louise Colet that he had begun his new novel, Flaubert accompanied his mother to London. They were going to visit the Great Exhibition. Flaubert was impressed with this boldest of all British imperial statements, proof of its cultural, scientific and political superiority, and packed his journals with minute details of the exhibits he saw. Even Nightingale, who was usually immune to patriotic jingoism, was seduced by the occasion. 'No other country could have produced the Great Exhibition,'[30] she wrote proudly to her mother. But we peer into the background of Flaubert's meticulously observed notes in vain. There is no mention of a recently returned, dark-haired, purposeful, thirty-one-year-old Englishwoman, nor even of a 'mother' looking like a sick parrot. By the time Flaubert reached London, Nightingale was back at Kaiserwerth.

'There is an old legend,' she wrote upon leaving the Institution in the summer of 1850, 'that the nineteenth century is to be the "century of woman"'. Whatever the wisdom, or the foolishness, of our forefathers may have meant by this, Englishwomen know but too well that, up to this time, the middle of the century, it has not been theirs.'[31] Nor did her new life at home look like being any different from the old, pre-Egypt existence. Much of the responsibility for this can be laid in the lap of her beloved Parthenope.

Her sister had suffered both physically and mentally in her absence. It is impossible, at this distance of time, to know how it came about, but Parthenope's physical and mental states were certainly linked, and their equilibrium seemed to depend on Florence being nearby and available. By the time she returned from Egypt, Parthenope was seriously ill. To improve the situation, Florence was forced to agree to devote the next months to her sister. She would have to be with her, do whatever she wanted to do, humour her, submit to her whims, not criticise her for enjoying the country-house life that Florence herself found so tedious. But far from being a balm to her sister's problems, Florence's presence seemed only to aggravate them. 'I can hardly open my mouth,' she wrote in a private note, 'without giving my dear Parthe vexation.'[32]

There were good reasons for this. However physically constrained Florence was by the obligation to stay close to Parthenope, no one could suppress her ambitions or stop her making plans. Her first brief stay at Kaiserwerth had convinced her of two things: that she was following the right path, doing 'God's work,' and that she must go back there. Within weeks of her return from Egypt, she confided this plan to her favourite aunt, Mai, Mary Shore Smith. Aunt Mai was at the forefront of a group within the family who thought Fanny Nightingale should allow her daughter to follow her vocation and who admired Florence for being so determined. But there was a personal price to pay for this obstinacy. Florence had left Kaiserwerth feeling 'so brave as if nothing could ever vex me again',[33] but her self-doubts and dreaming soon returned.

By Christmas, she was unable to hide her suffering from her parents. If anything, the journey to Egypt had made the tedium of life at home even harder to bear. Daytime was bad, but the evenings were worse. She could not bear the idea of a lifetime spent in the drawing room, waiting for the clock to announce that it was time to retire and seek oblivion in sleep. At Christmas, she told her family that she wished to die.

If Parthe was the problem, she also helped provide the cure. In spite of Florence's return, Parthe's health deteriorated – so much so that her physician recommended a cure at a German spa. Once it was agreed that Fanny and Florence would go with her, Florence began to agitate for permission to return to Kaiserwerth.

There had been other changes while she was away. Her struggle to find a fulfilling occupation for herself was taking place against a background of increasingly vociferous demands for social reform. In recent novels George Eliot and Charlotte Brontë had both agitated for a change in women's status. Equally important for Nightingale was the creation of several new Anglican nursing institutions. Her parents had disapproved of her having anything to do with hospitals run by Roman Catholics and, until recently, Baron Bunsen's Dalston hospital, run by deaconesses from Kaiserwerth, had been a solitary Protestant outpost. But Elizabeth Fry had founded her Institution of Nursing Sisters, inspired by Kaiserwerth, in 1840, while 1845 saw the opening of both the Park Village Community near London's Regent's Park and the Sisters of Mercy in Devonport. These medical institutions, run by genteel ladies, were the sort of places her parents ought not to have objected to her attending and yet they still considered this sort of work unsuitable for a Nightingale daughter. Not even the arrival at Embley of Elizabeth Blackwell could change that, they intimated.

Blackwell was a celebrity. The daughter of a trader from Bristol, she had decided to study medicine and, unable to do so in Britain, had emigrated to the United States, where she applied for a place at New York State Medical School. At that time there were no female medical students in the school, but it was a sign of the changing times that the college authorities stopped short of refusing her application. Instead they left it to the male students to decide if they wanted a female studying alongside them. The authorities assumed that the students would vote against her, but they did not, and Blackwell subsequently graduated top of her class.

American hospitals were not yet so enlightened and she failed to find one that would allow her to register. Instead she enrolled in a Parisian school for midwives and followed that, in October 1850, with a year's post-graduate study at St Bartholomew's in London. Nightingale saw Blackwell as a natural ally, someone who had gone ahead of her along the road. As they walked together through the gardens at Embley, Nightingale confided that whenever she looked in through the windows of the drawing room, 'I think how I should turn it into a hospital ward, and just how I should place the beds.'[34]

Blackwell's influence helped perhaps, as did Florence's care of family members during times of illness and distress. But the tipping point seems to have been the care she took over her father as his eyesight began to fail. She had had a special relationship with William since her childhood. He, after all, had been the one who had given her the education she now so longed to use.

There appears to be no document that pinpoints the exact moment that her father had a change of heart, no letters explaining it, no entries in Nightingale's notebooks. But at some point in that summer of 1851, William Nightingale finally understood that his younger daughter had a need for 'some great absorption'[35] and gave his blessing for her to go and find it.

Her return to Kaiserwerth was a significant moment. Parthenope recognised this as well and made one last stand. The two sisters had a fight in their hotel at Carlsbad, which ended with Parthenope throwing her bracelets at her sister and Florence passing out.

Kaiserwerth worked its magic, as she had known it would. After she had been there a month, she wrote to her mother that 'now I know what it is to live and to love life and really I should be sorry now to leave life'.[36] Things got even better. Three weeks later, she felt brave enough to try to tell her mother about the voice she had heard in Egypt, and earlier in her childhood. 'This may appear to you the passing fancy of a heated imagination . . . but little do you know how long that voice has spoken, how deep its tones have sunk within me.'[37]

Letters passed regularly between Kaiserwerth and the spas where Parthe and Fanny Nightingale were taking the waters, letters carrying words that none of them had been able to speak until now. And as the summer passed, so the tone of the letters became more conciliatory. Mr Nightingale was again the catalyst for this change: he wrote to warn his wife not to oppose Florence while she was at Kaiserwerth, perhaps fearing that she might then refuse to return home. This correspondence came to a head on 7 September 1851, when Fanny Nightingale wrote what must have been the hardest letter of her life, for in it she recognised her daughter's desire to leave them and her need for her mother's blessing upon her decision. 'Yes, my dear,' Fanny wrote from Franzensbad, 'take time, take faith & love with you, even though it be to walk in a path which leads you strangely from us all . . . I will do my best, I will indeed, to think you right, & let you follow the manner of man you are.' But she ended with a warning, or a plea, that Florence be merciful. 'You must not lay upon us more than we are able to bear.'[38]

The path that 'leads you strangely from us all' was clear now. The following year Nightingale travelled to Dublin in the hope of gaining experience at St Vincent's Hospital, run by the Sisters of Charity. She had suggested visiting this hospital back in 1844, but her father had then refused her permission. Now he agreed, but when she arrived in Dublin she found the place closed for refurbishment. She made up for this disappointment the following January when she went to visit a range of institutions in Paris and then entered the Maison de la Providence, another hospital run by the Sisters of Charity. But the real turning point came a couple of months later when her father was again the conduit of her happiness. This time he did two extraordinary things, without which she might not have gone any further down her chosen path. First, he gave his blessing for her to take up the position of Superintendent of the London Establishment for Gentlewomen during Illness, at Chandos Street initially and then at Harley Street. He also settled an allowance on her of £500 a year, worth around £30,000 today, to guarantee her financial and social independence.

Eleven months later Turkey and Russia went to war over the Crimea, and Britain, needing to ensure access to its Indian empire and nervous about Russian aspirations, sent 30,000 troops in support of Turkey. By the autumn, there were stories in *The Times* and elsewhere about the number of British soldiers dying from a lack of sanitation and medical care. It is at this point, just as she is swept away by history, that we have a last, clear glimpse of the young Florence Nightingale. It comes from the novelist Elizabeth Gaskell, who was staying at Lea Hurst. She described Nightingale as being 'tall; very slight & willowy in figure; thick, shortish rich brown hair, very delicate pretty complexion . . . grey eyes which are generally pensive and drooping, but when they choose can be the merriest eyes I ever saw; and perfect teeth making her smile the sweetest I ever saw . . . Dress her up in black glacé silk up to the long round white throat – and a black shawl on – & you may get *near* an idea of her perfect grace & lovely appearance.'[39]

On 27 October 1854, while the British cavalry's Light Brigade were camped near Balaclava awaiting their moment of destiny, this vision of grace and loveliness was standing on the quayside at Marseille. The Bracebridges were nearby: they would look after her in Turkey as they had done in Egypt. When the formalities were done, she and her companions and a party of 38 nurses boarded a steamer on a government-sponsored mission to the Scutari hospital in Constantinople. Nightingale was going back East.

Two years later, on 1 October 1856, the dual journey that had begun on a Cairo-bound ferry came to an end. On that day, Florence Nightingale was staying near Balmoral, the estate in Scotland where the royal family spent part of the summer. Queen Victoria wanted to meet the fêted Lady of the Lamp and to hear her plans for the reform of the British Army's medical services. That same day, a Thursday, the *Revue de Paris*, a literary magazine part-owned by Maxime Du Camp, carried the first of six instalments of a new novel, *Madame Bovary*. Gustave Flaubert had finally lost his 'virginity as an unpublished writer'. He thought that 'if my book is any good, it will gently tickle many a feminine wound'.[40] It did more than tickle. It caused a storm, established him as one of Europe's most important novelists and dragged him into court to face charges of offences against public morality, religion and decency.

When he sailed away from Alexandria, Gustave Flaubert had wondered whether he would return to Egypt. Neither he nor Florence Nightingale went back. And, pleasing as the idea would have been, there was really no need for them to return. They had lived out their dreams. And, in different ways, Egypt never left them, for there was always the writing it had inspired, the memory of the temptations it had presented, the thoughts it had provoked, and the luxury of travel to an unknown shore, leaving behind all that had constrained them.

The lingering scent of Egypt can most easily be traced on

Flaubert through the figure of Kuchuk Hanem. When he returned to France, he wished he had brought with him the shawl that she had tied around her hips while she danced for him. But although he knew that even if he had it, nothing would allow him to hold on to the woman, he was wrong when he wrote that her image would slowly fade from his memory. It clung to him for the rest of his life, as Louise Colet had known that it would.

She had challenged him about Kuchuk while he was writing *Madame Bovary* and he had attempted to soothe her by explaining that 'you and I are thinking of her, but she is certainly not thinking of us. We are weaving an aesthetic around her, whereas this particular very interesting tourist who was vouchsafed the honours of her couch has vanished from her memory completely.'[41] Whatever the truth, Flaubert used Kuchuk's memory to illuminate the heroine of *Salammbô*, the novel set in ancient Carthage that he wrote after *Madame Bovary*. Nor did Louise Colet forget. Twenty years after the Frenchmen had passed through Esna, long after Flaubert had severed all ties with her, she went to Egypt to attend the opening of the Suez Canal. And once there, she could not resist the opportunity of tracking down her ex-lover's lover and, with some satisfaction, afterwards reported that this most seductive of women was old, withered, shrivelled, and now no more tempting than a living mummy.

Florence Nightingale had no such passions to pursue. She had taken what she wanted from the journey. Yet Egypt stayed with her in her thoughts, her ideas, and through that most lingering of all the senses, taste: as an old woman she was still recommending Egyptian lentil soup 'as made every day by our Arab cook in Egypt, over a handful of fire not big enough to roast a mosquito'.[42] She was also still referring to Osiris in the same breath as Jesus Christ, as 'one who defied "the powers that be'",[43] just as she had. She was still being cheered by memories stirred by Edward Lear's paintings of Egypt. And she never lost sight of the contrast she had encountered on her last day there, the one that helped to define the course of her life: heaven or hell, the hospital or the harem.

Flaubert later took another view of the contrasts they had witnessed in Egypt. In a letter to Louise Colet in 1853, while in the middle of writing *Madame Bovary*, he confessed that, 'Until now we have understood the Orient as something that glitters, that screams, that is passionate, that is conflicting. We have seen only dancing girls and curved daggers, the fanaticism, the voluptuousness, etc. In a word, we remain still as Byron with it. Me, I have felt it differently; what I love in the Orient is a grandeur that is ignored, and a harmony between disparate things.'[44]

But the last word should be from Florence Nightingale. While sailing on the Nile, she had declared it impossible that people could return from Egypt and live their lives as they had done before. Flaubert would have agreed with her. Time proved her right.

NOTES

Introduction

1   Sattin, Anthony, ed., *Florence Nightingale: Letters from Egypt*, p.77.
2   Said, Edward, *Orientalism, Western Conceptions of the Orient*, p.184.
3   Hornby, Lady Emilia, *Constantinople During the Crimean War*, p.150.
4   Cook, Sir Edward, *Florence Nightingale*, Vol. I, p.304.
5   *Ibid.*, p.324.
6   Du Camp, Maxime, *Literary Recollections*, Vol. II, p.9.

1. Footfall

1   Sattin, Anthony, ed., *Florence Nightingale: Letters from Egypt*, p.23.
2   *Ibid.*, p.1.
3   McDonald, Lynn, ed., *Florence Nightingale's European Travels, Collected Works of Florence Nightingale*, p.329.
4   Martineau, Harriet, *Eastern Life: Past and Present*, Vol. I, p.86.
5   Sattin, p.24.
6   *Ibid.*, p.25.
7   Wilkinson, Sir John Gardner, *Modern Egypt and Thebes*, Vol. I, p.193.

8   Sattin, p.25.

9   *Ibid.*, p.24.

10 *Ibid.*, p.25.

11 *Ibid.*, p.23.

12 *Ibid.*, p.26.

13 *Ibid.*, p.26.

14 *Ibid.*, p.28.

15 *Ibid.*, p.24.

16 Vallée, Gérard, ed., *Florence Nightingale on Mysticism and Eastern Religions, Collected Works of Florence Nightingale*, Vol. 4, p.147.

17 *Ibid.*, p.151.

2. The Cairo Ferry

1   Bruneau, Jean, ed., *Flaubert: Correspondance*, Vol. I, p.524.

2   *Ibid.*

3   *Ibid.*, p.528.

4   De Biasi, Pierre-Marc, ed., *Flaubert: Voyage en Egypte*, p.173.

5   *Ibid.*, p.174.

6   Bruneau, Vol. I, p.531.

7   Du Camp, Maxime, *Le Nil*, p.36.

8   De Biasi, p.176.

9   *Ibid.*, pp.178–9.

10 *Ibid.*, pp.179–80.

11 *Ibid.*, p.180.

12 Bruneau, Vol. I, p.539.

13 Sattin, p.29.

14 De Biasi, p.184.

15 Sattin, p. 29.

16 Bostridge, Mark, *Florence Nightingale, The Woman and Her Legend*, p.184.

17 Sattin, pp.30–1.

18 Bostridge, p.185.

3. Words of God

1 Pope-Hennessy, James, *Monckton Milnes: The Years of Promise 1809–1851*, p.174.
2 *Ibid.*, p.176.
3 Bostridge, Mark, *Florence Nightingale, The Woman and Her Legend*, p.21.
4 *Ibid.*, p.36.
5 *Ibid.*, pp.52–3.
6 McDonald, Lynn, ed., *Florence Nightingale: An Introduction to Her Life, Collected Works of Florence Nightingale*, Vol. 1, p.90.
7 Bostridge, p.43.
8 McDonald, p.91.
9 *Ibid.*, p.15.

4. Coming Out

1 Bostridge, Mark, *Florence Nightingale, The Woman and Her Legend*, p.57.
2 *Ibid.*, p.66.
3 Letter from George Eliot to Sara Hennell, 16 July 1852.
4 McDonald, Lynn, ed., *Florence Nightingale: An Introduction to Her Life, Collected Works of Florence Nightingale*, Vol. 1, p.90.
5 Bostridge, p.64.
6 McDonald, p.413.
7 Simpson, M. C. M., *Letters and Recollections of Julius and Mary Mohl*, p.30.
8 Bostridge, p.73.
9 *Ibid.*, pp.105–6.
10 *Ibid.*, p.74.
11 *Ibid.*, p.96.
12 *Ibid.*, p.85.
13 *Ibid.*, pp.85–6.
14 McDonald, p.227.
15 Bostridge, p.101.

16 Woodham-Smith, Cecil, *Florence Nightingale*, p.52.

17 Bostridge, p.85.

18 Woodham-Smith, p.51.

19 Bostridge, p.83.

20 *Ibid.*

21 *Ibid.*, p.106.

22 Woodham-Smith, p.52.

23 *Ibid.*

24 Pope-Hennessy, James, *Monckton Milnes: The Years of Promise 1809–1851*, p.307.

25 Flaubert, Gustave, *Madame Bovary*, p.85.

26 Simpson, p.46.

27 Woodham-Smith, p.52.

28 George Eliot, letter to John Blackwood, 20 April 1859.

29 George Eliot, letter to John Blackwood, 22 September 1859.

30 Cook, Sir Edward, *The Life of Florence Nightingale*, Vol. I, p.70.

31 Keele, Mary, ed., *Florence Nightingale in Rome*, p.11.

32 *Ibid.*, p.5.

33 Quoted in O'Malley, I. B., *Florence Nightingale 1820–1856*, p.125.

34 Keele, p.27.

35 *Ibid.*, p.46.

36 *Ibid.*, p.34.

37 *Ibid.*, p.74.

38 *Ibid.*, pp.73–4.

39 *Ibid.*, p.207.

40 *Ibid.*, p.242.

41 *Ibid.*, p.208.

42 Quoted in Gill, Gillian, *Nightingales, Florence and Her Family*, p.219.

43 Bostridge, p.120.

44 *Ibid.*, p.121.

45 *Ibid.*, p.124.

46 *Ibid.*, p.126.

47 Pope-Hennessy, p.294.

48 *Ibid.*

49 *Ibid.*, p.297.

50 *Ibid.*, p.304.

51 Pope-Hennessy, p.165.

52 Mentioned in a note in Gill, p.230.

53 Bostridge, pp.126–7.

54 *Ibid.*, p.127.

55 Woodham-Smith, p.60.

56 Pope-Hennessy, p.307.

57 Bostridge, p.130.

58 Woodham-Smith, p.77.

5. Rabbit Stew

1   Bruneau, Jean, ed., *Flaubert: Correspondance*, Vol. I, p.230.

2   De Biasi, Pierre-Marc, ed., *Flaubert: Voyage en Egypte*, p.22.

3   Flaubert, Gustave, *Mémoires d'un Fou*, Maurice Nadeem, ed., p.265.

4   Flaubert, Gustave, *Dictionary of Received Ideas*, p.316.

5   Flaubert, Gustave, *Souvenirs, Notes et Pensées Intimes*, 25 January.

6   Du Camp, Maxime, *Literary Recollections*, Vol. I, p.224.

7   Flaubert, Gustave, *Trois Contes*.

8   Bruneau, Vol. I, p.214.

9   *Ibid.*, p.223.

10 *Ibid.*, p.224.

11 Flaubert, Gustave, *Notes de Voyage, April – May 1845*.

12 Bruneau, Vol. I, p.217.

13 *Ibid.*, p.263.

14 *Ibid.*, p.268.

15 *Ibid.*, p.270.

16 Du Camp, Vol. I, pp.224–5.

17 Enfield, D. E., *A Lady of the Salons: the Story of Louise Colet*, p.52.

18 *Ibid.*, p.53.

19 Bruneau, Vol. I, p.285.

20 *Ibid.*, p.272.

21 *Ibid.*, p.273.

22 *Ibid.*, p.287.

23 *Ibid.*, p.302.

24 *Ibid.*, p.307.

25 *Ibid.*

26 *Ibid.*, p.383.

27 Du Camp, Vol. I, p.230.

28 *Ibid.*

29 Bruneau, Vol. I, pp.452–3.

30 *Ibid.*, p.493.

31 *Ibid.*, pp.493–4.

32 *Ibid.*, p.497.

33 De Biasi, p.42.

34 Du Camp, Vol. I, p.284–5.

35 *Ibid.*, p.287.

36 Bruneau, Vol. I, p.505.

37 Du Camp, Vol. I, p.299.

38 *Ibid.*, p.300.

39 *Ibid.*

40 Flaubert, Gustave, *The Temptation of Saint Anthony*, p.1.

41 Du Camp, Vol. I, p.302.

42 *Ibid.*, p.301.

43 *Ibid.*

44 Du Camp, Vol. I, p.302.

45 *Ibid.*

46 *Ibid.*

47 *Ibid.*, p.301.

48 Steegmuller, FMB, p.167.

6. The Rose of Cities

1   Du Camp, Maxime, *Le Nil*, p.36.

2   De Biasi, Pierre-Marc, ed., *Flaubert: Voyage en Egypte*, p.185.

3   Sattin, Anthony, *Florence Nightingale: Letters from Egypt*, p.32.

4   *Ibid.*

5   *Ibid.*, p.37.

6   *Ibid.*, p.33.

7   *Ibid.*, p.39.

8   *Ibid.*, p.33.

9   *Ibid.*

10   *Ibid.*

11   *Ibid.*

12   *Ibid.*

13   *Ibid.*, p.36

14   *Ibid.*, p.34.

15   Bruneau, Jean, ed., *Flaubert: Correspondance*, Vol. I, p.544.

16   De Biasi, p.225.

17   Du Camp, p.41.

18   De Biasi, p.198.

19   Bruneau, Vol. I, p.538.

20   *Ibid.*

21   *Ibid.*

22   *Ibid.*, p.544.

23   *Ibid.*, p.542.

24   De Biasi, p.242.

25   *Ibid.*, p.231.

26   Bruneau, Vol. 1, p.570.

27   Flaubert, Gustave, *Mémoires d'un Fou*, Maurice Nadeem, ed., p.265.

28   Flaubert, Gustave, *Voyages et Carnets de Voyages, Oeuvres Complètes de Gustave Flaubert*, Vol. 10, p. 458.

29   *ibid.*

30   De Biasi, p.197.

31   Flaubert, *Oeuvres Complètes*, Vol. 10, p.459.

32   Bruneau, Vol. 1, p.541.

33   Sattin, p.41.

34   *Ibid.*

35   *Ibid.*, p.36.

36 *Ibid.*

37 Wilkinson, Sir John Gardner, *Hand-Book for Travellers in Egypt*, p.126.

38 *Ibid.*

39 Sattin, p.40.

40 *Ibid.*, p.41.

41 *Ibid.*, p.42.

42 De Biasi, p.219.

43 Bruneau, Vol. 1, p.562.

44 *Ibid.*, p.568.

45 *Ibid.*, p.563.

46 *Ibid.*, p.564.

47 *Ibid.*

7. The Stream of Time

1 Monckton Milnes, Richard, *Palm Leaves*, p.160.

2 Sattin, Anthony, *Florence Nightingale: Letters from Egypt*, p.68.

3 *Ibid.*, p.47.

4 *Ibid.*, p.42.

5 *Ibid.*, p.68.

6 *Ibid.*

7 *Ibid.*, p.42.

8 *Ibid.*, p.44.

9 *Ibid.*

10 *Ibid.*, p.48.

11 *Ibid.*

12 *Ibid.*, p.45

13 *Ibid.*, p.44.

14 *Ibid.*, p.61.

15 *Ibid.*, p.66.

16 *Ibid.*, p.53.

17 *Ibid.*

18 *Ibid.*, p.55.

19 *Ibid.*, p.54.

20 Champollion, Jean-François, *Egyptian Diaries*, p.108.

21 Wilkinson, Sir John Gardner, *Hand-Book for Travellers in Egypt*, pp.294–5.

22 Sattin, p.54.

23 *Ibid.*, p.56.

24 *Ibid.*, p.61.

25 *Ibid.*, pp.63–4.

26 Flaubert, Gustave, *Voyages et Carnets de Voyages, Oeuvres Complètes*, Vol. 10, p.483.

27 Vallée, p.218.

28 *Ibid.*, p.221.

29 *Ibid.*, p.234.

30 Sattin, p.79.

31 *Ibid.*, p.81.

32 *Ibid.*

33 *Ibid.*, p.77.

34 *Ibid.*, p.76.

35 *Ibid.*, p.79.

36 *Ibid.*

37 *Ibid.*, p.81.

8. Hunting the Bee

1 Du Camp, Maxime, *Literary Recollections*, Vol. I, p.334.

2 *Ibid.*, p.338.

3 *Ibid.*, p.337.

4 Flaubert, Gustave, *Voyages et Carnets de Voyages, Oeuvres Complètes*, Vol. 10, p.486.

5 Bruneau, Jean, ed., *Flaubert: Correspondance*, Vol. I, p.597.

6 Lane, Edward William, *An Account of the Manners and Customs of the Modern Egyptians*, p.325.

7 Wilkinson, Sir John Gardner, *Hand-Book for Travellers in Egypt*, p.406.

8   Du Camp, Maxime, *Le Nil*, p.131.

9   *Ibid.*, p.134.

10 Bruneau, Vol. II, p.448.

11 Bruneau, Vol. I, pp.605–6.

12 Flaubert, p.488.

13 *Ibid.*, p.489.

14 De Biasi, note on p.265.

15 *Ibid.*

16 Bruneau, Vol. I, p.606.

17 *Ibid.*, p.600.

18 Du Camp, p.134.

19 Bruneau, Vol. I, p.607.

20 *Ibid.*

21 Flaubert, p.490.

22 Said, Edward, *Orientalism, Western Conceptions of the Orient*, p.188.

23 Bruneau, Vol. I, p.605.

24 Vallée, Gérard, ed., *Florence Nightingale on Mysticism and Eastern Religions, Collected Works of Florence Nightingale*, Vol. 4, p.182–3.

25 Bruneau, Vol. I, p.601.

26 *Ibid.*, p.602.

27 Flaubert, Gustave, *Mémoires d'un Fou*, Maurice Nadeem, ed., p.265.

9. Grace and Truth

1   Vallée, Gérard, ed., *Florence Nightingale on Mysticism and Eastern Religions, Collected Works of Florence Nightingale*, Vol. 4, p.251.

2   Sattin, Anthony, *Florence Nightingale: Letters from Egypt*, p.86.

3   *Ibid.*, p.87.

4   *Ibid.*

5   Flaubert, Gustave, *Voyages et Carnets de Voyages, Oeuvres Complètes*, Vol. 10, p.492.

6   Du Camp, Maxime, *Literary Recollections*, Vol. I, p.338.

7   De Biasi, p.295.

8   Wilkinson, Sir John Gardner, *Hand-Book for Travellers in Egypt*,

p.419.

9 Sattin, pp.90–1.
10 Du Camp, pp.133–4.
11 Sattin, p.91.
12 *Ibid.*
13 *Ibid.*
14 *Ibid.*, p.95.
15 *Ibid.*
16 De Biasi, p.326.
17 *Ibid.*, p.328.
18 Sattin, p.105.
19 *Ibid.*, p.96.
20 *Ibid.*, p.95.
21 *Ibid.*, p.96.
22 *Ibid.*
23 *Ibid.*, p.98.
24 *Ibid.*
25 *Ibid.*, p.99.
26 *Ibid.*, pp.99–100.
27 *Ibid.*, p.100.
28 *Ibid.*
29 *Ibid.*, p.98.
30 *Ibid.*, p.101.
31 *Ibid.*, p.104.
32 *Psalms*, 91:4.
33 *St John*, 1:14.
34 Sattin, p.101.
35 *Ibid.*, p.103.
36 Wilkinson, p.440.
37 Du Camp, p.141.
38 De Biasi, p.317.
39 Du Camp, p.338.
40 De Biasi, p. 320.

41 Steegmuller, Francis, *Flaubert in Egypt*, p.136.

10. To the Holy Isle

1   Vallée, Gérard, ed., *Florence Nightingale on Mysticism and Eastern Religions, Collected Works of Florence Nightingale*, Vol. 4, p.283.

2   Sattin, Anthony, *Florence Nightingale: Letters from Egypt*, p.104.

3   *Ibid.*

4   Flaubert, Gustave, *Voyages et Carnets de Voyages, Oeuvres Complètes*, Vol. 10, p.510.

5   *Ibid.*

6   Thompson, Jason, *Sir Gardner Wilkinson and His Circle*, p.16.

7   *Ibid.*, p.19.

8   Vallée, p.288.

9   *Ibid.*, p.286.

10 *Ibid.*, p.287.

11 *Ibid.*, p.288.

12 Nightingale, Florence, *Cassandra*.

13 McDonald, Lynn, ed., *Florence Nightingale: An Introduction to Her Life, Collected Works of Florence Nightingale*, Vol. I, pp.90–1.

14 Flaubert, Gustave, *Madame Bovary*, p.61.

15 Woodham-Smith, Cecil, *Florence Nightingale*, pp.58–9.

16 Sattin, p.106.

17 Vallée, p.283.

18 Wilkinson, Sir John Gardner, *Hand-Book for Travellers in Egypt*, p.419.

19 Vallée, p.284.

20 *Ibid.*, p.294.

21 Griffiths, J. G., trs., Plutarch: *De Iside et Osiride*, p.20.

22 Sattin, p.113.

23 *Ibid.*, p.114.

24 Du Camp, Maxime, *Literary Recollections*, Vol. I, p.340.

25 Bruneau, Jean, ed., *Flaubert: Correspondance*, Vol. I, p.223.

26 Du Camp, p.338.

27 Bruneau, Vol. I, pp.612–13.

28 Du Camp, Vol. I, p.340.

29 Flaubert, Gustave, *Voyages et Carnets de Voyages, Oeuvres Complètes*, Vol. 10, p.514.

30 *Ibid.*

31 *Ibid.*

32 Vallée, p.301.

33 Sattin, p.114.

34 *Ibid.*

35 *Ibid.*

36 Vallée, p.303.

37 Flaubert, p.515.

38 Vallée, p.303.

39 *Ibid.*, pp.305–6.

40 *Ibid.*, p.312.

41 Thackeray, William Makepeace, *Notes of a Journey from Cornhill to Grand Cairo,* in *Sketch Books*, p.727.

42 Letter from Edward Stanley Poole to Joseph Bonomi, Cairo, undated (1847 folder) from the Private Collection of Ms Yvonne Neville-Rolfe in Emily Weeks, unpublished work on J. F. Lewis.

43 Sattin, p.114.

44 *Ibid.*, p.116.

45 *Ibid.*

46 *Ibid.*

47 *Ibid.*

48 *Ibid.*, p.120.

49 *Ibid.*

50 *Ibid.*, p.117.

51 Vallée, p.302.

52 *Ibid.*, p.298.

53 Sattin, p.119.

54 *Ibid.*, p.302.

11. Daydreams and Old Dust

1 Bruneau, Jean, ed., *Flaubert: Correspondance*, Vol. I, p.614.

2 Sattin, Anthony, *Florence Nightingale: Letters from Egypt*, p.123.

3 *Ibid.*

4 De Biasi, Pierre-Marc, ed., *Flaubert: Voyage en Egypte*, p.362.

5 *Ibid.*

6 *Ibid.*, p.363.

7 Bruneau, Vol. I, p.634.

8 *Ibid.*

9 Sattin, p.133.

10 *Ibid.*, p.126.

11 Wilkinson, Sir John Gardner, *Hand-Book for Travellers in Egypt*, p.337.

12 Sattin, p.137.

13 *Ibid.*

14 *Ibid.*, p.128.

15 *Ibid.*, p.129.

16 *Ibid.*, p.131.

17 *Ibid.*

18 *Ibid.*

19 *Ibid.*, p.136.

20 *Ibid.*, p.149.

21 *Ibid.*

22 Vallée, *Florence Nightingale on Mysticism and Eastern Religions, Collected Works of Florence Nightingale*, Vol. 4, p.335.

23 *Ibid.*, p.336.

24 *Ibid.*

25 *Ibid.*

26 Quoted in O'Malley, I. B., *Florence Nightingale 1820–1856*, p.125.

27 Sattin, p.137.

28 *Ibid.*, p.139.

29 Vallée, p.338.

30 *Ibid.*

31 Bruneau, Vol. I, p.627.

32 *Ibid.*, p.619.

33 *Ibid.*, p.621.

34 De Biasi, p.374.

35 Bruneau, Vol. I, pp.621–2.

36 Du Camp, Maxime, *Le Nil*, p.276.

37 Ibid., pp.260–1.

38 Weeks, Kent R., *The Illustrated Guide to Luxor, Tombs, Temples and Museums*, p.76.

39 Sattin, p.140.

40 *Ibid.*

41 *Ibid.*, p.152.

42 *Ibid.*, p.145.

43 Vallée, p.368.

44 *Ibid.*, p.389.

45 *Ibid.*, p.403.

46 Sattin, p.142.

47 Vallée, p.403.

12. Settling the Question

1 Bruneau, Jean, ed., *Flaubert: Correspondance*, Vol. I, p.619.

2 De Biasi, Pierre-Marc, ed., *Flaubert: Voyage en Egypte*, p.399.

3 Bruneau, Vol. I, p.622.

4 *Ibid.*, p.619.

5 *Ibid.*, p.623.

6 *Ibid.*, p.624.

7 *Ibid.*, p.635.

8 Sattin, Anthony, ed., *Florence Nightingale: Letters from Egypt*, p.162.

9 *Ibid.*, pp.162–3.

10 Vallée Gérard, *Florence Nightingale on Mysticism and Eastern Religions, Collected Works of Florence Nightingale*, Vol. 4, p.407.

11 Calabria, Michael D., *Florence Nightingale in Egypt and Greece, Her Diary and 'Visions'*, p.44.

12 Vallée, p.408.

13 *Ibid.*, p.409.

14 Sattin, p.164.

15 *Ibid.*

16 Bruneau, Vol. I, p.601.

17 *Ibid.*, p.627.

18 *Ibid.*

19 *Ibid.*, p.628.

20 Vallée, p.409.

21 *Ibid.*

22 Sattin, p.61.

23 *Ibid.*, p.165.

24 *Ibid.*, p.167.

25 *Ibid.*

26 Vallée, p.409.

13. Cairo and Alexandria

1   Vallée, Gérard, ed., *Florence Nightingale on Mysticism and Eastern Religions, Collected Works of Florence Nightingale*, Vol. 4, p.422.

2   *Ibid.*

3   *Ibid.*

4   Sattin, Anthony, ed., *Florence Nightingale: Letters from Egypt*, p.169.

5   De Biasi, Pierre-Marc, ed., *Flaubert: Voyage en Egypte*, p.218.

6   Sattin, p.170.

7   Vallée, p.427.

8   *Ibid.*

9   Sattin, p.181.

10 *Ibid.*

11 *Ibid.*, p.183.

12 *Ibid.*

13 *Ibid.*, p.184 .

14 *Ibid.*

15 Vallée, p,432.

16 Woodham-Smith, Cecil, *Florence Nightingale*, p.51.

17 Bostridge, Mark, *Florence Nightingale, The Woman and Her Legend*, p.140.

18 Vallée, p.421.

19 *Ibid.*, p.423.

20 *Ibid.*, p.435.

21 De Biasi, p.443.

22 Bruneau, Jean, ed., *Flaubert: Correspondance*, Vol. I, p.644.

23 De Biasi, p.445.

24 Bruneau, Vol. I, p.644.

25 Sattin, p.187.

26 *Ibid.*

27 *Ibid.*

28 Vallée, p.464.

29 Sattin, p.196.

30 *Ibid.*, p.188.

31 *Ibid.*

32 *Ibid.*, p.201.

33 *Ibid.*, p.202.

34 Vallée, p.463.

35 Bruneau, Vol. I, p.653.

36 *Ibid.*, p.647.

37 De Biasi, p.447.

38 Sattin, p.205.

39 *Ibid.*

40 *Ibid.*, p.165.

41 *Ibid.*, pp.207–8.

42 *Ibid.*, p.208.

14. Destiny

1 Calabria, Michael D., *Florence Nightingale in Egypt and Greece, Her Diary and 'Visions'*, p.82.

2 *Ibid.*, p.59.

3 *Ibid.*, p.63.

4 *Ibid.*, p.67.

5 *Ibid.*, p.68.

6 *Ibid.*, p.69.

7 *Ibid.*

8 *Ibid.*, p.72.

9 *Ibid.*, p.75.

10 Quoted in Wilson, A. N., *Eminent Victorians*, p.80.

11 McDonald, Lynn, ed., *Florence Nightingale on Women, Medicine, Midwifery and Prostitution, Collected Works of Florence Nightingale*, Vol. 8, p.118.

12 McDonald, Lynn, ed., *Florence Nightingale's European Travels, Collected Works of Florence Nightingale*, Vol. 7, p.461.

13 *Ibid.*, p.464.

14 *Ibid.*, p.461.

15 Calabria, p.77.

16 *Ibid.*, p.79.

17 McDonald, *European Travels*, p.466.

18 *Ibid.*, p.329.

19 De Biasi, p.128.

20 Bruneau, Jean, ed., *Flaubert: Correspondance*, Vol. I, p.756.

21 *Ibid.*, p.773.

22 *Ibid.*, p.777.

23 Bruneau, Vol. II, p.120.

24 Bruneau, Vol. I, p.707.

25 *Ibid.*, p.708.

26 De Biasi, Pierre-Marc, ed., *Flaubert: Voyage en Egypte*, p.80.

27 Bruneau, Vol. II, p.5.

28 *Ibid.*, p.31.

29 *Ibid.*, p.77.

30 McDonald, *European Travels*, p.686.

31 *Ibid.*, p.492.

32 Bostridge, Mark, *Florence Nightingale, The Woman and Her Legend*, p.149.

33 Woodham-Smith, Cecil, *Florence Nightingale*, p.66.

34 Bostridge, p.153.

35 *Ibid.*, p.158.

36 McDonald, Lynn, ed., *Florence Nightingale: An Introduction to Her Life, Collected Works of Florence Nightingale*, Vol. 1, p.128.

37 *Ibid.*, p.129.

38 Quoted in Bostridge, p.159.

39 Quoted in Gill, Gillian, *Nightingales, Florence and Her Family*, pp.292–3.

40 Bruneau, Vol. II, p.147.

41 Steegmuller, *Letters*, p.249.

42 McDonald, *Introduction*, p.739.

43 *Ibid.*, p.545.

44 Bruneau, Vol. II, p.283.

Bibliography

Barnes, Julian, *Flaubert's Parrot* (Jonathan Cape, London, 1984)

Bart, Benjamin F., *Flaubert* (Syracuse University Press, New York, 1967)

Bartlett, W. H., *The Nile Boat* (Arthur Hale, London, 1849)

Bostridge, Mark, *Florence Nightingale, The Woman and Her Legend* (Viking, London, 2008)

Brown, Frederick, *Flaubert: A Biography* (Heinemann, London, 2006)

Bunsen, Baroness Frances, *A Memoir of Baron Bunsen*, 2 Vols. (Longmans, Green & Co., London, 1868)

Calabria, Michael D., *Florence Nightingale in Egypt and Greece, Her Diary and 'Visions'* (State University of New York Press, New York, 1997)

Champollion, Jean-François, *Egyptian Diaries* (Gibson Square, London, 2001)

Clayton, Peter A., *The Rediscovery of Ancient Egypt: Artists and Travellers in the Nineteenth Century* (Thames & Hudson, London, 1982)

Cook, Sir Edward, *The Life of Florence Nightingale*, 2 Vols. (Macmillan, London, 1914)

Curtis, Lou, *Clarities and Obscurities: Gustave Flaubert's Expression of the Orient. Reality versus 'Imaginative Geography'*, in Proceedings of the Study Day held at Oxford Brookes University, 28 April 2005 (published online by the 2001 Group)

Dawson, Warren R. & Uphill, Eric P., *Who Was Who in Egyptology* (Egypt Exploration Society, London, 1995)

Du Camp, Maxime:
Le Nil: Egypte et Nubie, (Michel Lévy, Paris, 1853)
Literary Recollections, 2 Vols. (Remington, London, 1893)
Un Voyageur en Egypte: Le Nil de Maxime Du Camp, Michel Dewachter & Daniel Oster, eds. (Sand/Conti, Paris, 1987)

Eliot, George, *The George Eliot Letters*, 2 Vols., Gordon S. Haight, ed. (Yale University Press, New Haven & London, 1954)

Enfield, D. E., *A Lady of the Salons: the Story of Louise Colet* (Jonathan Cape, London, 1922)

Fagan, Brian M., *The Rape of the Nile: Tomb Robbers, Tourists, and Archaeologists in Egypt* (Macdonald & Janes, London, 1977)

Fairclough, Oliver, *The Grand Old Mansion: The Holtes and their Successors at Aston Hall 1618–1864* (Birmingham Museums and Art Gallery, Birmingham, 1984)

Flaubert, Gustave:
Correspondance, 10 Vols., Jean Bruneau, ed. (Gallimard, Paris, 1973)
En Egypte: lettres à sa mere (Collection Sépia, Paris, 2007)
Cinq Lettres d'Egypte (Editions Mille et Une Nuits, Paris, 2002)
The Letters of Gustave Flaubert 1830–1857, Francis Steegmuller, selected, trs & ed. (Harvard University Press, London, 1980)
Mémoires d'un Fou, Maurice Nadeem, ed. (Editions Rencontre, Lausanne, 1964)
Souvenirs, Notes et Pensées Intimes (Buchet-Chastel, Paris, 1965)
Madame Bovary (Everyman, London, 1993)

Dictionary of Received Ideas, in *Bouvard and Pécuchet* (Penguin, London, 1976)

Voyage en Egypte, Pierre-Marc de Biasi, ed. (Grasset, Paris, 1991)

Voyages, Dominique Barbéris, ed. (Arlea, Paris, 2007)

Gill, Gillian, *Nightingales, Florence and Her Family* (Hodder & Stoughton, London, 2004)

Gregory, Derek, 'Between the book and the lamp: imaginative geographies in Egypt, 1849–50', in *Transactions of the Institute of British Geographers*, Vol. 20, 1995

Griffiths, J.G., trs., Plutarch: *De Iside et Osiride* (OUP, Oxford, 1970)

Hay, Robert, *Illustrations of Cairo* (Tilt & Bogue, London, 1840)

Hobbs, Colleeen A., *Florence Nightingale* (Twayne, New York, 1997)

Hornby, Lady Emilia, *Constantinople During the Crimean War* (Richard Bentley, London, 1863)

Karl, Frederick, *George Eliot, A Biography* (HarperCollins, London, 1995)

Keele, Mary, *Florence Nightingale in Rome* (American Philosophical Society, Philadelphia, 1981)

Lane, Edward William, *An Account of the Manners and Customs of the Modern Egyptians* (Ward Lock, New York, 1890)

Lepsius, Dr Richard, *Letters from Egypt, Ethiopia, and the Peninsula of Sinai* (Henry G. Bohn, London, 1853)

Lesser, Margaret, *Clarkey, A Portrait in Letters of Mary Clarke Mohl* (OUP, Oxford, 1984)

Lewis, Michael, *John Frederick Lewis R.A.* (F. Lewis, Leigh-on-Sea, 1978)

Martineau, Harriet, *Eastern Life: Past and Present*, 3 Vols. (Edward Moxton, London, 1848)

Mojsov, Bojana, *Osiris: Death and Afterlife of God* (Blackwell, Oxford, 2005)

Monckton Milnes, Richard, *Palm Leaves* (Edward Moxon, London, 1844)

Mostyn, Trevor, *Egypt's Belle Epoque: Cairo and the Age of the Hedonists* (Quartet, London, 1989)

Nightingale, Florence:

Florence Nightingale: An Introduction to Her Life, Collected Works of Florence Nightingale, Vol. 1, Lynn McDonald, ed. (Wilfrid Laurier University Press, Ontario, Canada, 2001)

Florence Nightingale on Mysticism and Eastern Religions, Collected Works of Florence Nightingale, Vol. 4, Gérard Vallée, ed. (Wilfrid Laurier Press, Ontario, Canada, 2003)

Florence Nightingale's European Travels, Collected Works of Florence Nightingale, Vol. 7, Lynn McDonald, ed. (Wilfrid Laurier Press, Ontario, Canada, 2004)

Florence Nightingale on Women, Medicine, Midwifery and Prostitution, Collected Works of Florence Nightingale, Vol. 8, Lynn McDonald, ed. (Wilfrid Laurier Press, Ontario, Canada, 2005)

Florence Nightingale in Rome, Mary Keele, ed. (American Philosophical Society, Philadelphia, 1981)

Letters from Egypt, Anthony Sattin, ed. (Barrie & Jenkins, London, 1987)

Suggestions for Thought, Michael D. Calabria & Janet A. Macrae, eds. (University of Pennsylvania Press, Philadelphia, 1994)

Noel-Baker, Barbro, *An Isle of Greece: The Noels in Euboea* (Procopi, Greece, 1999)

O'Malley, I. B., *Florence Nightingale 1820–1856* (Thornton Butterworth, London, 1931)

Pope-Hennessy, James, *Monckton Milnes: The Years of Promise, 1809–1851* (Constable, London, 1949)

Oxford Dictionary of National Biography (OUP, Oxford, 2004)

Rees, Joan, *Writings on the Nile* (Rubicon, London, 1995)

Said, Edward, *Orientalism, Western Conceptions of the Orient* (Penguin, London, 1991)

Sattin, Anthony, *Lifting the Veil* (Dent, London, 1988)

(ed.) *Florence Nightingale: Letters from Egypt* (Barrie & Jenkins, London, 1987, Parkway, London, 1999)

Simpson, M. C. M., *Letters and Recollections of Julius and Mary Mohl* (Kegan Paul, London, 1887)

Steegmuller, Francis:
Flaubert and Madame Bovary (Robert Hale, London, 1939)
Flaubert in Egypt, trs & ed. (Bodley Head, London, 1972)
The Letters of Gustave Flaubert, selected, trs. & ed. (Picador, London, 2001)

Strachey, Lytton, *Eminent Victorians* (Continuum, London, 2002)

Thackeray, William Makepeace (aka M. A .Titmarsh), *Notes of a Journey from Cornhill to Grand Cairo,* in *Sketch Books* (Smith, Elder & Co., London, 1898)

Thompson, Jason, *Sir Gardner Wilkinson and His Circle* (University of Texas Press, Austin, 1992)

Adrianne Tooke, 'Flaubert: Views of the Orient', in *Eastern Voyages, Western Visions*, Margaret Topping, ed. (Peter Lang, Oxford, 2004)

Tuccelli, Nicole & Gérard Réveillac, *Le Nil en dahabieh 1850–1914* (Paris-Méditerranée, Paris, 2001)

Wall, Geoffrey, *Flaubert, A Life* (Faber, London, 2001)

Weeks, Emily M., 'Cultures Crossed, John Frederick Lewis and the Art of Orientalist Painting', in *The Lure of the East: British Orientalist Painting,* Nicholas Tromans, ed. (Yale University Press, New Haven, 2008)

Weeks, Kent R., *The Illustrated Guide to Luxor, Tombs, Temples and Museums* (AUC, Cairo, 2005)

Wheeler, Sara, *An Island Apart: Travels in Evia* (Little, Brown, London, 1992)

Wilkinson, Sir John Gardner:
Hand-Book for Travellers in Egypt (John Murray, London, 1847)
Manners and Customs of the Ancient Egyptians, 6 Vols. (John Murray, London, 1837)

Modern Egypt and Thebes, 2 Vols. (John Murray, London, 1843)

Wilkinson, Richard and Reeves, C. Nicholas, *The Complete Valley of the Kings* (Thames & Hudson, London, 1996)

Wilkinson, Richard, *The Complete Temples of Ancient Egypt* (Thames & Hudson, London, 2000)

Wilson, A. N., *Eminent Victorians* (BBC, London, 1989)

Woodham-Smith, Cecil, *Florence Nightingale* (Constable, London, 1950)

Index

INDEX

INDEX

FN's letters to 48, 51
Parthenope Nightingale to 239
Moses 28, 89, 102, 170, 198, 228, 229, 232
Mouriez, Paul 177, 232
Muhammad Ali Pasha, ruler of Egypt 9, 10, 18, 21, 29, 85, 88, 130, 132, 177
    tomb-mosque 88–9, 90, 93, 100
Muqattam Hills 85, 93
Murray, Captain 199–200
Murray, Charles (Consul) 86–7, 100, 95, 101, 110, 182, 183, 199, 200, 210, 233
Mustafa (cook) 219–20, 237
Mycerinus, Pharaoh 141, 152

Napoleon Bonaparte 18, 65, 88, 92, 95, 132, 179
Neith (goddess) 132
Nephthys (goddess) 172
New York State Medical School 252–3
New York Times xix, xx
Nicholson, Henry 41
Nightingale, Fanny (*née* Smith) xxii, 32–3, 34
    audience with Queen Victoria 40–1
    conflict with FN 6–7, 43, 45, 245
    on Continental tour 38–9, 40
    and daughters' education 29, 33–4, 37–8
    hopes for FN's marriage 47, 48, 49, 52–3, 58–9, 60–1
    removes opposition to FN's nursing career 254
Nightingale, Florence xviii, xx–xxi
    appearance 2–3, 38, 46, 255
    birth 32
    character traits xix, xx–xxi, 7, 25, 34, 110
    childhood and schooling 28–9, 31, 33–4, 89
    and children xxii, 56, 90–1
    conflict with family over desire to nurse 6–7, 42–7, 57
    on Continental tour with family 38–40
    early nursing experience 35, 42
    and her father *see* Nightingale, William
    and God's call 35–6, 39, 42–3, 56, *see also under* Egyptian journey (*below*)
    illnesses 24, 38
    love of music 39
    and her *madre* 56, *see* Sainte Colombe, Laure de
    meets Mary Clarke 39–40, *see* Mohl, Mary
    meets Herberts 55
    and the Nightingale School of Nursing, London xxiii
    and Palace visits 40–1
    in Rome 53–6
    suitors 41–2, *see also* Milnes, Richard Monckton
    teaches at local school 57
    tours with the Bracebridges *see* Bracebridge, Charles *and* Selina
    EGYPTIAN JOURNEY
        at Abukir Bay 10

at Abu Simbel 150–1, 152, 153–8, 161, 164
in Alexandria 2, 4–5, 8, 9, 10–14, 98–9, 234, 235–8
and ascent of cataracts at Aswan 144–6, 147–9
at Beni Hassan 115–17, 119
in Cairo 84, 85–92, 94, 99–102, 228, 229–30, 232–4
on Cairo ferry 23–7, 84–5
at Dakka Temple 164, 165, 166–70
her diaries xxv–xxvi, 114, 178, 185, 198–9, 205, 206, 218, 229–30
donkey riding 11, 87–8, 124, 125
and dreaming 121, 153, 169–70, 185, 199, 224–5
at Esna 189–90
finds happiness 144, 158, 197, 224, 229–30
at Girgeh 213, 214–15
at Giza 226–7
and God's call (*see also above*) xix, 8, 169, 206–7, 209, 214, 217–19, 223–4, 233
at Heliopolis 228–9
and Hermetic texts 165–6, 167, 168
illness 198–9
interest in funerary papyrus 101–2
at Karnak and Luxor 123–5, 187, 193, 194–200, 204–7, 209, 210, 240
learns hieroglyphs 33, 205
letters home 6, 7, 8, 13, 110–11, 112–13, 121, 153, 190, 206, 220, 227, 229, 244–5, 254
and life on the *dahabiya* 108–14, 163–4
at Lycopolis 119–20
makes decision to nurse 220–1, 222–4
at Memphis 224–5
at Philae 170–1, 174–5, 178–86, 209
at Ptah's cave 170
at Qena 214
socialises 86–7, 181, 182–5, 199–200, 219–20
and storms 212–13, 214, 217–18
thoughts on religions 101–2, 153–4, 156–7, 163, 164, 171, 174, 180, 186, 197, 204–5, 214, 233, 234, 257–8
at Valley of the Kings 198, 210
views on Egypt 90, 91, 115, 120, 121, 123–4, 184, 222, 227, 240, 257, 258
in Athens 241, 245
in Berlin 241–2
at Burlington Hotel, London 240–1
and Great Exhibition 250
at Kaiserwerth 244–5, 253–4, *see* Kaiserwerth Institute
life intolerable at Lea Hurst 241, 245, 250–2
opposition to nursing career removed 253–5
reads *Shirley* 242–3
at Scutari hospital xxi, 7, 255–6
Victoria's interest in xxii–xxiii, 256
and women's rights 243–4

MARK MORRIS

A Great and Terrible King:

Edward I and the Forging of Britain

*'Morris tells Edward's story fluently and conveys a compelling sense
of the reality, and the contingency, of personal rule'*
GUARDIAN

This is the first major biography for a generation of a truly for-
midable king. Edward I is familiar to millions as 'Longshanks',
conqueror of Scotland and nemesis of Sir William Wallace
('Braveheart'). Edward was born to rule England, but believed
that it was his right to rule all of Britain. His reign was one of
the most dramatic of the entire Middle Ages, leading to war
and conquest on an unprecedented scale, and leaving a legacy
of division that has lasted from his day to our own.

In his astonishingly action-packed life, Edward defeated and
killed the famous Simon de Montfort in battle; travelled across
Europe to the Holy Land on crusade; conquered Wales, extin-
guishing forever its native rulers, and constructed – at Conwy,
Harlech, Beaumaris and Caernarfon – the most magnificent
chain of castles ever created.

*'Marc Morris's new account of the life of Edward I is a splendid example of the
genre. Edward's life is in many ways an ideal subject for such an approach, full
of incident and action . . . An excellent, readable account of his reign'*
LITERARY REVIEW

*'Marc Morris has written the first full biography of Edward I for around 100
years, and uncommonly good it is too . . . Marc Morris does him justice, brings
him clearly before our eyes, and, like a true historian, judges him by the stan-
dards of his age, not ours. It's compelling stuff'*
DAILY TELEGRAPH